P9-CBZ-927

It is not easy to be dispassionate about this issue. Whose is the
'promised land', the land the Israelis call Israel, the Palestinians
call Palestine? What arguments, claims and counter-claims lie
behind the pioneer spirit of the settlers, the conflict, the
violence, the refugee problem, the uprooting of families?

This book outlines the claims, then traces the story behind
them, going right back to the time of the Bible, the basis for the
Jews' claims to the land. What do the Bible's prophecies mean?
How were the promises and prophecies made to ancient Israel
understood by Jesus and the first Christian community? How
should they be understood today? Is there a way forward?

Colin Chapman has been working with university students in
different countries in the Middle East since 1968. He has had to
face the issues first-hand. His aim in this book is to be fair in
facing the issues and constructive in putting forward a way of
peace.

MIDDLE EAST CHRISTIAN OUTREACH
P.O BOX 245
MISSISSAUGA ONTARIO L5A 3A1

(416) 276-5642

To Anne

Colin Chapman

WHOSE PROMISED LAND?

A LION
INTERNATIONAL PAPERBACK
Tring · Belleville · Sydney

Copyright © 1983 Lion Publishing plc

Published by
Lion Publishing plc
Icknield Way, Tring, Herts, England
ISBN 0 85648 956 5
Lion Publishing Corporation
10885 Textile Road, Belleville, Michigan 48111, USA
ISBN 0 85648 956 5
Albatross Books
PO Box 320, Sutherland, NSW 2232, Australia
ISBN 0 86760 644 4

First edition 1983
Reprinted 1983
Revised edition 1985

All Scripture quotations, unless otherwise specified,
from *The Holy Bible, New International Version,* copyright
© New York International Bible Society, 1978

Printed and bound in Great Britain by
Cox and Wyman, Reading

Contents

PREFACE

This book is an attempt to explain what the question **Whose Promised Land?** is all about, and to suggest one possible answer. I hope that the historical and biblical material may enable readers to work out their own answer to the question if they haven't already done so.

My own interest in the Middle East in general first came through the study of the Bible. But my first introduction to the problem of the Middle East came through the study of Hebrew. For four years at St Andrews University in Scotland I studied little else apart from Classical Greek and Hebrew (including biblical, rabbinic and modern Hebrew). When I graduated I spent a month touring Jordan, which in those days included the Old City of Jerusalem and the West Bank, and then a month hitch-hiking all round Israel. This was long before I had any idea that I would one day be working in the Arab world.

When I joined the Church Missionary Society in 1968, I had hoped to be sent to India where I was born, but was instead asked to go to Egypt to join the staff of the Anglican (Episcopal) cathedral in Cairo and to teach in a Presbyterian seminary. During this time I had the good fortune to meet Anne, my wife-to-be, who was working as a nurse at a centre for Palestinian refugees in Jordan. During 'Black September', the Civil War in Jordan in 1970, she was nursing both Palestinian and Jordanian casualties.

We were engaged in Cairo in December 1970, and married in Jordan in April 1971. When we first went to Beirut in October 1975, we found ourselves caught up in the Lebanese Civil War. The troubles which have continued since then have been a constant reminder of what the conflict of the Middle East is all about.

During this time I have visited Jerusalem twice to attend meetings of the Synod of the Episcopal Church, to which I belong, and have discussed the subject of the book with both Jews and Arabs.

The final draft has been prepared in Cyprus during the Israeli invasion of Lebanon in the summer of 1982, while waiting for an opportunity to return to our home and our work in West Beirut.

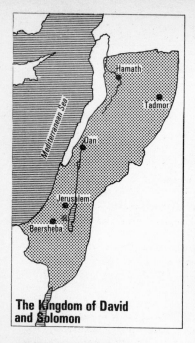

The Kingdom of David and Solomon

Hamath

Tadmor

Dan

Mediterranean Sea

Jerusalem

Beersheba

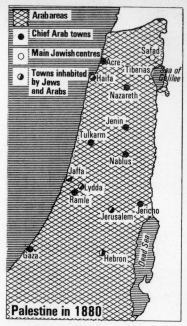

- ⊠ Arab areas
- ● Chief Arab towns
- ○ Main Jewish centres
- ◐ Towns inhabited by Jews and Arabs

Palestine in 1880

Safad
Acre
Tiberias
Sea of Galilee
Haifa
Nazareth
Jenin
Tulkarm
Nablus
Jaffa
Lydda
Ramle
Jerusalem
Jericho
Dead Sea
Gaza
Hebron

LEBANON
SYRIA
Sea of Galilee

- ⊠ To be under Jewish sovereignty
- □ To be under Arab sovereignty
- ◉ To be under international control

Jaffa
Jerusalem
Dead Sea
JORDAN
EGYPT

The UN Partition Plan 1947

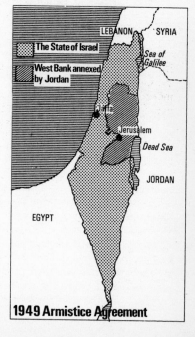

LEBANON
SYRIA
Sea of Galilee

- ⊠ The State of Israel
- ⊟ West Bank annexed by Jordan

Jaffa
Jerusalem
Dead Sea
JORDAN
EGYPT

1949 Armistice Agreement

INTRODUCTION

Conflicting Claims to the Land

Both Jews and Arabs today claim that the land of Palestine is theirs . . .

The Jews say that their ancestors first settled in Palestine some time around the twentieth century BC.

The Palestinian Arabs say they have been living in Palestine since at least the seventh century AD.

Many Jews base their claim to the land on God's promise that he would give the land to Abraham and his descendants as 'an everlasting possession'.

The Arabs argue that this promise gives them just as strong a claim on the land as the Jews, since Abraham had two sons; Isaac, who was the father of Jacob (i.e. Israel), and Ishmael, the ancestor of the Arabs.

The Jews say that the kingdom which lasted from the tenth century BC (under David) to the sixth century BC was the only independent nation state which has ever existed in the land (i.e. before 1948).

The Arabs say that if we accept claims which are based on possession of the land centuries ago, then Mexico would have a right to parts of the USA, the Spaniards could claim Mexico, and the Arabs could claim Spain.

The Jews say that although many of their ancestors were driven out of Palestine by the Romans in AD 135, groups of Jews remained in several centres in the land, and have continued to live there right up to the present time.

The Arabs do not deny this – and they add that for 1,300 years there was hardly any friction between these small Jewish communities and their Arab neighbours.

The Jews say that since 1882 they have constituted a majority in the city of Jerusalem.

The Arabs point out that the number of Jews living in the whole of Palestine in 1882 was 24,000 – which amounted to approximately 5 per cent of the total population.

Jews all over the world have always thought of Palestine as their ancestral homeland, and have continually expressed the hope that they will meet 'next year in Jerusalem'.

The Arabs insist that Palestine has a special significance for *all* of the three monotheistic religions – Judaism, Christianity, and Islam, and that none of them can lay exclusive claim to the land on purely religious grounds.

The Jews argue that when they started returning to Palestine from the 1880s onwards, they came in peacefully and acquired land by legal purchase.

The Arabs bitterly regret that land was often sold to Jews out of purely selfish motives. They also point out that much of the land was sold by absentee landlords living outside the land, many of whom were not Arabs, and that much of the land now owned by Jews was not acquired by legal purchase, but by expropriation or by war.

The Jews say that in settling in Palestine they had the approval of the Turkish government up to 1918, then the League of Nations, and finally of the British government, which was responsible for Palestine under the Mandate from 1920 to 1948.

The Arabs can point to historical documents which prove beyond doubt that during World War I the British government was making contradictory promises to the Jews and the Arabs. While assuring the Jews that they approved of the idea of a Jewish homeland in

Palestine (the Balfour Declaration), they were at the same time secretly promising to help the Arabs to establish their own independent states after the collapse of the Turkish Empire (The McMahon-Hussein Agreement). Moreover, although the Balfour Declaration and the League of Nations' Mandate included safeguards to protect the civil and political rights of the non-Jewish population, all the promises made to the Arabs were subsequently broken.

After centuries of persecution which led eventually to the killing of 6 million Jews under the Nazis in Germany, European Jews *had* to find a refuge – and Palestine was the obvious place to choose, because of all that the land had meant to them in the past.

The Arabs insist that at first they welcomed the Jewish immigrants, and lived peacefully alongside them for many years. They only began to be more hostile when they realized that many of the immigrants were seeking greater political power. Hostility inevitably led to violence, because the Arabs saw that the Jews would eventually become a majority and take control of the land. The Arabs point out that they were not in any way responsible for the persecution of the Jews in Europe, and wonder why *they* should have had to suffer for the crimes of Europe.

The Jews say they have a right to the land because of all that they have invested in it; they have drained the swamps and made the desert 'blossom like a rose'.

To which the Arabs reply: since when has an argument like this been accepted in a court of law as a valid claim to ownership?

How can we hope to decide between these conflicting claims to the same piece of land?

We begin with history. Part 1, **Facts and Figures** is a brief historical survey of the land from the twentieth century BC to the twentieth century AD. Bare facts, however, can hardly give us the 'feel' of history. Part 2, therefore, **Call the Next Witness**, sets out some of the questions we may want to ask, together with answers from different sources, especially from those who have been involved in the conflict over the land.

We then turn to the Bible. Part 3, **The land before and after Christ**, traces the theme of the land through the Old and New Testaments, while Part 4, **Is there any word from the Lord**? attempts to explore other themes in the Bible which may shed light on the problem of the land today.

The Epilogue, **Whose Promised Land**? One possible answer, puts forward a personal answer to the question.

1

FACTS AND FIGURES

66One can be sure that in time the world will
become conscious of what has happened . . . **99**
John H. Davis

Who has lived in the land and who has ruled it in the past? How and
why have so many Jews returned to the land in the last 100 years and
established the State of Israel?

Part 1 is not a complete history of the land, but simply an outline of
the basic facts about the land and its inhabitants from the twentieth
century BC to the present day.

1·1 The Patriarchs – Abraham, Isaac and Jacob (about 2000 – 1700 BC)

Some time after 2000 BC (it is difficult to know precisely when), Abraham, the head of a small tribe, or perhaps just an extended family, migrated from Harran in Syria to the hill country of Palestine. He didn't settle permanently in any one place, but moved between Shechem, Beersheba and Hebron. The inhabitants of the land at that time, who were of Semitic and other stock, are named by the writer of Genesis as 'the Kenites, Kenizzites, Kadmonites, Hittites, Perizzites, Rephaites, Amorites, Canaanites, Girgashites and Jebusites' (Genesis 15:19–21).

During a time of famine he lived in Egypt, and on a later occasion took refuge in Gerar in the northern Negev. The only piece of land he bought was the field containing the cave in which he buried his wife Sarah.

Abraham's son Isaac may have settled more permanently in one place in the hill country. But during another severe famine Isaac's son, Jacob, moved to Egypt with his whole family at the invitation of Joseph who had by this time become, in effect, the prime minister of Egypt. Their descendants stayed in Egypt for over 400 years.

1·2 The Exodus and the Conquest of the Land (about 1280 – 1050 BC)

After a time of severe oppression under one of the pharaohs in Egypt, the twelve tribes of Israel made their escape under the leadership of Moses. After crossing the Red Sea, they spent forty years in different parts of the Sinai Peninsula. Somewhere around 1280 BC Joshua led them across the River Jordan.

The conquest of the land began with the capture of Jericho, and continued with several campaigns in the hill country to the south and north. The boundaries of the land which Joshua believed had been promised by God to the children of Israel ran from (approximately) the Mediterranean coast east to Mt Hermon, then to the southern end of the Dead Sea, and west to the Mediterranean. The east bank of the Jordan was allocated by special request to two-and-a-half tribes.

It is somewhat misleading, however, to speak of 'the conquest of the land', since the Israelites didn't conquer anything like the whole land. One tribe after another attempted to occupy the territory allotted to it, but not all the tribes were successful, and large areas remained under the control of the Canaanites and others who were living in the land.

There then followed a period of decline during which the tribes came under the control of neighbouring peoples like the Philistines, but from time to time they were able to establish their independence under their own leaders or 'judges'.

1·3 The Kingdom under Saul, David and Solomon (1050 – 931 BC)

Saul, the first king (about 1050 – 1011 BC), rallied many of the tribes in an attempt to push back the Philistines who occupied most of the coastal plain and controlled most of the hill country. When he was killed in battle, he was succeeded by King David (about 1011 – 971 BC), who was more successful, and after breaking the power of the Philistines on the coast, turned his attention to the area east of the Jordan, where he defeated three smaller kingdoms: Edom in the south, Moab to the east of the Dead Sea, and Ammon to the north of the Dead Sea. He then defeated the states of Aram further to the north.

During the reign of his son, King Solomon (about 971 – 931 BC), the kingdom enjoyed a period of peace and prosperity, and its power extended further than at any other period in its history ('from Dan to Beersheba . . .').

1·4 The Kingdoms of Israel and Judah (931 – 587 BC)

After the death of Solomon in about 931 BC, the ten northern tribes revolted against his successor King Rehoboam, and two separate kingdoms came into being – the northern kingdom with its capital at Samaria, and the southern kingdom with its capital at Jerusalem.

The northern kingdom continued under its own kings for 200 years, until it was threatened by the growing power of Assyria in the north. It finally came to an end when Samaria was captured in 722 BC and a large proportion of the population was deported.

This deportation was very thorough, and large numbers of immigrants from other conquered territories were brought in to take their place. Those who settled in the province of Samaria eventually adopted the religion of the Israelites who had remained in the land. But this community, later called 'the Samaritans', were despised by the people of Judah to the south because of their mixed ancestry and because their religion was no longer considered to be pure.

The deported Israelites were settled in several different places within the Assyrian Empire – in what is today NE Syria, SE Turkey and the western part of Iran. This was part of a deliberate policy aimed at making them lose their identity and assimilate more easily with the local population. Most historians seem to accept that the Assyrian policy must have achieved its aim, and that the vast majority of the exiles were fully absorbed in the communities where they settled and never returned to their land.

1·5 The Babylonian Exile (597–539 BC)

When the northern kingdom of Israel was absorbed within the Assyrian Empire, the southern kingdom of Judah was able to defend itself and retain some measure of independence. By the beginning of the sixth century, however, the Babylonians had taken over control of the whole area from the Assyrians, and were now threatening the small kingdom of Judah on their south-western border.

In 597 BC Nebuchadnezzar of Babylon captured Jerusalem, despoiled the temple and deported the cream of the population to Babylon.

When the people left in the land rose up in revolt against the Babylonians in 586 BC, the Babylonian army attacked and destroyed much of the city of Jerusalem and took many of the remaining people into exile.

When Cyrus, king of Persia, captured Babylon in 539 BC, his policy was to repatriate the different groups of exiles in the country. The first group of exiles therefore returned in 537 BC under Zerubbabel, while other groups returned over a period of many years – some as much as seventy or eighty years later under Ezra and Nehemiah.

1·6 Palestine under the Babylonians, Persians and Greeks (597–63 BC)

At some periods after the return from the exile, the Jews enjoyed a considerable measure of independence, but they were never able to establish the kind of sovereign state which had existed from the tenth century to the sixth century BC. So from 597 BC onwards the Jewish community in Palestine lived under the control of one foreign power after another.

The Babylonian Empire controlled the whole of Palestine after 597 BC.

The Persian Empire dominated Palestine after Cyrus' victory in 539 BC.

Alexander the Great conquered the coastal plain in 330 BC, although he didn't interfere with the Jewish community around Jerusalem.

The Ptolemies (who were Greek) took control of Palestine after the death of Alexander the Great in 323 BC.

The Seleucids (of Syria), who were also Greek, took over control of Palestine from the Ptolemies in 200 BC. It was during this period that Antiochus Epiphanes tried to stamp out the Jewish religion – for example, by setting up an altar to Zeus in the temple. Jewish resistance was led by Judas Maccabeus, and after three years of intense guerilla warfare, the Syrians were driven out of Jerusalem and the temple was purified (165 BC).

Thus for a short period of two or three years, the Jews had a fully independent Jewish state based in Jerusalem. But the Syrians soon regained control, re-established pagan worship in the temple, and nominated their own candidate as high priest. In the years that followed, the Jews were ruled by a succession of their own priest-kings, and enjoyed a certain measure of independence.

1·7 Palestine under the Romans
(63 BC – AD 330)

The Romans took over Palestine in 63 BC when Pompey invaded at the head of the Roman army. At times they ruled the country through local puppet kings such as Herod the Great (37–4 BC); at other times they ruled through Roman procurators like Pontius Pilate (AD 26–36); or through direct Roman rule (AD 135–330). Resistance to Roman rule led to the Jewish revolt of AD 66, which ended in AD 70 when Jerusalem was captured and the temple destroyed. Some Jews made a final stand at Masada near the Dead Sea, but the Romans captured the stronghold in AD 73.

Although Roman rule was not oppressive, resistance continued. A further Jewish revolt in AD 132 was led by Bar Cochba, who rallied an army of 200,000 men and proceeded to drive the Romans out of Jerusalem. When the Roman army recaptured Jerusalem in AD 135 the Jews were slaughtered. The Emperor Hadrian now turned Jerusalem into a Roman colony and called it Aelia Capitolina. He built a pagan temple in honour of Jupiter on the site of the temple, and forbade the Jews to enter Jerusalem on pain of death. Although these repressive actions killed all hopes of Jewish national independence, communities of Jews continued to live in different centres in Palestine (e.g. on the coastal plain and in Galilee.)

1·8 Palestine under the Byzantine Empire *(330–632)*

In AD 330 the Roman Emperor Constantine, who had made Christianity the official religion of the Roman Empire, founded a new capital city for the eastern half of his empire at Byzantium, which was therefore known as Constantinople. In 395 the Roman Empire was officially divided into two halves and the eastern half became known as the Byzantine Empire; Palestine was thus a province of the Byzantine Empire for some three-and-a-half centuries.

Treatment of the Jews (in Palestine and elsewhere) by the Byzantine emperors varied: in 438 the Empress Eudocia removed the ban on Jews praying at the temple site, but the Emperor Justinian (527–65) organized attempts to convert Jews to Christianity by force and from that time onwards Byzantine treatment of the Jews deteriorated.

In 614 the Persians invaded the Byzantine Empire and occupied Syria, Palestine and Egypt. For three years Jerusalem was in the hands of the Jews, until the Byzantines defeated the Persians in 617 and re-asserted their control over Palestine.

1·9 Palestine under the Arabs and Seljuk Turks *(632–1096)*

In 632, only two years after the death of the prophet Muhammad, the Arab armies invaded Palestine and captured Jerusalem. Palestine thus became part of the Muslim Empire for the next 450 years.

From 661 this empire was ruled by the Umayyads, an Arab dynasty which ruled from Damascus.

Then from 750 it was ruled by the Abbasids, a dynasty which ruled from Baghdad.

The Arab Muslims came to Palestine as conquerors; but since there was no attempt either to expel the people of the land or to convert them to Islam they remained as Christians or Jews. Gradually, however, the population began to convert to Islam, since that was the path to social advancement, and Arabic quickly became the most widely-spoken language. Islam, however, did not become the religion of the majority of the population of Palestine until the thirteenth century.

1·10 Palestine under the Crusaders and the Mamluks

(1096–1517)

In 1099 the Crusaders, Christian knights from western Europe, recaptured Jerusalem from the Muslims (and massacred the entire population of the city, Jewish and Muslim). The Crusaders established a kingdom in Palestine, based on Jerusalem, but in 1187 they were defeated and expelled from Jerusalem by Saladin. Although they retained a certain amount of territory, they were finally expelled altogether from Palestine in 1291, when their last stronghold, the port of Acre, was recaptured by the Muslims. Palestine remained under Muslim rule thereafter, ruled by various dynasties of Mamluks, slave-soldiers, mostly of Turkish descent, until its conquest by the Ottoman Turks in 1516.

1·11 Palestine under the Ottoman Turks (1517–1918)

In 1516 the Ottoman Turks conquered Palestine.

At the beginning of this period there were approximately thirty Jewish communities in different parts of Palestine, with their centre in Safed. There was very heavy taxation on Jews.

In 1880 the total population of Palestine was approximately 480,000.

Of these the total number of Arabs was around 456,000.

The total number of Jews was around 24,000 (i.e. approximately 5 per cent of the population).

The first *Aliyah* (return of Jews) took place in 1881. Most of the new immigrants established new Jewish colonies.

The number of Jews gradually increased through further waves of immigration particularly during World War I.

In 1914 there were 60,000 Jews (approximately 11 per cent of the total).

1·12 Palestine under the Mandate (1922–48)

The Turks were defeated during World War I and were driven out of Palestine in 1918 by the combined efforts of the British, the French and the Arabs. It was in November 1917 that the British government issued the famous Balfour Declaration, in which it expressed support for the idea of 'a national homeland for the Jewish people'.

A Peace Conference of the victorious powers was held at Versailles in 1919 to decide the future of the region.

Under the terms of the Mandate, which came into effect in 1922, Britain was given responsibility for Palestine, while France was given responsibility for Syria.

The terms of the Mandate were as follows:

> The Mandatory shall be responsible for placing the country under such political, administrative and economic conditions as will secure the establishment of the Jewish National Home, as laid down in the preamble, and the development of self-governing institutions and also for safeguarding the civil and religious rights of all the inhabitants of Palestine, irrespective of race and religion.

During the twenties and thirties there were many violent clashes between the Arab communities and the more recently arrived Jewish settlers. In 1936 the Arabs rose in revolt against the British in protest at the continued Jewish immigration. The revolt was crushed. The Peel Commission sent out by the British government in 1937 concluded that the Mandate was no longer workable, and recommended that the country should be partitioned into two states, one Jewish and one Arab.

In 1939 a British White Paper proposed a joint Arab-Jewish state and a limit on Jewish immigration of 75,000 in the next five years. This was seen by the Jews as a breach of the Balfour Declaration and the Mandate.

The period of World War II saw a great deal of legal and illegal Jewish immigration and further polarization of the two communities. During the holocaust in Europe, Britain and the USA would not accept Jewish immigrants and their sole hope was Palestine. As a result, the Jews numbered 31 per cent of the total population in 1947.

During these years the Jews acquired more land by purchase from the Arabs:

— In 1918 the Jews owned 2 per cent of the land.
— In 1935 they owned about 5½ per cent of the land
(equivalent to 12 per cent of the cultivable land).
— By 1947 they owned 6 per cent of the land.

1·13 The UN Partition Plan (1947)

In 1947 the British government announced that it intended to give up the Mandate, and to hand the whole problem of Palestine over to the United Nations (the successor to the League of Nations).

A special commission of the UN in 1947 made detailed recommendations for the creation of two separate states:

● a Jewish state, which would include 52 per cent of the land, with a population of 497,000 Arabs and 498,000 Jews
● an Arab state which would include the remaining 48 per cent of the land, with 725,000 Arabs and 10,000 Jews
● Jerusalem and the area surrounding it, would become an 'international zone'

The General Assembly approved the Partition Plan by a 2 to 3 majority, largely through the influence of the USA.

While the Jews in Palestine accepted the plan, the Palestininian Arabs totally rejected it. A state of civil war developed, with both sides increasing their terrorist activities. These were the most widely publicized episodes in a series of attacks and counter-attacks, random killings and military operations that cost several thousand lives among the Palestinian Arabs and Jews:

● On 9 April 1948, the Irgun, a Jewish underground group, killed 254 Arab men, women and children in the village of Deir Yassin south-west of Jerusalem.
● On 12 April 1948, as a reprisal for Deir Yassin, the Arabs attacked a convoy travelling to the Hadassah Hospital north-east of Jerusalem and killed seventy-seven Jewish doctors, nurses, university teachers and students.

1·14 The Founding of the State of Israel (1948)

When the British Mandate ended on 14 May 1948, Dr Chaim Weizmann raised the flag of David and proclaimed the new state of Israel.

The Arabs had no plans for establishing the Arab state called for by the UN Partition Plan, and were determined to destroy the new

Jewish state. Therefore, within hours of the creation of the State of Israel, Arab forces from Jordan, Syria, Egypt, Lebanon and Iraq launched an attack. In the fighting which followed during the next seven months, the Jewish forces defeated the Arab armies and took over large areas in the north (Galilee) and in the south (the Negev), which, according to the Partition Plan, should have formed part of the Arab state. Jerusalem was divided with the old, walled city including the holy sites falling under Arab rule, and west Jerusalem being held by the Jews.

By the time of the ceasefire in January 1949, Israel had occupied 77 per cent of the land (i.e. one third more than it would have had if the Arabs had accepted the UN plan). The territory on the West Bank, including East Jerusalem, which was supposed to form part of the Arab state, was annexed by Jordan.

1·15 Conflicts since 1948

Suez 1956

The nationalization of the Suez Canal by President Nasser of Egypt in 1954 created an international crisis which gave Israel the opportunity to attack Egypt, and so put an end to terrorist attacks across the border.

After concluding a secret treaty with Britain and France, Israel invaded Sinai on 26 October 1956, and in less than a week took the whole of Sinai. Britain and France then launched an airborne attack on the Suez Canal.

As a result of strong pressure from America, however, Britain and France were forced to withdraw their forces, and Israel agreed to withdraw from Sinai after receiving assurances that Egypt would not attack Israel or interfere with Israeli shipping in the Gulf of Aqaba.

The June War 1967

By the end of 1966 the clashes between Israel and its Arab neighbours had reached serious proportions. Condemnation of these incidents by the UN Security Council had little effect.

President Nasser, goaded on by the propaganda from other Arab countries, especially Syria, requested the UN to withdraw its emergency forces from the border between Israel and Egypt in Sinai, and moved Egyptian forces down to the border.

In order to forestall any Arab attack, Israel struck first and destroyed most of the Egyptian airforce while still on the ground at their air bases. In less than a week Israel had occupied the whole of Sinai, the West Bank (including the Old City of Jerusalem), and the Golan Heights.

The Security Council Resolution of 22 November 1967 called on Israel to withdraw from territories occupied in the 1967 war. Israel refused to comply with this resolution, and instead began building settlements on the West Bank, the Golan Heights and Gaza.

The October/Yom Kippur War 1973

The Egyptian army crossed the Suez Canal on 6 October 1973 in a surprise attack, and succeeded in penetrating some distance into Sinai. The Israeli counter-attack, however, resulted in the encirclement of a large part of the Egyptian army, and a cease-fire came into effect on 24 October.

Although Egypt did not achieve its aim of recovering Sinai, the psychological effect of the initial victory in the war enabled President Sadat in 1977 to make his historic visit to Jerusalem to propose a peace plan with Israel.

This initiative culminated in the Camp David Treaty of 1979, in which Israel, Egypt and the USA agreed:
- that Israel would withdraw from Sinai
- that Israel and Egypt would seek to normalize relations
- and that these agreements would be 'linked' with negotiations between Israel and Egypt which would lead to 'full autonomy' for the Palestinians in the West Bank and the Gaza Strip.

The Invasion of Lebanon 1978

In March 1978 the Israeli army invaded southern Lebanon in an attempt to crush the Palestinian forces who were using it as a base to launch attacks across the border into Israel. The Israelis withdrew in June 1978 as a result of strong pressure from the United Nations, but established a buffer zone under Major Saad Haddad instead of turning over all occupied territory to the UN forces.

The Annexation of the Golan Heights 1981

Although UN Security Council Resolutions after the 1967 war had demanded that Israel should give the Golan Heights back to Syria, the Israeli Knesset passed a law in December 1981 officially annexing the area.

The Invasion of Lebanon 1982

On 6 June 1982 the Israeli army launched a full-scale invasion of Lebanon, following the attempted assassination of the Israeli ambassador in London. The operation had a number of objectives, but the removal of the PLO forces from Lebanon and the security of Israel's northern border were uppermost. The southern Palestinian camps were effectively destroyed and Beirut besieged for two months before the exodus of the PLO militia and leadership. This was followed by Israel's entry into West Beirut and the massacre of

Palestinian civilians by Lebanese militia in the camps of Sabra and Chatila.

1·16 Some Conclusions

If we are to try to settle the question Whose Promised Land? simply by appealing to past history, these are some of the questions we must ask and answer:

Q How long have the Jews been living in the Land?

The ancestors of the Jews first entered the land in the about twentieth century BC. They controlled much of the hill country from around 1280—1011 BC. They controlled most of Palestine and had an independent kingdom from 1011—931 BC.

They had two separate states with their own kings from 931—721 BC. They had the small kingdom of Judah centred on Jerusalem from 721—587 BC. From 587 BC the Jews living in a small area around Jerusalem came under the control of one foreign power after another – the Babylonians, Persians, Greeks and Romans.

When the Jews were expelled from Jerusalem by the Romans in 135 AD, communities of Jews continued to live in Galilee and on the coastal plain.

This situation remained basically unchanged for centuries. There was a regular flow of pilgrims and immigrants from Jewish communities in Europe, and the fortunes of the Jewish community rose or declined according to the severity of the pressures from the ruling powers, and according to the amount of financial and moral support received from Jews elsewhere.

Jews therefore base their historical claim on the land not only on their occupation of the land during the biblical period, but also on the unbroken Jewish occupation of certain towns since then and the unbroken links maintained throughout the centuries between Jews of the Diaspora (Dispersion) and Jews in Palestine.

Q How long have the Arabs been living in the land?

The Arabs, who came to Palestine in the seventh century and made it part of the Islamic Empire, settled *alongside* the existing population (whose roots could be traced back to the Canaanites, the Phoenicians, the Philistines and the descendants of some of the tribes of Israel, etc.), and inter-married with them.

The Arab rulers made a permanent impression on the country because all the indigenous population accepted the language of Arabic, and the majority accepted the religion of Islam. The population since then has therefore always thought of itself as being 'Arab'.

Other foreign invaders and rulers who lived in the country for longer periods – like the Crusaders and the Turks – intermarried to a certain extent with the population of the country.

Therefore, while the Palestinian Arabs today cannot claim to be 'pure Arabs', they can maintain without any doubt that their ancestors – however mixed racially they may be – have been living in the land for thirteen centuries at the very least (i.e. since the seventh century AD), and since the time of the Romans have constituted the majority of the population.

Q How far are we to go back in history?

How was the land divided between the Jews and the rest of the population in 1000 BC, AD 135, AD 1880, AD 1947, AD 1948, AD 1967 . . .?

Are we to go back to 1000 BC and the undivided kingdoms of Saul, David and Solomon?

Are we to go back to AD 135 when the Jews were expelled from Jerusalem?

Are we to go back AD 1880 when

- the Jews were 5 per cent of the population, owning less than 2 per cent of the land; and
- the Arabs were 95 per cent of the population, owning or settled in 98 per cent of the land?

Are we to go back to AD 1947 and the UN Partition Plan in which

- the Jews (who were 31 per cent of the population owning 6 per cent of the land) were given 52 per cent of the land; and
- the Arabs (who were 69 per cent of the population and owned or were settled in 94 per cent of the land) were given 48 per cent of the land?

Are we to go back to AD 1948,

- when the Jews occupied a further 25 per cent of the land as a result of the fighting after Partition, and thus came to possess 77 per cent of the land?

Are we to go back to AD 1967,

- when Israel occupied Sinai, the West Bank, the Gaza Strip and the Golan Heights, but were later required by the United Nations to withdraw from 'occupied territories'?

2

CALL THE NEXT WITNESS

❝ Two important phenomena of the same nature and yet in direct conflict, which have so far escaped all attention, are at present developing in the Asiatic part of Turkey. They are the awakening of the Arab nation and the hidden attempts of Jews to re-establish the ancient kingdom of Israel on a very large scale. These two movements are destined to be in permanent conflict, until one gains the upper hand over the other. The fate of the whole world will depend on the eventual outcome of the conflict between these two peoples who represent two conflicting principles. ❞

Najib Azuri, a Palestinian Arab, writing in 1905

❝ It was evident twenty years ago [i.e. in 1891] that the day would come when the Arabs would stand up against us. ❞

Asher Ginsberg (Ahad Ha'Am), a Jew, writing in 1911

❝ We are doomed to live in a constant state of war with the Arabs and there is no escape from sacrifice and bloodshed. This is perhaps an undesirable situation, but it is a fact. If we are to proceed with our work against the wishes of the Arabs we shall have to expect such sacrifices. ❞

Moshe Dayan, an Israeli Jew, writing in 1968

What happens if we try to look at the events of the last 100 years not just as detached spectators or observers, but through the eyes of those who lived through them?

Part 2 is a kind of anthology of quotations. Instead of trying to argue a particular case, it presents different kinds of source material to enable readers to make up their own minds about the history of the land in recent years.

2·1 Anti-Semitism

Q What is anti-Semitism?

It is a strange irony of history that although both Jews and Arabs are Semitic peoples, the word 'anti-Semitism' has come to be used exclusively for feelings or actions against the Jewish people.

Theodor Herzl (1860—1904), the founder of the modern Zionist movement, explained his understanding of anti-Semitism:

> I understand what anti-Semitism is about. We Jews have maintained ourselves, even if through no fault of our own, as a foreign body among the different nations. In the ghetto, we have taken on a number of anti-social characteristics . . . Anti-Semitism is a consequence of the emancipation of the Jews. The peoples about us who lack a historical understanding . . . do not see us as a historical product . . . When we came out of the ghetto, we were . . . 'ghetto Jews'. We should have been allowed time to accustom ourselves to freedom.

Max Nordau, at the First Zionist Congress in Basle in 1897, described the effects of anti-Semitism on Jews in Europe in a speech which was later described as 'a monument of our age':

> Jewish misery has two forms, the material and the moral. In Eastern Europe, North Africa and western Asia – in those very regions where the overwhelming majority, probably nine-tenths of all Jews, live – there the misery of the Jews is to be understood literally. It is a daily distress of the body, anxiety for every day that follows, a tortured fight for bare existence. In Western Europe . . . the question of bread and shelter, and the question of security of life and limb concerns them less. There the misery is moral. It takes the form of perpetual injury to self-respect and honour and of a brutal suppression of the striving for spiritual satisfactions which no non-Jew is obliged to deny himself . . .

He went on to speak of the pogroms in eastern Europe in the early 1880s:

> [After] a slumber of thirty to sixty years, anti-Semitism broke out once more from the innermost depth of the nations and his real situation was revealed to the mortified Jew . . . He has lost the home of the ghetto, but the land of his birth is denied to him as his home. He avoids his fellow Jew because anti-Semitism has made him hateful. His countrymen repel him when he

wishes to associate with them. He has no ground under his feet
and he has no community to which he belongs as a full
member. He cannot reckon on his Christian countrymen
viewing either his character or his intentions with justice, let
alone with kindly feelings. With his Jewish countrymen he has
lost touch. He feels that the world hates him and he sees no
place where he can find warmth when he seeks it . . .

The emancipated Jew is insecure in his relations with his
fellow beings, timid with strangers, even suspicious of the secret
feelings of his friends. His best powers are exhausted in the
suppression, or at least the difficult concealment, of his own
real character. For he fears that this character might be
recognized as Jewish, and he never has the satisfaction of
showing himself as he is in all his thoughts and sentiments. He
becomes an inner cripple.

Q How did Christianity contribute to the growth of anti-
Semitism?

Dagobert D. Runes, a Jew, expresses the feelings of many Jews who
believe that Christianity is largely responsible for anti-Semitism:

Anti-Semitism was born with Christianity; to be sure, not with
Jesus, a Jew Himself, whose followers took conviction in His
descendancy from the House of David, but rather with those
who, on the basis of sermons flowing from the lips of the gentle
Nazarene, created an organized church . . .

A new era began, the era of Christianity not as the solemn
teachings of a gentle Jew, but as a powerful body of involved
edicts, codes and doctrines that affected the whole Western
world. The nations of the Roman Empire, without leadership
and broken in spirit, submitted to the wishes of the Bishop of
Rome, all except the Jews. The Jew would not surrender,
neither in Judea nor in Egypt, neither in Persia nor in Lybia.
Not even in Rome.

So the Bishop of Rome, who in the 4th century became the
master of the souls of Europe, put the mark of perfidy on the
name and title of every Jew in his realm and elsewhere. And
this blot he willed should remain upon the children and
children's children of the House of Israel; and because of this
stigma, for more than 1500 years Christians have always found
it easy to deal with Jews as non-beings. *Judai monstra sunt.* [Jews
are monsters]

It was the Bishop of Rome who in the 13th century directed
that the blot which was placed upon the Jew should also be
carried on his clothing, visible to all.

It was the Bishop of Rome who ordered in the 15th century that the marked people be confined to ghettos so that they might not soil the Christians around them.

It was the Bishop of Rome who used the Crusades against the Moslems as an occasion to heap blemish upon the Jews.

It was the Bishop of Rome who was the spiritual head of the *auto-da-fé* [Inquisition] in which in Spain alone nine thousand Jewish patricians were burned *ad majorem Christi gloriam* [for the greater glory of Christ]. And in our time, it was the Bishop of Rome who refused to utter a single sentence of horror, nay, disapproval, of the choking to death by German Christians of one million Jewish children and five million Jewish women and unarmed men.

The crucifixon of the Jew Jesus by order of the whole Jewish community has been made a cornerstone of all Christian theology, supported by the implication that in the eyes of God the Jews are forever accursed, and that every Jewish child in your town, and every Jewish woman in your town, and every man, is a congenital sinner and criminal.

Runes quotes the following passages from the writings of John Chrysostom, Augustine, Thomas Aquinas and Martin Luther to show how Christians have often been encouraged to think about the Jews:

The Jews are the most worthless of all men – they are lecherous, greedy, rapacious – they are perfidious murderers of Christians, they worship the devil, their religion is a sickness . . .
The Jews are the odious assassins of Christ and for killing God there is no expiation possible, no indulgence or pardon. Christians may never cease vengeance, and the Jews must live in servitude forever. God always hated the Jews, and whoever has intercourse with Jews will be rejected on Judgment Day. It is incumbent upon all Christians to hate the Jews.
John Chrysostom (AD 344—407)

The true image of the Hebrew is Judas Iscariot, who sells the Lord for silver. The Jew can never spiritually understand the Scriptures and forever will bear the guilt for the death of Jesus because their fathers killed the Saviour.
Augustine (AD 354—430)

It would be perfectly licit to hold the Jews, because of their crucifying the Lord, in perpetual servitude.
Thomas Aquinas (AD 1225—1274)

Set their synagogues on fire, and whatever does not burn up should be covered or spread over with dirt so that no-one may ever be able to see a cinder or stone of it . . . in order that God may see that we are Christians . . . Their homes should likewise be broken down and destroyed . . . They should be put under one roof or in a stable, like gypsies, in order that they may realize that they are not masters in our land as they boast, but miserable captives, as they complain of us incessantly before God with bitter wailing . . . They should be deprived of their prayer books and Talmuds, in which such idolatry, lies, cursing, and blasphemy are taught . . . their rabbis must be forbidden to teach under the threat of death.

  Martin Luther (AD1483—1546)

Q What forms did anti-Semitism take in nineteenth-century Europe?

James Parkes, an English historian, describes the development of modern anti-Semitism in his book *The Emergence of the Jewish Problem* (1879—1939). He begins by describing some of the basic attitudes towards Jews in the nineteenth century:

Modern anti-Semitism is a political weapon deliberately invented and artificially developed for ends which have nothing to do with the Jewish people or the Jewish religion. Its salient characteristic is that the material out of which it is forged is not only false, but known by its artificers to be false. The actual problems, prejudices, difficulties, and jealousies which arise out of the presence of actual Jewish communities are too diverse and too diffuse to have any practical value as a general weapon of the kind which anti-Semites desired. They had, however, this essential value. They provided the background of susceptibility on which the anti-Semite was able to paint his vast chimeras, and gave to the most improbable creations of his fancy the similitude of probability.

Among the peasants and the proletariat, and among the ignorant of all classes, there had survived into the nineteenth century relics of the religious intolerance of the Middle Ages, and memories of the exactions of Jewish usurers; and they were familiar with Jews as strange, ragged and 'foreign' pedlars dealing with trumpery, or as old-clothes merchants, ridiculous with their evil-smelling sacks, and the three or four old hats beloved of nineteenth-century cartoonists.

Among the middle classes and the urban artisanate the word 'Jew' stood for something quite different. It stood for the rival and competitor. The urbanization and industrialization of

Europe had opened all kinds of new occupations to the more enterprising members of the Jewish population. The place which they came to occupy, if never so powerful as anti-Semites represented it, was yet a prominent one in many walks of urban life, and quite sufficient to attract jealousy among the non-Jewish urban population of similar standing, and desiring to obtain similar advantages from the expanding capitalism of the time.

To the aristocrat, the landowner, and the cleric, 'Jews' appeared in still a third light. The urbanized, capitalistic, liberal, secularist, and 'democratic' bourgeois state, which had deprived these classes of their authority and privileges, had emancipated the Jews, and given them every opportunity for influencing the public life of what had been 'Christendom'. To them the Jew was the parvenu, the sceptic, the desecrator of traditions.

Without this triple background of dislike, suspicion, or hostility arising out of actual Jewish problems the whole vast structure of anti-Semitism would have crumbled . . .

He goes on to describe how anti-Semitism was used as a political weapon:

The common enemy for which, in different countries, the weapon of anti-Semitism was forged, was precisely the liberal, secular, urbanized, and capitalistic state of the period; and though it proved no more than a Mrs Partington's mop in the effort to restore the aristocratic and clerical society which had perished, it was most adroitly chosen for the discomfiture of nineteenth-century politicians. In the first place Jews alone could be described by *all* the adjectives used above to describe the nineteenth-century state. Their politics were almost universally *liberal*, for it was liberalism which had secured their political emancipation, and it was in liberal circles that they were most at home. The Jewish generation which had first profited by emancipation was largely in revolt against the traditions of the Synagogue, and was by temperament *secularist*; for the alternative of a modernized and reformed Judaism had scarcely appeared. They had for centuries been an *urban* population. And they were better equipped for the nineteenth-century *capitalist* development than any similar class of non-Jewish society. They were cosmopolitan, accustomed to handling money, and versed in all forms of commercial practice. Whatever aspect of modern society was under attack, it was therefore possible to give it the name of 'Jewish'. Anti-

Semitism united 'the enemies of dissent, the enemies of wealth as well as the enemies of the alien and the enemies of the upstart – clericals, nationalists, socialists, and aristocrats'. But that was not all. A concentration on the 'Jewish' aspect of society allowed the attack to be made simultaneously on all fronts, and to bring together the most diverse elements of opposition. The traditional hostility to the Jews of the Churches, whether Roman, Protestant, or Orthodox, brought together the aristocratic prelate who disliked the diminution of his privileges, the sincere Christian who hated the secularist opportunism of the new society, and the poor rural or urban curate whose parishioners were ruthlessly exploited by the selfishness of capitalist enterprise; the old landowner and the non-Jewish industrialist united in opposing the Jewish rival of the latter; and the Christian and the freethinking intellectual found common ground in hostility to the cultural influence of Jews in the arts and professions. But even among the *petite bourgeoisie* in the towns and cities it was useful; for it brought together the jealous, the unsuccessful, and the displaced in a common movement. Only the Socialist movement resisted the temptation and refused to fall into the trap of distinguishing a Jewish from a non-Jewish capitalist. The 'Christian' Socialists, on the other hand, whether Roman or Protestant, were in the forefront of the movement.

These are some specific examples he gives of how anti-Semitism was used:

Not only could the weapon of anti-Semitism draw together the most diverse elements in society; it could also be wielded in any one of a number of ways. The charge that opponents were 'Jewish' could be used simply as a stick with which to beat them. It was in this way that organized political anti-Semitism was first used by Bismarck in his attack on the National Liberals in 1879. The Jews could be used as a scapegoat for the failings of an unpopular regime, as they were used by the Russian bureaucracy from 1881 to 1917. Alternatively the scapegoat technique could be used to persuade people that their misery was neither the fault of their rulers, as in nineteenth-century Rumania, nor of themselves, as in the propaganda which brought the National Socialists to power in twentieth-century Germany. The Jewish bogy could be used to undermine confidence in a regime too strong for direct attack, as in the case of the French Third Republic in the period between 1880 and 1914. Finally, a concentration on supposedly anti-social or unpopular activities of Jews provided a most satisfactory smoke-screen to divert attention from the equally anti-social or unpopular activities of non-Jews engaged in similar occupations. Hence the considerable support given to fascist movements of the Mosley type by non-Jewish capitalists who have been only too glad to have attention diverted from themselves in a period in which socialism, or advanced radicalism, has been 'in the atmosphere'.

There is then nothing surprising in the emergence of anti-Semitism in the nineteenth-century picture. To present it as an unexpected return to medieval prejudice in a period of rationalism and toleration is to ignore the opportunism of modern political struggles.

2·2 Zionism

Q Why have the Jews felt such a strong attachment to the land throughout their history?

Denys Baly, an Englishman who lived and worked in Palestine for many years before and after the creation of Israel in 1948, describes how for many centuries Jews have expressed their longing to return to the land:

The famous cry of hope, 'Next year in Jerusalem', which year by year is uttered at the feast of the Passover is not the only expression of this longing for return. Three times a day, at the morning, afternoon and evening services the following words are spoken, 'Sound the great horn for our freedom; lift up the ensign to gather our exiles, and gather us from the four corners of the earth. Blessed art thou, O Lord, who gatherest the banished ones of the people of Israel. Restore our judges as at the first, and our counsellors as at the beginning; remove from us sorrow and sighing; reign thou over us, O Lord, thou alone in loving-kindness, and tender mercy, and justify us in judgment. Blessed art thou, O Lord, the King who lovest righteousness and judgment. And to Jerusalem, thy city, return in mercy, and dwell therein as thou hast spoken; rebuild it soon in our days as an everlasting building, and speedily set up therein the throne of David. Blessed art thou, O Lord, who rebuildest Jerusalem'. Nor are these the only occasions. Running throughout the liturgical services, like one of the threads of which the pattern is made, is this earnest longing and hope, and this certainty that the day will come in which the hope will be fulfilled.

He goes on to explain the unbroken contact between the Jews of the Dispersion and the Jews of Palestine over many centuries:

Equally impressive is the unbroken contact which the Jews of the Dispersion maintained with the land of Palestine, and that not only as a place of pious pilgrimage but as a continuing centre of Jewish life. The Jewish community in Palestine was not always numerous, was from time to time in severe straits of poverty and privation, and on occasions was kept in existence only by the timely charity of their fellow Jews in other lands. Yet the gifts that in return went out from them to the Jews throughout the world were such that it would be true to say that had they not been given, then Judaism as we know it today would never have been. From Palestine in the grim period after the destruction of Jerusalem came the Mishnah and from Palestine also, some five hundred years later, came the Massoretic text of the Hebrew Scriptures, the sole authority for the Hebrew text until the dramatic discovery of the Dead Sea Scrolls in the bloody twilight of the Mandate. The contribution of Tiberias to the development of the Talmud takes second place to the work of the Babylonian scholars of the time, but it has its place in that development. These three things, the *Tanakh* or Old Testament, definitively edited by the Massoretes, the Mishnah and the Talmud, are the foundation and the basis of the Jewish way of life, and if Judaism had no other debt to Palestine than that two of them had taken shape there, the Dispersion would still have had to own that Palestine was their mother.

The Jews in Palestine continued to maintain a precarious existence there throughout the succeeding centuries, surviving the massacres of the Crusades and the fitful intolerance, indifference, and magnanimity of the Muslim rulers. Left to themselves, they would probably have died out altogether or become merged in the surrounding Muslim flood, or have been preserved as a tiny fossil like the Samaritan community of Nablus. That this did not happen was due to the continual flow, irregular but never entirely ceasing, of Jews from other countries. Devout rabbis who wished to spend their final years in prayer and study in the Holy Land, desperate exiles fleeing before some new persecution, great names like that of Nahmanides, lesser men whose names today are lost for ever – they constitute a fact of history to which the Zionists may rightly call attention. After the expulsion of the Jews from Spain the life of the Jewish community in Galilee was once again vigorous and effective. At the beginning of the seventeenth century, when religious life there was already on the decline, Safad had eighteen talmudic colleges and twenty-one synagogues. Joseph Caro, the author of the authoritative code-book of Jewish conduct, the *Shulhan Arukh*, lived for forty years in Safad, dying there in 1575. Isaac Luria, who through his disciple Haim Vital, a native of Safad, was to have a tremendous effect on the development of Jewish mysticism, came to Safad in 1570, though he was destined to live there for only two more years. These names, though the most important, are not the only ones. During their time, in fact, the Palestinian community was among the most dynamic sections of Jewry . . .

. . . The enduring continuity of Jewish contact with some part of what they believe to be their historic homeland is seen to be more impressive than it is popularly held to be . . . It is this enduring contact of the Jewish people with Palestine, together with the deep-seated religious and emotional ties with the country, which are the strength of the Zionist case. When in the nineteenth century the Jews began to look for somewhere to live in safety, Palestine was the only country which could stir the general interest.

Q What are the origins of Zionism?

Although the prayer 'Next year in Jerusalem' had for centuries expressed the hope that the Jews would one day return to the land, few believed that it could ever become reality. The first significant development in the nineteenth century, however, was that after the emancipation of Jews in western Europe, some wealthy Jews like the philanthropist Sir Moses Montefiore, began to work for the revival of the struggling Jewish communities in Palestine. Then in 1881 the programs among the Jewish communities in western Russia led to a new upsurge of Zionist feeling.

Moshe Leib Lilienblum (1843—1910), a Russian Jew, argued that the root of the problem was that the Jew was always made to feel a 'stranger'. This is how his ideas are summed up by David Vital, professor of political science at Tel Aviv University, in his book *The Origins of Zionism*:

> The 'Middle Ages' are once again upon us, with the sole difference that it is no longer religion that is the criterion for distinguishing the native from the stranger, but nationality and race. It is these that are now the household gods of Europe in both the West and the East. The Jew is not a Teuton of the German nation, or a Magyar of the Hungarian nation, or a Slav, but a son of Shem and therefore, whether he wills it or

not, a 'stranger'. Thus, in the final analysis, nothing has
changed . . . We, the Jews, may not think of ourselves as
strangers, but others do. There is therefore nothing that we
ourselves can do to avoid the conflict . . . There is only one way
out of the predicament: the Jews must cease to be strangers.
But how?

He totally rejected the idea that Jews should be assimilated in the
countries where they lived:

The petty-minded and the small of heart propose final and
absolute assimilation – a despicable and unjustifiable solution in
principle, an unworkable one in practice. There was no
evidence to suggest that the surrounding people wished to
accept the Jews and, in any case, there was no reason to believe
that it was a matter subject to deliberate decision. 'I do not
speak of the flight of individuals; there have always been
blackguards in mind and deed. They have never done anything
to improve the condition of the Jews, on the contrary: . . . they
have reduced the ranks of the beaten and increased the ranks
of the beaters.' But assimilation *in toto* was another matter:
assimilation was national death; a nation could not commit
suicide. If it occured, it would be as a consequence of history,
which is to say of processes and events over which we ourselves
have no control.

Lilienblum went on to propose a return to Erez-Israel as the only
solution to the problem:

No, the solution to the troubles of the Jews and to the fears and
resentments of the Gentiles was to find a place where the Jews
'would no longer be strangers but citizens and masters of the
land themselves' . . . It might take a century for the Jews to
evacuate Europe, but a beginning must be made. Where to?
Not to America, where, once again, they would be strangers,
but to Erez-Israel 'to which we have a historic right which was
not lost with our (lost) rule of the country, any more than the
peoples of the Balkans lost their rights to their lands when they
lost their rule over them'.

Leon Pinsker (1821—91) was influenced by Lilienblum's writings,
and in 1882 published a very significant book entitled *Auto-
emancipation*, in which he argued that the problems of the Jews
could only be solved if they were able to live as a nation in their own
homeland. This is David Vital's summary of Pinsker's ideas:

The heart of the problem, says Pinsker, is that the Jews

comprise a distinctive element in every one of the nations in which they are found, an element that cannot be entirely absorbed and therefore cannot be readily and comfortably tolerated, but is, on the contrary, feared and hated and denied equality of status and treatment . . . By the standards of others, once they had lost their country the Jewish people should have fallen into decay long ago. But instead, uniquely, they continued to maintain themselves as a nation and, by so doing, became in the eyes of others an uncanny and frightening people . . . As such the Jews aroused superstitious fear; fear led to hatred; hatred to a psychosis which has now, after almost twenty centuries, become a malady passed down from father to son . . . There is, generally, little love for strangers. But not all strangers are alike. All have a home somewhere – except the Jew . . . 'The Jews are aliens who have no representatives, because they have no country . . .'

It cannot be denied that the emancipation of the Jews, where instituted, is a great achievement. But it is only legal emancipation, not social. Its basis is in reason, not in natural and unencumbered feeling . . . Equality can be attained only by the recreation of full Jewish nationaity, by the collective return of the Jews to the ranks of the nations as a people living in their own homeland. This will not be achieved by the efforts of others, but by self-help. The Jews must not look to others to emancipate them; they must strive for *auto*-emancipation.

Pinsker's solution is a territorial solution. He does not propose a Return. At one point he says plainly that it is not the Holy Land that the Jews need but *a* land. At another point he makes clear that he does not object to Erez-Israel; but nor does he believe it a suitable country for settlement . . . It is the fact of territory that is crucial.

Whereas earlier in the nineteenth century only a few individuals and groups of Jews had settled in Palestine, after the publication of *Auto-emancipation*, Pinsker became the leader of a movement known as 'Hibbat Zion' (Love of Zion), which encouraged Jews from Europe to settle in Erez-Israel. This movement is described by Vital as 'Proto-Zionism . . . a somewhat inchoate movement devoted to the resettlement of the Jews in Erez-Israel/Palestine . . . Institutionally it was weak. In character and ethos it was philanthropic rather than political.'

This first period of immigration lasted from 1882 to 1903. Accor-ding to **Noah Lucas** in his *Modern History of Israel,* it

resembled subsequent Zionist immigration in that it was a

minuscule trickle alongside the mass emigration to the west
prompted by the outbreak of pogroms and intensified
persecution of the Jews in Russia after 1882 . . . Most (of the
early immigrants who actually reached Palestine) were of the
middle class with substantial property which enabled many of
them to acquire land and develop citrus plantations and
vineyards. In the event the majority settled in the cities,
especially Jerusalem where their livelihood was at best
precarious . . . The Zionism of these settlers was construed in
terms of personal emancipation rather than a clear vision of
national redemption, and their efforts contributed little to the
regeneration of Jewish national life in Palestine. By the end of
the century their settlements had degenerated into effete
charitable foundations.

Lucas also describes the way in which the movement Hibbat Zion
was influenced by Ahad Ha'Am, (Asher Ginsberg), one of its most
outstanding leaders:

The settlement attempt in Palestine, although it was small in
scale, did accustom the Jews of eastern Europe to consider
immigration to Palestine as a possible concrete solution for
their immediate plight. On the other hand the failures of the
immigrants provoked scepticism about the efficacy of
'practical' Zionism (as the settlement effort was dubbed) and
led to vigorous debate among Zionist writers and followers as to
the proper strategy for the national movement. The first
influential criticism of the Lovers of Zion and the early settlers
came from the pen of Ahad Ha'Am (1856—1927), himself a
Russian leader of the movement and possibly the most acute
thinker of Zionism.

In his essay *This Is Not The Way*, published in 1889, Ahad
Ha'Am presented the kernel of what became with subsequent
elaboration a sophisticated doctrine of Zionism, advocated by a
critical school of thought within the mainstream of the
movement. Ahad Ha'Am suggested in his essay that the
approach of the Lovers of Zion with the haphazard settlement
activities it sponsored was bound to fail so long as it appealed to
self interest and the desire for personal emancipation rather
than to the inspiring vision of national regeneration with its
cultural potentiality. The development of the national
movement required the reinvigoration of Jewish education in
the diaspora for the revivial of Jewish spiritual unity and
creativity. Settlement in Palestine was of crucial importance
because it would eventually establish a centre of leadership for

such creativity but not if cultural quality was subordinated to quantity.

This was the basic line of argument of 'spiritual' or 'cultural' Zionism: it selected the crisis of Judaism rather than that of the Jews as the core issue.

Q How did Zionism become a political movement?

The person who drew together the many different strands of Zionism and made them into a coherent political movement was **Theodor Herzl** (1860—1904), a Hungarian Jew, who was born and brought up in Budapest. At the age of 18 he moved with his parents to Vienna, where he studied law. After finding that because he was a Jew he couldn't practise law, he became a civil servant. He soon started to write, and when he moved to Paris in 1891, became a correspondent for a newspaper in Vienna. In 1894 he reported in detail the trial of Alfred Dreyfus, the French Jew who was condemned on the basis of false evidence, and this experience made him painfully aware of the problem of anti-Semitism.

In his first book, *The Jewish State, An Attempt at a Modern Solution to the Jewish Question*, written immediately after the Dreyfus affair and published in 1896, he attempted to outline a purely political solution to the problems facing Jewish communities in Europe. This was his analysis of the Jewish question:

> The Jewish question exists wherever Jews live in perceptible numbers. Where it does not exist, it is carried by Jews in the course of their migrations . . . This is the case in every country, and will remain so, even in those highly civilized – for instance France – until the Jewish question finds a solution on a political basis. The unfortunate Jews are now carrying the seeds of anti-semitism into England; they have already introduced it into America . . .
>
> We are one people – our enemies have made us one in our respite, as repeatedly happens in history. Distress binds us together, and, thus united, we suddenly discover our strength. Yes, we are strong enough to form a State, and, indeed a model State. We possess all human and material resources necessary for the purpose . . .

He proposed that Jews should create their own state as a way of solving these problems:

> Let the sovereignty be granted us over a portion of the globe large enough to satisfy the rightful requirements of a nation; the

rest we shall manage for ourselves.

The creation of a new State is neither ridiculous nor impossible. We have in our day witnessed the process in connection with nations which were not in the bulk middle class, but poorer, less educated, and consequently weaker than ourselves. The Governments of all countries scourged by anti-semitism will be keenly interested in assisting us to obtain the sovereignty we want.

He described how organizations such as The Jewish Society could be set up to work towards the creation of the Jewish state:

Should the Powers declare themselves willing to admit our sovereignty over a neutral piece of land, then the Society will enter into negotiations for the possession of this land. Here two territories come under consideration, Palestine and Argentina. In both countries important experiments in colonization have been made, though on the mistaken principle of a gradual infiltration of Jews. An infiltration is bound to end badly. It continues till the inevitable moment when the native population feels itself threatened, and forces the Government to stop a further influx of Jews. Immigration is consequently futile unless based on an assured supremacy.

The Society of Jews will treat with the present masters of the land, putting itself under the protectorate of the European Powers, if they prove friendly to the plan. We could offer the present possessors of the land enormous advantages, take upon ourselves part of the public debt, build new roads for traffic, which our presence in the country would render necessary, and do many other things. The creation of our State would be beneficial to adjacent countries, because the cultivation of a strip of land increases the value of its surrounding districts in innumerable ways.

He then discussed the relative merits of Argentina and Palestine – two countries which had been suggested as possible locations for a Jewish homeland:

Shall we choose Palestine or Argentina? We shall take what is given us, and what is selected by Jewish public opinion. The Society will determine both these points.

Argentina is one of the most fertile countries in the world, extends over a vast area, has a sparse population and a mild climate. The Argentine Republic would derive considerable profit from the cession of a portion of its territory to us. The present infiltration of Jews has certainly produced some discontent, and it would be necessary to enlighten the Republic on the intrinsic difference of our new movement.

Palestine is our ever-memorable historic home. The very name of Palestine would attract our people with a force of marvellous potency. Supposing His Majesty the Sultan were to give us Palestine, we could in return undertake to regulate the whole finances of Turkey. We should there form a portion of the rampart of Europe against Asia, an outpost of civilization as opposed to barbarism. We should as a neutral State remain in contact with all Europe, which would have to guarantee our existence. The sanctuaries of Christendom would be safeguarded by assigning to them an extra-territorial status such as is well known to the law of nations. We should form a guard of honour about these sanctuaries, answering for the fulfilment of this duty with our existence. This guard of honour would be the great symbol of the solution of the Jewish Question after eighteen centuries of Jewish suffering.

Because of the enthusiastic response to his book, Herzl organized a Zionist Congress in Basle in August 1897. It is hard to over-estimate the significance of this congress, which was attended by 200 Jews from all over Europe, and was the very first gathering of its kind. The Congress formally adopted The Basle Programme, which stated:

Zionism strives for the establishment of a publicly and legally secured home in Palestine for the Jewish people.

For the attainment of this aim the Congress considers the following means:

1. The appropriate promotion of colonization with Jewish agriculturalists, artisans and tradesmen.

2. The organization and gathering of all Jews through suitable local and general institutions, according to the laws of the various countries.

3. The promotion of Jewish national feeling and consciousness.

4. Preparatory steps for the attainment of such Government consent as is necessary in order to achieve the aim of Zionism.

This is how **Ahad Ha'Am** summed up the significance of the Congress:

For three days, from morning to evening, some two hundred Jews from all countries and of all tendencies had debated in the open and before all the nations the matter of the foundation of a secure home for the Jewish people in the land of their fathers.

Thus the *national* answer had burst the bounds of 'modesty' and been made public. It had been expounded to all the world aloud, in clear language, and with a straight back – something which had not occured since Israel was exiled from the land.

David Vital explains why the Congress was so crucial for the Zionist movement:

> Zionism re-created the Jews as a political nation; and by so doing it revolutionized their collective and private lives. It did not do so immediately or completely or equally . . . It seems beyond question that this movement for revival and radical change in Jewry did attain results which may fairly be called revolutionary and, further, that its definitive form dates from 1897. For that reason alone the First Zionist Congress must now be judged one of the pivotal events in the modern history of the Jews.
>
> [The Congress] established a precedent – and the principle – of unity, bringing together virtually all the diverse strains of which the movement was composed: romanticists and pragmatists, orthodox and secularists, socialists and bourgeois, easterners and westerners, men whose minds and language were barely influenced by the non-Jewish world and those who were largely products of it, and, above all, those whose primary concern was with the condition of the Jews as opposed to those, like Ahad Ha'Am, whose eyes were on the crisis of Judaism.

The key to Herzl's influence lay in his great organizing ability and his belief that he could use the great powers to assist Jewish settlement in Palestine. He brought to the Zionist movement a drive and a confidence which the Lovers of Zion and the eastern European Jews didn't have at that time. In his own diary he summed up what he believed he had achieved at this first Zionist Congress:

> Were I to sum up the Basle Congress in a word – which I shall guard against pronouncing publicly – it would be this: at Basle I founded the Jewish State . . . If I said this out loud today, I would be answered by universal laughter. Perhaps in five years and certainly in fifty everyone will know it.

Like most of the other leaders of the Zionist movement in his time he seemed to be more concerned about the problems of the Jews in Europe than about the possible consequences of his dreams for the people who were living in Palestine. In his diary he explained how he thought the Jewish immigrants would have to treat the Arabs:

> We shall have to spirit the penniless population across the

border by procuring employment for it in the transit countries, while denying it any employment in our own country. . . Both the process of expropriation and the removal of the poor must be carried out discreetly and circumspectly.

The second great leader of the Zionist movement was **Chaim Weizmann**, a Russian Jew, who came to settle in England in 1904. After teaching chemistry at the University of Manchester for several years, he moved to London in 1916 and began working in the Admiralty under the supervision of Lord Balfour. During this time he did a great deal to explain and commend the idea of a Jewish national homeland to officials in the British government, and he was therefore one of the main architects of the Balfour Declaration (see section 2·5).

Some months *before* the Balfour Declaration, Weizmann wrote these words about his hopes for the gradual creation of a Jewish homeland in Palestine:

> States must be built up slowly, gradually, systematically and patiently. We, therefore, say that while the creation of a Jewish Commonwealth in Palestine is our final ideal . . . the way to achieve it lies through a series of intermediary stages. And one of those intermediary stages, which I hope is going to come about as a result of the war, is that the fair country of Palestine will be protected by such a mighty and just Power as Great Britain. Under the wing of this Power, Jews will be able to develop, and to set up the administrative machinery which . . . would enable us to carry out the Zionist scheme.

In his autobiography he later explained how he thought of the Balfour Declaration merely as 'a framework' within which Jews could achieve their ultimate goals in Palestine:

> The Balfour Declaration was no more than a framework, which had to be filled in by our own efforts. It would mean exactly what we would make it mean – neither more nor less. On what we could make it mean through slow, costly and laborious work would depend whether and when we should deserve to attain statehood.

In an address to a Jewish audience in London two years after the issue of the Declaration, he said:

> I trust to God that a Jewish state will come about; but it will come about not through political declarations, but by the sweat and blood of the Jewish people . . . [The Balfour Declaration] is the golden key which unlocks the doors of Palestine and gives

you the possibility to put all your efforts into the country . . .
We were asked to formulate our wishes. We said we desired to
create in Palestine such conditions, political, economic and
administrative, that as the country is developed, we can pour in
a considerable number of immigrants, and finally establish such
a society in Palestine that Palestine shall be as Jewish as
England is English, or America is American . . . I hope that the
Jewish frontiers of Palestine will be as great as Jewish energy
for getting Palestine.

On many occasions of this kind he gave assurances that the Zionists
would do nothing to harm the Arabs in Palestine:

All fears expressed openly or secretly by the Arabs that they are
to be ousted from their present position are due either to a
fundamental misconception of Zionist aims or to the malicious
activities of our common enemies.

I need hardly say that we Jews will be meticulously and
scrupulously careful to respect the sentiments of any religious
group or sect in Palestine.

The Zionists are not demanding in Palestine monopolies or
exclusive privileges . . . It always was and remains a cardinal
principle of Zionism as a democratic movement that all races
and sects in Palestine should enjoy full justice and liberty.

Palestine must be built up without violating the legitimate rights
of the Arabs – not a hair of their heads shall be touched.

It is not our objective to seize control of the higher policy of the
province of Palestine. Nor has it ever been our objective to turn
anyone out of his property.

Sir Charles Webster, a British diplomat who knew Weizmann well
during these years, has described his impressions of his brilliant
diplomacy in promoting the Zionist programme:

With unerring skill he adapted his arguments to the special
circumstances of each statesman. To the British and Americans
he could use biblical language and awake a deep emotional
undertone; to other nationalities he more often talked in terms
of interest. Mr Lloyd George was told that Palestine was a little
mountainous country not unlike Wales; with Lord Balfour the
philosophical background of Zionism could be surveyed. For
Lord Cecil the problem was placed in the setting of a new
world organization; while to Lord Milner the extension of

imperial power could be vividly portrayed. To me, who dealt with these matters as a junior officer of the General Staff, he brought from many sources all the evidence that could be obtained of the importance of a Jewish National Home to the strategical position of the British Empire, but he always indicated by a hundred shades and inflections of the voice that he believed that I could also appreciate better than my superiors other more subtle and recondite arguments.

This skilful presentation of facts would, however, have been useless unless he had convinced all with whom he came into contact of the probity of his conduct and the reality of his trust in the will and strength of Britain.

2·3 Jewish Settlement in the Land

Q How did the Jewish settlers acquire land?

David Hirst, an English journalist who has been the Middle East correspondent of *The Guardian* for many years, describes how land was sold to Jews in the period before 1929 in his book *The Gun and the Olive Branch*:

The great bulk of the land that the Zionists acquired came from large, predominantly absentee, landowners. As resistance built up, the area relinquished by small farmers, 42.7 per cent of the total from 1891 to 1900, fell to a mere 4.3 per cent from 1900 to 1914.

The name Sursock occupies an invidious and recurrent place in this story. The Sursocks were a Levantine family of high breeding and immense wealth who spent much of their time in Western Europe. They also owned some of the richest land in Palestine. In a series of transactions from 1891 to 1920 they sold it all to the Zionists, as unmoved by high appeals to their sense of Arab history as by workaday calls on their conscience. In 1910 they sold the region of Foule, with its Crusader castle made famous by Saladin, in the fertile Vale of Esdraelon; in 1920 they disposed of the rest of their holdings, along with 8,000 peasants in twenty-two villages who made a living from them. They had acquired the whole area in 1872 from corrupt Ottoman officials for the derisory sum of £18,000 to £20,000. It brought in a revenue of £12,000 to £40,000 a year. They sold it for ten times the price they had paid for it, but subsequently complained bitterly that they had let it go so cheap – as indeed they had. The fate of the 8,000 peasants was never determined; the tenants among them – but not the labourers – received 'compensation' of £28,000 – precisely £3.5 per head for the lot. The Sursock sale was a famous and much-deplored transaction. But there were many others.

He goes on to explain why the Arabs had only themselves to blame for the ways in which land was sold to Jews after 1929:

Although there have been many and often fortuitous circumstances to which the Zionists owe their astonishing success, by no means the least have been the incompetence and irresponsibility of the Arab leaders, the frivolity and egoism of the privileged classes. The frailties which the Haifa newspaper *Carmel* had first denounced a quarter of a century earlier were all the greater now. About nine-tenths of all land acquired by the Jews up to 1929 was sold by absentee landlords. But after that, the ever-growing 'Zionist peril' notwithstanding, the main culprits were resident landlords. It was at this time, too, that Arab usurers came most offensively into their own; smallholders were forced to borrow at interest rates of up to 50 per cent; they would cling desperately to their little plots of land, but in the end, under a crushing burden of debt, were forced to abandon them to the land-hungry Jews. There were mouth-watering profits to be made; the price of a dunum near Rishon-le-Zion, originally eight shillings, had reached £10 to £25 by the early thirties. Officially, of course, the willing squanderers of the Arab heritage were becoming the pariahs of society. They were ritually condemned on every suitable occasion – at conferences convened to consider the 'Zionist peril', in the campaign statements of rival political parties, in the anathemas issued by religious authorities. Thus in 1932, the Independence Party issued a proclamation declaring that 'there is no future for the nation unless the gates are closed on immigration, and the sale of land prohibited; the delegates reaffirm their dissatisfaction at the middle-men and the landsellers, and consider that the time has come to punish and oppose them . . .' In Palestinian vocabulary *simsar* – 'middle-man' – has established itself ever since as a word of abuse. In 1935, when immigration and land sales were surpassing all limits, Haj Amin Husseini, the Mufti, assembled some 400 men of God, imams, qadis, muftis, preachers and teachers, who issued a *fatwa*, or religious edict, outlawing the sale of land to Jewish immigrants and denouncing its perpetrators as apostates to be denied burial in Moslem cemeteries.

These land sales revealed fatal weaknesses within the Arab community:

> However – and here is the real measure of the Palestinian
> leadership – although the landsellers and agents might suffer all
> manner of verbal abuse, they rarely suffered much worse.
> Landselling, branded as 'treason', was a characteristic
> accusation which one faction of notables hurled at another. It
> made for an immense hypocrisy. There was no real social
> ostracism, let alone any condign punishment. The very people
> who most vociferously condemned the practice were not
> infrequently the ones who most indulged in it. In 1928, the
> delegates to the Seventh Palestine Congress were described by
> a contemporary as a very odd assortment who included 'spies
> and middlemen selling land to the Jews'. In 1932, the
> newspaper *al-Arab* found it strange indeed that the Arab
> Executive should wax so indignant about the sale of Arab land
> when some of its own members were doing the selling. No
> wonder a British fact-finding team's efforts to uncover the full
> extent of these odious transactions met with resistance from the
> Arab as well as the Jewish leadership. If, by 1948, the
> landsellers had only allowed some 6.6 per cent of physical
> Palestine to fall into Jewish hands – though that represented a
> much higher proportion of its cultivable area – the damage they
> inflicted on the Palestinian psyche is less easy to calculate. But
> it was undoubtedly great. The landsellers typified the
> Palestinians' response to Zionism at its most self-destructive.
> They were the most unhealthy part of a body politic so diseased
> that, instead of achieving that self-renewal which, under strain,
> an even slightly healthier one might have achieved, it
> degenerated still further. It did not immunize itself against the
> sickness which the landsellers represented; it let the sickness
> spread. The disloyalty of a few, rather than fortifying the
> constructive patriotism of the majority, aggravated the
> factionalism, recrimination and mistrust which poisoned the
> whole Palestinian struggle, and the behaviour of the politicians
> in particular.

Q What was the official Jewish policy regarding settlement in the land and the establishment of a Jewish state?

David Ben-Gurion, who became the first Prime Minister of Israel in 1948, explained:

> The Debate has not been for or against the indivisibility of the

Land of Israel. The Debate concerned which of the two routes would lead quicker to the common goal.

He summed up the goals of the Zionist movement in the introduction to *The History of the Haganah*:

At the present time we speak of colonization, and only of colonization. It is our short-term objective. But it is clear that England belongs to the English, Egypt to the Egyptians and Judea to the Jews. In our country there is room only for Jews. We will say to the Arabs: 'Move over'; if they are not in agreement, if they resist, we will push them by force.

Joseph Weitz, a Jewish government official responsible for Jewish colonization, wrote the following words in 1940:

. . . after the [Second World] war the question of the land of Israel and the question of the Jews would be raised beyond the framework of 'development' amongst ourselves. It must be clear that there is no room for both peoples in this country. No 'development' will bring us closer to our aim, to be an independent people in this small country. If the Arabs leave the country, it will be broad and wide-open for us. And if the Arabs stay, the country will remain narrow and miserable. When the War is over and the English have won, and when the judges sit on the throne of Law, our people must bring their petitions and their claim before them; and the only solution is Eretz Israel, or at least Western Eretz Israel, without Arabs. There is no room for compromise on this point! The Zionist enterprise so far, in terms of preparing the ground and paving the way for the creation of the Hebrew State in the land of Israel, has been fine and good in its own time, and could do with 'land-buying' – but this will not bring about the State of Israel; that must come all at once, in the manner of a Salvation (this is the secret of the Messianic idea); and there is no way besides transferring the Arabs from here to neighbouring countries, to transfer them all; except maybe for Bethlehem, Nazareth and Old Jerusalem, we must not leave a single village, not a single tribe. And the transfer must be directed to Iraq, to Syria, and even to Transjordan. For that purpose we'll find money, and a lot of money. And only with such a transfer will the country be able to absorb millions of our brothers, and the Jewish question shall be solved, once and for all. There is no other way out.

Moshe Dayan, a hero in the wars of 1948 and 1956, who later served as Minister of Foreign Affairs in the Israeli government, described in

1967 how the state needs to be expanding continually for the sake of its own security:

> People abroad ought to realise that, quite apart from their strategic importance to Israel, Sinai, the Golan Heights, the Tiran Straits and the hills west of the Jordan lie at the heart of Jewish history. Nor has the 'restoration of historical Israel' ended yet. Since the return to Zion a hundred years ago a double process of colonization and expansion of frontiers has been going on. We have not yet reached the end of that road. It is the people of Israel who will determine the frontiers of their own state.

2·4 Arab Reactions to Jewish Settlement

Q How did the Arabs react to Jewish settlement?

Najib Azuri, writing in 1905, reveals how he, as a Palestinian Arab, understood the goal of the Jewish settlers in Palestine at that time:

> The Jews of our time have understood very well the mistake made by their forefathers. They are trying carefully to avoid it in the restoration of what they call their ancient fatherland. They want to get hold of a part of Palestine which their forefathers were never able to occupy, and in particular to take possession of all the natural boundaries of the country. These are two of the most important points in the Zionist plan of action.
>
> They regard as these natural boundaries Mount Hermon in the north, the source of the Jordan, and the Leontes valley, with the territory which lies between Rasyaya and Sidon; in the south the Suez Canal and the Sinai peninsula; in the east the Arabian desert, and as a western frontier the Mediterranean. With these frontiers, and in the hands of a people that can defend them, Palestine would be impregnable.

Asher Ginsberg (known as Ahad Ha'Am, 1856—1927) was a Russian Jew who visited Palestine many times from 1891 onwards. He finally settled there in 1922 and died in 1927. After a visit to Palestine in 1891 he recorded some of the problems which the Jewish settlers in Palestine were facing and some of the problems which they were creating:

> Palestine is not an uninhabited country and can offer a home

only to a very small proportion of the Jews who live scattered throughout the world. Those who settle in Palestine must above all seek to win the friendship of the Palestinians, by approaching them courteously and with respect. But what do our brothers in Palestine do? Precisely the opposite. They were slaves in the land of their exile, and suddenly they find themselves with unlimited freedom, an unbridled freedom of the kind that can be found only in Turkey. This sudden change has aroused in them a tendency to despotism, which is what always happens when slaves come to power. They treat the Arabs with hostility and cruelty, rob them of their rights in a dishonest way, hurt them without reason and then pride themselves on such actions; and no one attacks this despicable and dangerous tendency . . .

We abroad have a way of thinking that Palestine today is almost desert, an uncultivated wilderness, and that anyone who wishes to buy land there can do so to his heart's content. But this is not in fact the case. It is difficult to find any uncultivated land anywhere in the country . . . We abroad have a way of thinking that the Arabs are all savages, on a level with the animals, and blind to what goes on around them. But that is quite mistaken. The Arabs, especially the townsmen, see through our activities in their country, and our aims, but they keep silent and make no sign, because for the present they anticipate no danger to their own future from what we are about. But if the time should ever come when our people have so far developed their life in Palestine that the indigenous population should feel more or less cramped, then they will not readily make way for us.

In 1911 he wrote to a friend in Jaffa:

As to the war against the Jews in Palestine, I was a spectator from afar with an aching heart, particularly because of the want of insight and understanding shown on our part to an extreme degree. As a matter of fact, it was evident twenty years ago, that the day would come when the Arabs would stand up against us.

The **Emir Faisal**, son of Sherif Hussein of Mecca, and **Chaim Weizmann** met in January 1919, and signed an agreement in which they pledged their good faith in 'carrying into effect the British Government's Declaration of the 2nd of November, 1917' (i.e. the Balfour Declaration). This document shows the willingness of a prominent Arab leader at the time to allow Jews to settle in Palestine:

All necessary measures shall be taken to encourage and

stimulate immigration of Jews into Palestine on a large scale,
and as quickly as possible to settle Jewish immigrants upon the
land through close settlement and intensive cultivation of the
soil. In taking such measures the Arab peasant and tenant
farmers shall be protected in their rights, and shall be assisted in
forwarding their economic development.

After signing the agreement, however, Faisal added a proviso in his
own handwriting in Arabic to qualify his position:

Provided the Arabs obtain their independence as demanded in
my Memorandum dated the 4th February, 1919, to the Foreign
Office of the Government of Great Britain, I shall concur in the
above articles. But if the slightest modification of departure
were to be made I shall not be bound by a single word of the
present Agreement which shall be deemed void and of no
account or validity . . .

Three months later he expressed his fear of what would happen if
the Jews wanted to establish a state:

Let the unhappy Jews find refuge there . . . under a Moslem or
a Christian government . . . But if the Jews desire to establish a
state and obtain sovereign rights in the country, I foresee
serious dangers and conflicts between them and other races.

Some Zionist leaders expressed their understanding of the Arab
reaction to what the Jews were doing in Palestine.

Moshe Sharett, in speeches to the Mapai Political Committee in
1936:

There is no Arab in Palestine who is not harmed by Jewish
immigration; there is no Arab who does not feel himself part of
the Great Arab Nation which includes Iraq, the Hedjaz, and
Yemen. For him Palestine is an independent unit that had an
Arab face. That face is now changing. In his eyes Haifa was an
Arab town, and now it is Jewish. His reaction cannot but be
resistance.
    I am convinced that the Arabs genuinely fear Jewish growth
and domination. If this is not true, then all the years I studied
Arabic and have met with Arabs were in vain. And if I am
wrong on this fundamental question I am not fit to be here.

David Ben-Gurion, commenting on Arab terrorism in a speech to the
same committee in 1938:

I want to destroy first of all the illusion among our comrades that the [Arab] terror is a matter of a few gangs, financed from abroad . . . We are facing not terror but a war. It is a national war declared upon us by the Arabs. Terror is one of the means of war . . . This is an active resistance by the Palestinians to what they regard as a usurpation of their homeland by the Jews – that's why they fight. Behind the terrorists is a movement, which though primitive is not devoid of idealism and self-sacrifice . . .

In our political argument abroad, we minimize Arab opposition to us. But let us not ignore the truth among ourselves. I insist on the truth, not out of respect for scientific but political realities. The acknowledgement of this truth leads to inevitable and serious conclusions regarding our work in Palestine . . . let us not build on the hope the terrorist gangs will get tired. If some get tired, others will replace them. A people which fights against the usurpation of its land will not tire so easily . . . it is easier for them to continue the war and not get tired than it is for us . . . The Palestinian Arabs are not alone . . .

But the fighting is only one aspect of the conflict which is in essence a political one. And politically we are the aggressors and they defend themselves. Militarily, it is we who are on the defensive, who have the upper hand . . . but in the political sphere they are superior. The land, the villages, the mountains, the roads are in their hands. The country is theirs, because they inhabit it, whereas we want to come here and settle down, and in their view we want to take away from them their country, while we are still outside.

British officials in Palestine explained how they understood the Arab reaction:

Commander Hogarth sent the following report to the Foreign Office in 1918;

Weizmann's disclaimers of political aims are not credited, partly because associates of his at home and in Palestine have not always endorsed them . . . Anti-Jew feeling is as strong as – perhaps stronger than ever among all classes of Arabs . . .

Herbert Samuel, a British Jew, who was appointed in 1920 by the British government as High Commissioner for Palestine, wrote the following in a personal letter to Weizmann in 1921:

After a year in Palestine I have come to the conclusion that the importance of the Arab factor had been underestimated by the Zionist movement: unless there is very careful steering it is upon the Arab rock that the Zionist ship may be wrecked.

Gilbert Clayton, one of Weizmann's chief advisers among the British military, wrote the following in 1924:

> In general, a year in Palestine has made me regard the whole adventure with apprehension. We have become an alien and detested element into the very core of Islam, and the day may well come when we shall be faced with the alternative of holding it there by the sword or abandoning it to its fate; the Arabs are under-dogs for the moment but they will bide their time and wait.

Maxime Rodinson, writing in *Israel and the Arabs* (1982):

> The origin of the conflict lies in the settlement of a new population on a territory already occupied by a people unwilling to accept that settlement. This is as undeniable as it is obvious. The settlement may be justified in whole or in part; but it cannot be denied. Likewise the refusal of the indigenous population to accept it may be thought justifiable, or it may not.

2·5 The Role of Britain

Q What promises did Britain make to the Jews?

Britain's promises to the Jews were contained in the Balfour Declaration which was a letter written on 2 November 1917 by **Arthur Balfour**, the British Foreign Secretary, to Lord Rothschild, a prominent English Jew. Since Palestine at that time was still part of the Ottoman Empire, the British government had no authority to decide the future of the country, but hoped to be able to do so after the defeat of Turkey in World War I.

> Foreign Office
> November 2nd, 1917
>
> Dear Lord Rothschild,
> I have much pleasure in conveying to you, on behalf of His Majesty's Government, the following declaration of sympathy with Jewish Zionist aspirations which has been submitted to, and approved by the Cabinet:
>   'His Majesty's Government view with favour the establishment in Palestine of a national home for the Jewish people, and will use their best endeavours to facilitate the achievement of this object, it being clearly understood that nothing shall be done which may prejudice the civil and

religious rights of the existing non-Jewish communities in
Palestine, or the rights and political status enjoyed by Jews in
any other country.'

I should be grateful if you would bring this declaration to
the knowledge of the Zionist Federation.
Yours sincerely,

Arthur Balfour

In making this declaration the British government hoped to
encourage Jews both in America and in Russia to support the cause
of the Allies in the war against Germany. There was also the hope
that a Jewish homeland established in Palestine with the support of
Britain would protect the Suez Canal and thus safeguard British
interests in India and the East.

Another motive which prompted this letter was the desire to
avoid a large influx of Jewish refugees into Britain. Balfour had
expressed this desire several years earlier when he supported the
introduction of an Aliens Act, which was intended to restrict Jewish
immigration into Britain:

A state of things could easily be imagined in which it would not
be to the advantage of the civilization of the country that there
should be an immense body of persons who, however patriotic,
able and industrious, however much they threw themselves into
the national life, still, by their own action, remained a people
apart, and not merely held a religion differing from the vast
majority of their fellow-countrymen, but only intermarried
among themselves.

Arthur Koestler once described the Balfour Declaration as:

. . . a document in which one nation solemnly promises to a
second nation the country of a third nation.

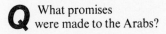 What promises
were made to the Arabs?

During World War I the British government made several promises
to Arab leaders in order to enlist their support in the war against the
Turks. Some of these promises were contained in letters written by
Sir Henry McMahon, the British High Commissioner in Egypt, to
Sherif Hussein of Mecca. The following are extracts from two of
these letters:

We hereby confirm to you the declaration of Lord Kitchener
. . . in which was manifested our desire for the independence of
the Arab countries and their inhabitants, and our readiness to

approve an Arab Caliphate upon its proclamation . . .

(dated 30 August 1915)

. . . I am authorised to give you the following pledges on behalf of the Government of Great Britain, and to reply as follows to your note:

(1) That, subject to the modifications stated above, Great Britain is prepared to recognise and uphold the independence of the Arabs in all the regions lying within the frontiers proposed by the Sharif of Mecca; [i.e. the area now corresponding to the Arabian Peninsular, Iraq, Syria, Lebanon, Jordan and Palestine].

(2) That Great Britain will guarantee the Holy Places against all external aggression, and will recognise the obligation of preserving them from aggression;

(3) That, when circumstances permit, Great Britain will help the Arabs with her advice and assist them in the establishment of governments to suit those diverse regions . . .

I am confident that this declaration will convince you, beyond all doubt, of Great Britain's sympathy with the aspirations of her friends the Arabs; and that it will result in a lasting and solid alliance with them, of which one of the immediate consequences will be the expulsion of the Turks from the Arab countries and the liberation of the Arab peoples from the Turkish yoke which has weighed on them all these long years.

(dated 24 October 1915)

The following Anglo-French Declaration, dated 7 November 1918, was publicized widely all over Palestine:

The goal envisaged by France and Great Britain in prosecuting in the East the War set in train by German ambition is the complete and final liberation of the peoples who have for so long been oppressed by the Turks, and the setting up of national governments and administrations that shall derive their authority from the free exercise of the initiative and choice of the indigenous populations.

In pursuit of those intentions, France and Great Britain agree to further and assist in the setting up of indigenous governments and administrations in Syria [i.e. Syria and Palestine] and Mesopotamia which have already been liberated by the Allies, as well as in those territories which they are endeavouring to liberate, and to recognise them as soon as they are actually set up.

Far from wishing to impose this or that system upon the populations of those regions, their [i.e. France's and Great Britain's] only concern is to offer such support and efficacious help as will ensure the smooth working of the governments and administrations which those populations will have elected of their own free will to have; to secure impartial and equal justice for all; to facilitate the economic development of the country by promoting and encouraging local initiative; to foster the spread of education; and to put an end to the dissensions which Turkish policy has for so long exploited. Such is the task which the two Allied Powers wish to undertake in the liberated territories.

Q How could the promises made to the Jews and the Arabs be reconciled?

Sir Edward Grey, who had been the British Foreign Secretary from 1905 to 1916, admitted the inconsistency between the promises made to the Jews and the Arabs in a speech to the House of Lords in March 1923:

A considerable number of these engagements, or some of them, which have not been officially made public by the Government, have become public through other sources. Whether all have become public I do not know, but I seriously suggest to the Government that the best way of clearing our honour in this matter is officially to publish the whole of the engagements relating to the matter, which we entered into during the war. If they are found to be not inconsistent with one another our honour is cleared. If they turn out to be inconsistent, I think it will be very much better that the amount, character and extent of the inconsistencies should be known, and that we should state frankly that, in the urgency of the war, engagements were entered into which were not entirely consistent with each other.

I am sure that we cannot redeem our honour by covering up our engagements and pretending that there is no inconsistency, if there really is inconsistency. I am sure that the most honourable course will be to let it be known what the engagements are, and, if there is inconsistency, then to admit it frankly, and, admitting that fact, and having enabled people to judge exactly what is the amount of the inconsistency, to consider what is the most fair and honourable way out of the impasse into which the engagements may have led us. Without comparing one engagement with another, I think that we are placed in considerable difficulty by the Balfour Declaration itself. I have not the actual words here, but I think the noble Duke opposite will not find fault with my summary of it. It promised a Zionist home without prejudice to the civil and religious rights of the population of Palestine. A Zionist home, my Lords, undoubtedly means or implies a Zionist Government over the district in which the home is placed, and if 93 per cent of the population of Palestine are Arabs, I do not see how you can establish other than an Arab Government, without prejudice to their civil rights. That one sentence alone of the Balfour Declaration seems to me to involve, without over-stating the case, very great difficulty of fulfilment . . .

Q How did Britain attempt to carry out these promises?

In a secret memorandum submitted to the British cabinet in 1919, **Lord Balfour** made it very clear that the British government had no intention of applying the principle of self-determination and allowing the Arabs in Palestine to decide their own future:

Do we mean, in the case of Syria, to consult principally the wishes of the inhabitants? We mean nothing of the kind . . . The contradiction between the letter of the Covenant and the policy of the Allies is even more flagrant in the case of the 'independent nation' of Palestine than in that of the 'independent nation' of Syria. For in Palestine we do not propose even to go through the form of consulting the wishes of the present inhabitants of the country . . . The Four Great Powers are committed to Zionism. And Zionism, be it right or wrong, good or bad, is rooted in age-long traditions, in present needs, in future hopes, of far profounder import than the desires and prejudices of the 700,000 Arabs who now inhabit that ancient land . . . In short, so far as Palestine is concerned, the Powers have made no statement of fact which is not admittedly wrong, and no declaration of policy which, at least in the letter, they have not always intended to violate.

He made the same admission in a letter to Lloyd George:

The weak point of our position is of course that in the case of Palestine we deliberately and rightly decline to accept the principle of self-determination.

Erskine Childers, an English journalist and writer, has described the frame of mind in which **Lloyd George**, then the British Prime Minister, approached the question of Palestine at the Peace Conference in Versailles in 1919 following the defeat of Germany and its ally, Turkey, in World War I. His main concern was to do all he could to implement the Balfour Declaration:

> Lloyd George, without whose personal support the Balfour Declaration certainly could never have been obtained, was almost lyrical in his Welsh scriptural romanticism about Zionism. We know from documents that he had it fixed in his mind that he was being given the chance to recreate the Holy Land of the scriptures, as he constantly put it, 'from Dan to Beersheba'. And if I may digress into greater detail for a moment, it is only because I think that what this led to provides both a fascinating and perhaps tormenting glimpse of the way in which our Western notions and emotions, played out in the hands of men wielding total military supremacy, have so gravely injured Arabs.
>
> In the first place, Foreign Office experts in London tried to explain very tactfully to the Prime Minister that there simply was no such place as Dan on any twentieth-century map of Palestine. It did not matter. It is a fact of documentary record that Lloyd George went to the Peace conference at Versailles determined to draw upon the Palestine of 1919, political boundaries for a new Hebrew State 'from Dan to Beersheba'. It is a fact of documentary record that the Zionists themselves were placed in an extremely delicate situation over this: because they in fact wanted very much more territory than from Dan to Beersheba – they also wanted most of the Sinai Peninsula, all of Transjordan, the whole southern portion of what is today Lebanon, and all south-westerm Syria almost to the edge of Damascus. Yet the Prime Minister on whose enthusiasm they so counted kept on saying 'Dan to Beersheba', like a kind of ritual incantation . . .
>
> I believe that I can state with a degree of absolute, mathematical certainty, that no other indigenous people in this century has been disposed of by European Powers and a European settler movement on the basis of a map reputedly showing the area of a tribal kingdom that had briefly existed there three thousand years earlier. To come upon these facts in the sober archives of twentieth-century government is to have one's brain reel and – in my case at least – to be filled with a sense of shame.

In the end, therefore, British and French promises to the Arabs were totally disregarded, and the Versailles Peace Conference gave Britain the Mandate for Palestine, and France the Mandate for Syria.

2·6 The UN Partition Plan (1947)

Q How did the UN come to
accept this plan?
What was the background?

David Hirst describes some of the diplomacy which prepared the
way for the acceptance of the Partition Plan:

> The United Nations, to which a despairing Britain had handed
> over the whole problem, ruled in favour of partition. That vote
> was a story of violence in itself – albeit diplomatic violence – in
> which the United States went to the most extraordinary lengths
> of backstage manipulation on behalf of its Zionist protégés.
> Partition went against the better judgment of many of those
> nations which cast their vote in favour of it. America too – at
> least its State Department officials who knew something about
> the Middle East – had grave misgivings. But the White House,
> which knew a good deal less, overruled them. It sanctioned
> what a deeply distressed James Forrestal, the Secretary of
> Defense, described as 'coercion and duress on other nations'
> which 'bordered on scandal'. President Truman warned one of
> his secretaries that he would demand a full explanation if
> nations which normally lined up with the United States failed to
> do so on Palestine. Governments which opposed partition,
> governments which could not make up their minds, were
> swayed by the most unorthodox arguments. The Firestone Tyre
> and Rubber Company, with plantations in Liberia, brought
> pressure to bear on the Liberian Government. It was hinted to
> Latin American delegates that their vote for partition would
> greatly increase the chances of a pan-American road project.
> The Philippines, at first passionately opposed to partition,
> ended up ignominiously in favour of it: they had too much at
> stake in seven bills awaiting the approval of Congress.
> Important Americans were persuaded to 'talk' to various
> governments which could not afford the loss of American good
> will.

President Truman had earlier admitted that he was under strong
pressure from Jewish voters in the USA. In an address to American
ambassadors to Arab countries in 1945 he said:

> I am sorry, gentlemen, but I have to answer to hundreds of
> thousands who are anxious for the success of Zionism; I do not
> have hundreds of thousands of Arabs among my constituents.

In his memoirs he speaks of the intense pressure put on him in 1947 by Zionists who wanted the USA to support the resolution recommending the establishment of the State of Israel:

> The facts were that not only were there pressure movements around the United Nations unlike anything that had been seen there before but that the White House, too, was subject to a constant barrage. I do not think that I ever had so much pressure and propaganda aimed at the White House as I had in this instance. The persistance of a few of the extreme Zionist leaders – actuated by political motives and engaging in political threats – disturbed and annoyed me. Some were even suggesting that we pressure sovereign nations into favourable votes in the General Assembly.

Q What did the Jews and the Arabs think of the plan?

David Hirst sums up Jewish and Arab reactions:

> For the Zionists the Partition Plan ranked, as a charter of legitimacy, with the Balfour Declaration which, in their view, it superseded and fulfilled. Certainly, it was a no less partisan document. Palestine comprises some 10,000 square miles. Of this, the Arabs were to retain 4,300 square miles while the Jews, who represented one-third of the population and owned some 6 per cent of the land, were allotted 5,700 square miles. The Jews also got the better land; they were to have the fertile coastal belt while the Arabs were to make do, for the most part, with the hills. Yet it was not the size of the area allotted to the Jews which pleased them – indeed, they regarded it as the 'irreducible minimum' which they could accept – it was rather the fact of statehood itself. Conversely it was not merely the size of the area they were to lose, it was the loss of land, sovereignty and an antique heritage that angered the Arabs. The Partition Plan legitimized what had been, on any but the most partisan interpretation of the Balfour Declaration and the Mandate, illegitimately acquired. The past was, as it were, wiped out. Overnight, the comity of nations solemnly laid the foundations of a new moral order by which the Jews, the great majority of whom had been in Palestine less than thirty years, were deemed to have claims equal, indeed superior, to those of the Arabs who had lived there from time immemorial.

Maxime Rodinson, a French Jew, who is a Professor of Old Ethiopic and Old South Arabian languages at the Sorbonne in Paris, explains how the UN Partition Plan was received by the Arab states:

For the Arab masses, the acceptance of the UN resolutions meant an unconditional surrender to a European *Diktat*, of the same kind as the capitulation of black or yellow kings in the nineteenth century to the gunboats which had fired shots on their palaces.

European countries had supported colonists with the intention of gaining control of part of the national territory. During the period when the native population could have forced out these colonists easily enough, they had been prevented from reacting by the British police and the British army, who had received their mandate from the nations of Europe and America. Their reaction was also morally hamstrung by the fallacious assurance that what was going on was no more than the peaceful settlement of a number of unfortunate people with no evil intentions, who in any case would remain in the minority.

When the real concerns of the colonists became known publicly and when it became evident how they had gradually developed collective strength under the protection of the mandate, the European and American world wanted to force the Arabs to accept the *fait accompli* (for all their internal differences, all following the same line, from the socialist Soviet Union to the ultra-capitalist USA).

For the Arabs, the aftermath of the Second World War was a bitter repetition of the deception of the First. Once again, people had made all kinds of promises to them in order to secure their collaboration or at least their neutrality. But after the war was won, the promises were broken by a malevolent confederacy of Europeans, agreed in their rich nations' complicity against the people that had had confidence in them.

Did not the 1922 mandate stipulate that 'there should be no infringement of the rights and the position of other parts of the population' (euphemistically called non-Jews)? Had not the America Presidents Roosevelt and Truman promised Ibn Saud, in their letters of 5 April 1945 and 28 October 1946, that they would not make any decision about Palestine without full consultation with the Arabs and the Jews, and that nothing would be resolved which went against Arab interests?

All these promises were now broken. There was not an Arab who could openly contradict the statement made by the Arab High Committee: 'Any attempt by the Jews or any other group of powers to set up a Jewish state on Arab territory is an act of oppression which will be met with force on grounds of justified self-defence.'

Q How are we to explain the role played by the great powers in the passing of the Partition Plan?

The British Council of Churches Report entitled *Towards Understanding the Arab-Israeli Conflict* explains how the holocaust influenced world opinion:

> The most significant and terrible action by an outside power which contributed to the establishing of the State of Israel (and consequently the Arab-Israeli conflict) was the Holocaust in Europe. It was the experience of persecution in Europe, culminating in the Nazi attack on the Jews, which gave the longings for a state practical form. Persecution amounting to threatened genocide motivated the Jews to make a life or death attempt to create a state of their own. The European Holocaust precipitated an irresistible surge of world opinion and support and put what the major powers of the day (though not the Arabs) regarded as an undeniable authority behind the claim to the land.
>
> The Yad Vashem museum, memorial to the victims of the Holocaust, reminds all who visit it of the dreadful details. 'Yad Vashem' is a quotation from Isaiah 56, verse 5; it means a 'place – or a memorial – and a name' and it commemorates those millions of victims who in death by gas, or bullet or hanging had neither memorial nor name. Its grim stone, monochrome photographs and shelves full of the books which record the names of the dead, still being added to as more details become known, leave one aware of how once Europe treated its Jews, and of their determination never to leave their fate to others again.

Edward W. Said, a Palestinian who is Professor of Comparative Literature at the University of Columbia in the USA, sums up the role of the great powers in the fulfilment of the vision of Zionism in the following words:

> For indeed it was the world that made the success of Zionism possible, and it was Zionism's sense of the world as supporter and audience that played a considerable practical role in the struggle for Palestine.

The Quaker Report *Search for Peace in the Middle East* points out how the Palestinian Arabs feel that *they* have had to suffer for the sins of the great powers of the 'Christian West':

> How many of the Jews who went to Palestine in the 1930s and 1940s would have migrated to some other country if they had been given encouragement cannot be known. In any case, the Christian West was able to escape in large measure from its accumulated centuries of anti-Semitic guilt, by co-operating with the dedicated Zionist' leadership in helping displaced Jews find refuge in a predominantly Arab land.
>
> At the time the UN partition plan was adopted, the Jewish third of the population of Palestine owned about six per cent of the land. The Arab two-thirds of the population owned about a third of the land, and felt they had good claim on that major portion of public lands listed as Government domain. At partition the Palestinian Arabs saw themselves being forced to give up much of their lands, private and communal, to Jewish settlers as part of a grand-scale international effort at restitution and compensation to the Jews. The Palestinian Arabs, a Semitic and largely Muslim people, concluded that they were being required to pay for the anti-Semitic sins of the Christian West.
>
> This is obviously a simplified and only partial explanation of how the Zionist movement and the present state of Israel came to gain broad Western support, but it will be impossible to understand current Arab attitudes apart from this unflattering interpretation of why the United States and Western Europe gave support to the creation of Israel and have continued to support it. In fact, some Arabs came to feel that in Western nations pro-Zionism for Jews abroad was the natural corollary of continued anti-Semitism at home.

Erskine Childers, makes the same point in commenting on the way Jews have been treated by Christians over the centuries:

> The ironies here are scarcely to be contemplated. Who in fact pleaded with the Arabs to cross the Pillars of Hercules – straits of Gibraltar – into Spain? The Jews of Spain who were being persecuted by their Visigothic rulers. Some decades earlier, when the Arabs had first arrived outside the gates of Jerusalem, they had signed a treaty with its inhabitants guaranteeing Christians and Jews alike complete autonomy and freedom of worship. When our Crusader ancestors arrived outside Jerusalem some centuries later, they entered by a trick, and as they made the streets run red – to quote an eyewitness – they assembled all Jews in the synagogue and burned them alive. The first great wave of anti-Semitism in Europe followed the

Crusades, which had carried out perhaps the first mass incineration of Jews, nearly a thousand years before Hitler, in Palestine. And a thousand years later we, the descendants of those Crusaders, decided that Arab-inhabited Palestine should be taken from its Arabs and given to a Jewish settler movement to pay for our latest crimes in Europe.

2·7 Partition and War (1948–49)

Q How did the Jews and Arabs prepare for partition?

Denys Baly describes how both the Jews and the Arabs prepared for the implementation of the UN Partition Plan in May 1948:

> There seems little point in spending much time upon the question of whether the Arabs were the aggressors in 1948, except that it is an accusation which the Arabs themselves resent bitterly. Anyone who lived in Palestine during the last five years of the Mandate and had the good fortune to be intimate with both Arabs and Jews could not but be aware that both sides had every intention of fighting, *if necessary*. The Jewish prepartions, as one might expect of them, were better organized, more thorough and more efficient, and had been going on for a longer time than those of the Arabs, who do not normally exhibit efficiency as one of their virtues.

Glubb Pasha (John Bagot Glubb), who served in the Middle East for thirty-six years, mainly with the Jordanian government, describes an incident which indicates how some of the Jews were preparing for partition:

> In December 1947, two British officers and a Jewish official in the mandatory government were discussing the newly published UN partition plan over an evening drink. One of the British officers asked the Jewish official whether the Jewish state would not have a great deal of trouble, in view of the fact that there would be as many Arabs in it as Jews. 'Oh no!' replied the Jewish officer. 'A few calculated massacres will soon get rid of them.' This was five months before the 'Arab Invasion'.

Jon and David Kimche, the Zionist historians, have described the aim of the so-called Dalet Plan of the Jewish underground in the months before partition:

> to capture strategic heights dominating the most likely lines of

advance of the invading Arab armies, and to fill in the vacuum left by the departing British forces in such a way as to create a contiguous Jewish-held area extending from the north to the south.

David Ben-Gurion sums up what the Jewish underground group known as the Haganah had achieved before partition:

> Until the British left, no Jewish settlement, however remote, was entered or seized by the Arabs, while the Haganah . . . captured many Arab positions and liberated Tiberias and Haifa, Jaffa and Safad . . . So, on the day of destiny, that part of Palestine where the Haganah could operate was almost clear of Arabs.

Menachem Begin a leader of the Irgun, the other main group of the Jewish underground, has described in detail the objectives which they set for themselves in the months between January and March 1948:

> In the months preceeding the Arab invasion . . . we continued to make sallies into the Arab area. In the early days of 1948, we were explaining to our officers and men, however, that this was not enough . . . It was clear to us that even the most daring sallies carried out by partisan troops would never be able to decide the issue. Our hope lay in gaining control of territory. At the end of January 1948, at a meeting of the Command of the Irgun in which the planning section participated, we outlined four strategic objectives: (1) Jerusalem, (2) Jaffa, (3) the Lydda-Ramleh plain, (4) the Triangle [the towns of Nablus, Jenin and Tulkarm], comprising the bulk of the non-desert area west of Jordan.

Q What kind of atrocities were committed?

David Hirst describes the fate of the Arab village of Deir Yassin on the night of 9 April 1948:

> In 1948 Deir Yassin had a particularly peaceable reputation. For months, as Arab-Jewish clashes intensified throughout the country, it had lived 'in a sort of agreement' with neighbouring Jewish settlements; it was practically the only village in the Jerusalem area not to complain to the Arab authorities that it was in danger; it had on occasion collaborated with the Jewish Agency; it was said by a Jewish newspaper to have driven out some Arab militants. On the night of 9 April 1948, the villagers went to sleep, as usual, in the comforting knowledge that they

were among the least likely of Jewish targets. Just as a
precaution, however, and in accordance with ancient custom,
the village elders had appointed a score of night watchmen.
These sported a few old Mausers and Turkish muskets whose
main function, till then, had been the shooting of rabbits and
the furnishing of a noisy backdrop for village weddings and
feasts.

At 4.30 the following morning, a combined force of *Irgun*
and *Stern*, 132 strong, descended on the sleeping village. By
noon they had slaughtered two-thirds of the inhabitants. For
this operation, as for the blowing up of the King David, the
Irgun was acting in collaboration with the *Haganah* and the
official Jewish leadership . . .

Although it took place on the very edge of Palestine's
biggest city, very few people, apart from its perpetrators and
surviving victims, actually witnessed the massacre or its
immediate aftermath. The perpetrators did not consider it an
atrocity at all; people who did had fallen for 'lying propaganda'
designed to besmirch their name. According to Begin, his men
had fought a clean fight against fierce resistance; they had
sought 'to avoid a single unnecessary casualty'; and, by using a
loudspeaker to warn all women, children and old men to take
refuge in the hills they had deprived themselves, in a spirit of
humanity, of the elements of complete surprise.

It seems, however, that the loudspeaker was as ineffectual
as the claimed half-hour advance warning to the occupants of
the King David Hotel; the armoured car on which it was
mounted fell into a ditch well short of the first houses, and only
the car's crew could hear the message which it blared into the
night. The surviving victims certainly told a very different story,
although, mostly women and children, they were apparently
very reluctant to tell it at all to the British police who
interrogated them. Twelve-year-old Fahmi Zidan survived the
first mass killing of about thirty-five villagers. He recalled: 'The
Jews ordered all our family to line up against the wall and they
started shooting us. I was hit in the side, but most of us children
were saved because we hid behind our parents. The bullets hit
my sister Kadri (four) in the head, my sister Sameh (eight) in the
cheek, my brother Mohammad (seven) in the chest. But all the
others with us against the wall were killed: my father, my
mother, my grandfather and grandmother, my uncles and aunts
and some of their children.' Halim Eid saw 'a man shoot a
bullet into the neck of my sister Salhiyeh who was nine months
pregnant.' Then he cut her stomach open with a butcher's

knife. She said that another woman, Aisha Radwan, was killed trying to extract the unborn infant from the dead mother's womb. In another house, Naaneh Khalil, sixteen, saw a man take 'a kind of sword and slash my neighbour Jamil Hish from head to toe then do the same thing on the steps of my house to my cousin Fathi'. The attackers killed, looted, and finally they raped. They dynamited the houses; and when the dynamite ran out they systematically worked through the remaining buildings with Sten guns and grenades. By noon they had despatched 254 people; as for their own casualties, what Begin described as 'murderous' fire from the old Mausers and muskets had cost them four dead.

Jacques de Reynier was a Swiss official of the Red Cross who entered the village shortly after the massacre. This is his account of what he saw:

> . . . the Commander of the *Irgun* detachment did not seem willing to receive me. At last he arrived, young, distinguished, and perfectly correct, but there was a peculiar glitter in his eyes, cold and cruel. According to him the *Irgun* had arrived 24 hours earlier and ordered the inhabitants by loudspeaker to evacuate all houses and surrender: the time given to obey the order was a quarter of an hour. Some of these miserable people had come forward and were taken prisoners, to be released later in the direction of the Arab lines. The rest, not having obeyed the order, had met the fate they deserved. But there was no point in exaggerating things, there were only a few dead, and they would be buried as soon as the 'cleaning up' of the village was over. If I found any bodies, I could take them, but there were certainly no wounded. This account made my blood run cold.
>
> I went back to the Jerusalem road and got an ambulance and a truck that I had alerted through the Red Shield . . . I reached the village with my convoy, and the Arab firing stopped. The gang was wearing country uniforms, with helmets. All of them were young, some even adolescents, men and women, armed to the teeth: revolvers, machine-guns, hand grenades, and also cutlasses in their hands, most of them still blood-stained. A beautiful young girl, with criminal eyes, showed me hers still dripping with blood; she displayed it like a trophy. This was the 'cleaning up' team, that was obviously performing its task very conscientiously.
>
> I tried to go into a house. A dozen soldiers surrounded me, their machine-guns aimed at my body, and their officer forbade

me to move. The dead, if any, would be brought to me, he said. I then flew into one of the most towering rages of my life, telling these criminals what I thought of their conduct, threatening them with everything I could think of, and then pushed them aside and went into the house.

The first room was dark, everything was in disorder, but there was no-one. In the second, amid disembowelled furniture and covers and all sorts of debris, I found some bodies cold. Here, the 'cleaning up' had been done with machine-guns, then hand grenades. It had been finished off with knives, anyone could see that. The same thing in the next room, but as I was about to leave, I heard something like a sigh. I looked everywhere, turned over all the bodies, and eventually found a little foot, still warm. It was a little girl of ten, mutilated by a hand grenade, but still alive . . . everywhere it was the same horrible sight . . . there had been 400 people in this village; about fifty of them had escaped and were still alive. All the rest had been deliberately massacred in cold blood for, as I observed for myself, this gang was admirably disciplined and only acted under orders.

After another visit to Deir Yassin I went back to my office where I was visited by two gentlemen, well-dressed in civilian clothes, who had been waiting for me for more than an hour. They were the commander of the *Irgun* detachment and his aide. They had prepared a paper that they wanted me to sign. It was a statement to the effect that I had been very courteously received by them, and obtained all the facilities I had requested, in the accomplishment of my mission, and thanking them for the help I had received. As I showed signs of hesitation and even started to argue with them, they said that if I valued my life, I had better sign immediately. The only course open to me was to convince them that I did not value my life in the least . . .

Larry Collins and **Dominique Lapierre**, American journalists, in their book *O Jerusalem!* describe the Arab ambush of a convoy on its way to the Hadassah Hospital on Mt Scopus north-east of Jerusalem:

Packed into the buses and ambulances . . . was an astonishing assembly of professors, doctors, researchers and scholars, the most precious cargo a Haganah convoy could carry through the dangerous curves of Sheikh Jarrah to Mount Scopus. Distinguished products of the most famous faculties of Europe, they fled the persecutions of the Continent to come here and found a prestigious array of hospitals, laboratories and research centres . . .

The convoy's most prestigious passenger, the director of Hadassah Hospital, the world-renowned ophthalmologist Chaim Yassky, had characteristically taken one of the most exposed seats, beside the driver of the first ambulance. Behind him were his wife, six other doctors, a nurse and a wounded man on a stretcher . . .

Crouched in a ditch alongside the road, his fingers fixed on the plunger of an electric mine, a tailor named Mohammed Negger watched the convoy's approach, calculating the instant at which to fire his explosives. Forty-eight hours before, in a bar he frequented, Negger had been given the date and the hour of the convoy's passage by a British officer. Moreover, the Britisher had told Negger that if the men attacked the convoy, they would not be molested as long as they did not fire on British patrols.

His words were an invitation to attack it. To the Arabs, Mount Scopus also represented a Haganah strongpoint from which their foes sometimes launched assaults on their rear. All the next day in the back room of his tailor shop, while Neggar shuttled in and out to give his customers fittings, his aides had planned the ambush. Counting on British indifference, they had decided to strike from the roadside ditch near a clump of cypress trees beyond the Orient House Hotel. The road began to flatten out there, and the Jews might be expected to relax their vigilance.

The din of the convoy's motors rose, and finally the lead armored car appeared around a bend on the road. Tensely, Neggar watched it crawl toward him. It seemed to the tailor like 'an enormous black beetle'. He tightened his fingers until he heard the click of the plunger. An explosion shook his ditch, and a cloud of smoke enveloped the armored car. When it cleared, Neggar blinked. He had pushed his plunger too soon. Instead of destroying the vehicle, he had blown an enormous crater in the road. Unable to stop in time, the heavy vehicle had lumbered into the hole. Behind the car, the rest of the convoy ground to a halt . . . For a moment, the concerned passengers sat in their darkened vehicles, wondering what was happening outside. A signal from Neggar to the score of men with him in his ditch gave them the answer. A rain of gunfire swept into the stalled convoy.

The explosion, the gunfire, attracted the attention of all Jerusalem. By the scores, then by the hundred, Arab irregulars poured toward the ambush site from the villages nearby and the walls of the Old City. In the suffocating darkness of their metallic prisons, the passengers began to hear a new sound mingling with the din of the gunfire. It was a gutteral clamor, a furious call for vengeance, the name of the Arab village the two wounded men in Esther Passmann's ambulance had helped to assault three days earlier: 'Deir Yassin!' . . .

By the side of the road, a thirteen-year-old Arab boy named Jamil Bazian watched the men beside him soaking rags in gasolene to hurl at the trapped cars.

At three-fifteen, Dr Yassky turned to peer from the slit by the driver's seat of the ambulance. A hundred yards behind him he saw the first results of the scene Jamil Bazian had just witnessed. Great sheets of orange flame were sweeping over the two buses crowded with his friends and colleagues. He turned toward his wife. '*Shalom*, my dear,' he said. 'It is the end.'

Then Yassky pitched forward and tumbled to the floor of the ambulance. His wife rushed to his side. The director of Hadassah Hospital was dead. He had been struck by a bullet passing through the ambulance at the moment he had turned to address his wife . . .

By nightfall it was over. A ghastly silence reigned at last on the bend in the road to Mount Scopus where Mohammed Neggar had detonated his mine. A few ribbons of smoke, the putrid stench of burned flesh, and the carbonized remains of the convoy's trapped vehicles remained to greet the falling dusk. Dr Moshe Ben-David had been faithful to his appointment in Samarra. The bus after which he had so faithfully run had been his coffin. At least seventy-five others, most of them men and women who had come to Palestine to heal, not to kill, had died with him. So completely had the flames devoured their victims that twenty-four of their bodies would never be identified.

The following morning, Moshe Hillman, the Haganah man who had cleared the convoy's departure, picked through the ruins, removing a skull, an arm, a hat, a stethoscope, a pair of glasses . . .

Q Why did so many Arabs leave their homes?

Edgar O'Ballance, writing in a semi-official history of the 1948 war entitled *The Arab-Israeli War of 1948*:

It was Jewish policy to encourage the Arabs to quit their homes and they used psychological warfare in urging them to do so. Later, as the war wore on, they ejected those Arabs who clung to their villages. This policy, which had such amazing success, had two distinct advantages. First, it gave the Arab countries a vast refugee programme to cope with, which their elementary economy and administrative machinery were in no way capable of attacking, and secondly ensured that the Jews had no Fifth Column in their midst.

I.F. Stone, an American Jewish journalist who was decorated by the Irgun in 1948:

> The argument that the refugees ran away 'voluntarily' or because their leaders urged them to do so until after the fighting was over, not only rests on a myth but is irrelevant. Have refugees no right to return? Have German Jews no right to recover their properties because they had to flee?
>
> Jewish terrorism, not only by the Irgun in such savage massacres as Deir Yassin, but in milder forms by the Haganah itself, 'encouraged' Arabs to leave areas the Jews wished to take over for strategic or demographic reasons. They tried to make as much of Israel as free of Arabs as possible.

Menachem Begin, who had been the leader of the Irgun group which attacked Deir Yassin, later described the effects of what had happened there:

> Arab headquarters at Ramallah broadcast a crude atrocity story, alleging indiscriminate massacre by *Irgun* troops of about 240 men, women and children in Deir Yassin. The official Zionist bodies, apprehensive of the *Irgun*'s growing strength and popular support, eagerly seized upon this Arab accusation and, without even trying to check their veracity, accepted them at their face value and bestirred themselves to denounce and smear the *Irgun*. This combined Arab-Zionist *Greuelpropaganda* produced, however, unexpected and momentous consequences. Arabs throughout the country, induced to believe the wild tales of 'Irgun butchery', were seized with limitless panic and started to flee for their lives. This mass flight soon developed into a maddened, uncontrollable stampede. Of the about 800,000 Arabs who lived on the present territory of the State of Israel, only some 165,000 are still there. The political and economic significance of this development can hardly be over-estimated.

In Jerusalem, as elsewhere, we were the first to pass from the defensive to the offensive . . . Arabs began to flee in terror . . . Haganah was carrying out successful attacks on other fronts, while all the Jewish forces proceeded to advance through Haifa like a knife through butter. The Arabs began to flee in panic shouting 'Deir Yassin'.

Yigal Allon, one of the main heroes of the war of 1948, later recorded in the *Book of Palmach* some of the tactics which he and other Jews used in the months before the UN Partition Plan was due to come into effect:

> There were left before us only five days, before the threatening date, the 15th of May. We saw a need to clean the inner Galilee and to create a Jewish territorial succession in the entire area of the upper Galilee. The long battles had weakened our forces, and before us stood great duties of blocking the routes of the Arab invasion. We therefore looked for means which did not force us into employing force, in order to cause the tens of thousands of sulky Arabs who remained in Galilee to flee, for in case of an Arab invasion these were likely to strike us from the rear. We tried to use a tactic which took advantage of the impression created by the fall of Safed and the [Arab] defeat in the area which was cleaned by Operation Metateh – a tactic which worked miraculously well.
>
> I gathered all of the Jewish mukhtars, who have contact with Arabs in different villages, and asked them to whisper in the ears of some Arabs, that a great Jewish reinforcement has arrived in Galilee and that it is going to burn all of the villages of the Huleh. They should suggest to these Arabs, as their friends, to escape while there is still time. And the rumours spread in all the areas of the Huleh that it is time to flee. The flight numbered myriads. The tactic reached its goal completely. The building of the police station at Halsa fell into our hands without a shot. The wide areas were cleaned, the danger was taken away from the transportation routes and we could organise ourselves for the invaders along the borders, without worrying about the rear.

Allon admitted that if the Arab armies had not invaded, the Jews would have seized even more territory than they in fact did before the final cease-fire in early 1949:

> . . . there would have been no stop to the expansion of the forces of *Haganah* who could have, with the same drive, reached the natural borders of western Israel, because in this stage most of the local enemy forces were paralysed.

Chaim Weizmann, speaking later about the fighting which took place between 1948 and 1949 described its results in the following terms:

> It was a miraculous clearing of the land: the miraculous simplification of Israel's task.

John H. Davis, an American who was Commissioner-General of the United Nations Relief and Works Agency for Palestine Refugees (UNRWA) for five years, explains his understanding of why so many Arabs fled from their homes:

> The cause of the panic flight of nearly three-quarters of a million men, women and children from their homes has been obscured by veils of propaganda. It is only recently that careful sifting of the evidence has helped to clarify the picture. For long, a widely publicised view was that the refugees left voluntarily or because the Arab authorities themselves ordered them to leave, to clear the way for the advancing armies of the Arab States. As General Glubb has pointed out, voluntary emigrants do not leave their homes with only the clothes they stand up in, or in such a hurry and confusion that husbands lose sight of wives and parents of their children. Nor does there appear to be one shred of evidence to substantiate the claim that the fleeing refugees were obeying Arab orders. An exhaustive examination of the minutes, resolutions and press releases of the Arab League, of the files of leading Arabic newspapers, of day-by-day monitorings of broadcasts from Arab capitals and secret Arab radio stations, failed to reveal a single reference, direct or indirect, to an order given to the Arabs of Palestine to leave. All the evidence is to the contrary; that the Arab authorities continuously exhorted the Palestinian Arabs not to leave the country . . .
>
> What now seems clear . . . is that the Arab Governments, by inept and exaggerated publicising of Jewish atrocities in press and radio in an effort to justify to the world the impending arrival of their troops in Palestine to 'restore order', in fact unwittingly added to the panic and confusion in a population that had for years witnessed the spectacle of Jewish terrorists holding the armed might of the Mandatory Power to ransom and therefore had cause to fear the ruthless efficiency of their tactics.
>
> Panic and bewilderment thus played decisive parts in the flight. But the extent to which the refugees were savagely driven out by the Israelis as part of a deliberate master-plan has been insufficiently recognised.

2·8 The Voice of Israel

Q How do Jews in Israel express
the philosophy of the state?

David Ben-Gurion, speaking about the Law of Return in 1951:

It [Israel] is not a state for its citizens alone, but for the whole
Jewish people, for every Jew whoever he be, who chooses to
live in his homeland, who chooses Israeli independence in
preference to life in the Diaspora. The peculiar sign that singles
out the State of Israel and fixes its central mission, the Zionist-
Jewish mission, is the 'Law of Return', the foundation scroll of
the rights of the Jewish people in Israel. This law has its origins
in the Declaration of Independence of 14th May 1948, which
says 'The State of Israel shall be open to immigration and to the
Ingathering of the Exiles'. It may be said that for that purpose
the State was founded. The Law of Return establishes that it is
not the State that confers upon the Jew abroad the right to
settle in Israel, this right being inherent in his being a Jew, if he
only has the desire to join the population of the State.

Abba Eban, writing in *An Autobiography* (1978):

Zionism and Israel made great promises to the Jewish people.
They may even have promised too much. There has always
been a Utopian element in our national movement. The higher
the expectation, the greater the possibility of disappointment.
We have restored our nation's pride. We have given the Jewish
people a renewed sense of its collective creativity. We have
created a sanctuary in which our special legacy can be
preserved and enlarged. We have taken Jewish history out of
provincialism and caused it to flow into the mainstream of
human culture. We have given mankind a special
communication of social originality and intellectual vitality. We
have revealed an immense power of Jewish recuperation.
Above all, we have fulfilled our human vocation by redeeming
hundreds of thousands of our kinsmen from sterility,
humiliation and death. So Israel has no cause for
comprehensive apology. It is a society inspired by a positive
vision, a nation in which tomorrow is more vivid than
yesterday, and in which it seems more important to build than
to destroy . . . it is in Israel alone that the Jew can face the world
in his own authentic image, and not as a footnote in the story of
other societies. It is only as a nation in its own soil, its own

tongue and its own faith that the Jewish people can hear what it has to hear, say what it has to say – do what it has to do.

Moshe Davis, Executive Director of the Office of Britain's Chief Rabbi, in the book *I am a Jew* (1978):

> Israel is the only country in the world which is a Jewish country, and where the majority of the citizens are Jewish. The mere fact of its existence causes many Jews to sleep more peacefully in their beds. It represents an ultimate asylum, should it be needed. And few Jews would ever categorically guarantee that Jews – in any country – will always live where they are safely. They would not rule out as absurd the possibility that, one day, they or their children might indeed buy that air ticket, for whatever reasons. The uncertainty of the Jew in the world – even in the closing decades of the 20th Century – is still a very real factor in determining Jewish attitudes towards Israel.
>
> I know that when I went to visit the State of Israel for the first time twenty-seven years ago [i.e. 1951] (I was the first of my family for many generations to do so), I felt that I was returning home for myself and also for countless others before me whose great dream it was to see the Land but who were never so privileged. I have been back many times since, and each time I find there is something special about it. I always find it an emotional and spiritual experience, a return to roots, drinking from the ancient wells of my tradition and my history.
>
> The religious aspect of the contemporary Jewish State – notwithstanding its many real problems – seems to have Biblical undertones. A measure of prophetic fulfilment is apparent in its achievements. The Hebrew language has been revived. A unique system of social justice embraces the total living system of that quarter of a million of its inhabitants who live in the Kibbutzim and co-operative settlements. Israel has become the home of one-fifth of the Jewish people. The country has resisted the combined and repeated attacks of all its neighbours to destroy it. Half a million of its Jewish population derive from the backward countries of the Middle East, whose civilizations are several hundred years behind the West. They have been absorbed into the modern, twentieth century culture and technology of Israel.

One of those present during the independence ceremony (May 14, 1948) was **Golda Meyerson** (Golda Meir), who later recalled how, when Ben Gurion spoke the words 'the State of Israel':

> My eyes filled with tears and my hands shook. We have done it.

We had brought the Jewish state into existence – and I, Golda Mabovitch Meyerson, had lived to see the day. Whatever price any of us would have to pay for it, we had recreated the Jewish national home.

The long exile was over. From this day on, we would no longer live on sufferance in the land of our forefathers. Now we were a nation like other nations, masters – for the first time in twenty centuries – of our own destiny. The dream had come true – too late to save those who had perished in the Holocaust, but not too late for the generations to come.

Moshe Dayan, describing his feelings on hearing of the 1947 UN Resolution partitioning the country:

The U.N. decision recognizing Israel's right to statehood was an historic event. The successful passage of the resolution represented an enormous political achievement, in which Ben-Gurion had played the major role. However, underlying our expression of joy was a far deeper emotion, one that I felt as a Jew – indeed, more as a Jew than I had ever known before. I felt in my bones the victory of Judaism, which for two thousand years of exile from the Land of Israel had withstood persecutions, the Spanish Inquisition, pogroms, anti-Jewish decrees, restrictions, and the mass slaughter by the Nazis in our own generation, and had reached the fulfillment of its age-old yearning – the return to a free and independent Zion.

Q How do non-Jews who are sympathetic towards Israel explain and defend its ideals?

W. Laqueur, writing in one of the standard histories of Zionism:

The Arab-Jewish conflict was inevitable, given the fact that Zionism wanted to build more than a cultural centre in Palestine. Nor is it certain that a cultural centre would not have encountered Arab resistance. Zionism, the transplantation of hundreds of thousands of Jews, was bound to effect a radical change in Palestine, as a result of which the Palestinian Arabs were bound to suffer. It was not the Arabs' fault that the Jews were persecuted in Europe, that they had awakened to the fact that they wanted again to be a nation and therefore needed a state in the country in which they had lived two thousand years before.

The effects of Zionism on the Arabs should not be belittled. The fact that they derived economic and other benefits from Jewish immigration is immaterial in this context. This is not to say that Zionism was bound to result in the evacuation or expulsion of many Palestinian Arabs from Palestine. Had the Arabs accepted the Peel Plan in 1937, the Jewish state would have been restricted to the coastal plain between Tel Aviv and Haifa. Had they not rejected the UN partition of 1947, most of Palestine would still have remained in their hands. The Arab thesis of inevitable Zionist expansion is a case of self-fulfilling prophecy: the Arabs did everything in their power to make their prophecy come true, by choosing the road of armed resistance – and losing. The Zionist movement and the yishuv matured in the struggle against the Arab national movement. Eventually it reached the conclusion that it was pointless to seek Arab agreement and that it could achieve its aims only against the Arabs.

Arab intransigence was the natural reaction of a people unwilling to share its country with another. For European Jewry the issue was not an abstract one of preserving a historical connection, religious and national ties. With the rise of Hitler it became a question of life or death, and they felt no pangs of conscience: the danger facing the Jews was physical extinction. The worst fate that could befall the Arabs was the partition of Palestine and minority status for some Arabs in the Jewish state. Zionism is guilty no doubt of many sins of commission and omission in its policy on the Arab question. But whichever way one looks at it, the conflict on immigration and settlement could not have been evaded since the basis for a compromise did not exist. Zionism could and should have paid more attention to Arab grievances and aspirations. But despite all concessions in the cultural or economic field, the Arabs would still have opposed immigration with an eye to the inevitable consequences of mass immigration.

Seen from the Arab point of view, Zionism was an aggressive movement, Jewish immigration an invasion. Zionists are guilty of having behaved like other peoples – only with some delay due to historical circumstances. Throughout history nation-states have not come into existance as the result of peaceful development and legal contracts. They developed from invasions, colonisation, violence and armed struggle. It was the historical tragedy of Zionism that it appeared on the international scene when there were no longer empty spaces on the world map. Wherever the Jews would have chosen to settle, they would have sooner or later come into conflict with the native population. The creation of nation-states meant the perpetration of acts of injustice. The native population was either absorbed and assimilated or it was decimated or expelled. The expulsion of ten million Germans from Eastern Europe was almost immediately accepted as an established fact by the outside world and those unwilling to put up with it were denounced as revanchists and war-mongers. Given the realities of Soviet power, it was clear that the new order in eastern Europe could not be challenged except through a new world war. But Zionism was not in a position of such strength, nor was there a danger of world war. Hence the fact that the territorial changes in eastern Europe have been accepted as irreversible, while those in the Middle East continue to be challenged by many.

A resolution of the General Assembly of the United Nations on 10 November 1975 condemned Zionism as 'a form of racism and racial discrimination'. The Ecumenical Theological Research Fraternity in Israel responded immediately by issuing an appeal to churches around the world, in which it attempted to explain and defend Zionism against this criticism:

> Christians should be aware that Zionism, far from being itself a racist movement, was for most Jews the only viable answer to anti-Jewish racism culminating in the destruction of European Jewry during the Nazi holocaust. Christians have to acknowledge that the Church's age-long teaching of contempt for the Jewish people, and the long history of Christian anti-Jewish practices, have in a large measure contributed to the perpetration of terrible crimes against Jews. Recognizing this fact, the least that Christians can do is to attempt a fair and proper assessment of what Zionism is and what it means to the Jewish people.
>
> For this reason, it is impossible to present Judaism and Zionism as two entirely different things. There is only a very thin line between anti-Zionism and anti-Semitism or anti-Judaism. Zionism has to be seen as an important and valid expression of a fundamental dimension of Judaism. The basic aspiration of Zionism is to free and unite the Jewish people; free it from alienation, oppression and persecution, and unite it in the Land from which it has been exiled but which it has never abandoned . . . Zionism is an attempt of the Jewish people to give contemporary expression to its identity, and to take its place in freedom, dignity and co-operation among the community of nations, and make its contribution to the one world of which the prophets have spoken.
>
> When we come to the political implications of Zionism and

the Jewish-Arab conflict, it should be borne in mind that the main-stream of the Zionist movement never had the intention to deprive the Arab population living in the land of their rights, but desired to live in peace with them. If there was an underestimation of the Arab position towards Zionist settlement in the country, and even insensitivity to their fears and their feelings, this did not originate from ill-will or bad intentions, but from human limitations and weaknesses.

The fundamental Zionist principles enshrined in Israel's Declaration of Independence of 1948 include the following: 'The State of Israel will be open for Jewish immigration and for the Ingathering of the Exiles; it will foster the development of the country for the benefit of all its inhabitants; it will be based on freedom, justice and peace according to the vision of the prophets of Israel; it will ensure complete equality of social and political rights for all its citizens, irrespective of religion, conscience, language, education and culture; it will safeguard the Holy Places of all religions; and it will be faithful to the principles of the Charter of the United Nations'.

2·9 Other Jewish Voices

Q Are all Jews Zionists? Why have some Jews rejected the idea of a Jewish state?

In May 1917 (six months before the Balfour Declaration) the Board of Deputies of British Jews and the Anglo-Jewish Association published a joint manifesto in *The Times*:

Zionist theory regards all the Jewish communities of the world as constituting one homeless nationality incapable of complete social and political identification with the nations among whom they dwell and it is argued that for this homeless nationality a political centre and an always available homeland in Palestine are necessary. Against this theory, the conjoint committee strongly and earnestly protest. Emanicapted Jews in this country regard themselves primarily as a religious community, and they have always based their claims to political equality with their fellow citizens of other creeds on this assumption – that they have no separate aspirations in a political sense.

The second point in the Zionist programme which has aroused the misgivings of the conjoint committee is the proposal to invest the Jewish settlers in Palestine with certain special rights in excess of those enjoyed by the rest of the population . . . Any such action would prove a veritable calamity for the whole Jewish people. In all the countries in which they live the principle of equal rights for all religious denominations is vital for them.

Asher Ginsberg (Ahad Ha'Am) became the leader of the movement known as 'Moral Zionism', which was critical of the 'Political Zionism' of Weizmann and others. In 1922 he wrote the following letter to the Tel Aviv newspaper *Haaretz*, after hearing that a group of Zionists had killed an Arab as a reprisal for anti-Jewish riots:

Is this the goal for which our fathers have striven and for whose sake all generations have suffered? Is this the dream of a 'Return to Zion', to stain its soil with innocent blood? Many years ago I wrote an essay in which I stated that our people will willingly give their money to build up their state, but they will never sacrifice their prophets for it. This was to me an axiomatic truth. And now God has afflicted me to have to live and to see with my own eyes that I apparently erred. The people do not part with their money to rebuild their national home, but instead, their inclination grows to sacrifice their prophets on the altar of their 'renaissance': the great ethical principles for the sake of which they have suffered, and for the sake of which alone it is worthwhile to return and become a people in the land of our fathers. For without these principles, my God, what are we and what can our future life in this country be, that we should bring all the endless sacrifices without which this land cannot be rebuilt? Are we really doing it only to add in an Oriental corner a small people of new Levantines who vie with other Levantines in shedding blood, in desire for vengeance, and in angry violence? If this be the 'Messiah', then I do not wish to see his coming.

Albert Einstein:

I should much rather see reasonable agreement with the Arabs on the basis of living together in peace than the creation of a Jewish State. Apart from practical considerations, my awareness of the essential nature of Judaism resists the idea of a Jewish State, with borders, an army, and a measure of temporal power, no matter how modest. I am afraid of the inner damage Judaism will sustain – especially from the development of a narrow nationalism within our own ranks, against which we have already had to fight strongly, even without a Jewish State. We are no longer the Jews of the Maccabean period. A return to a nation in the political sense of the word would be equivalent to turning away from the spiritualization of our community which we owe to the genius of our prophets.

Q Why have some orthodox Jews opposed the idea of a Jewish state and criticized its policies and actions?

Rabbi Benjamin, former editor of the magazine *Ner*:

In the end we must come out publicly with the truth; that we have no moral right whatever to oppose the return of the Arab refugees to their land . . . that until we have begun to redeem our sin against the Arab refugees, we have no right to continue the Ingathering of Exiles. We have no right to demand that American Jews leave their country to which they have become attached, and settle in a land that has been stolen from others, while the owners of it are homeless and miserable. We had no right to occupy the house of an Arab if we had not paid for it at its value. The same goes for fields, gardens, stores, workshops. We had no right to build a settlement and then to realize the ideal of Zionism with other people's property. To do this is robbery. I am surprised that Rabbi Herzog and all those who speak in the name of Jewish ethics and who always quote the Ten Commandments should consent to such a state of affairs. Political conquest cannot abolish private property.

. . . In the end we must speak the truth. We are faced with this choice: to listen to the voice of truth for the sake of our own good and genuine peace, or, not to listen to it, and to bring evil and misfortune upon us and the future generations.

Rabbi Yosef Becher claims to speak for around 100,000 orthodox Jews in New York who describe themselves as anti-Zionist. In an article published in a Beirut magazine in 1981, he described how he understood the thinking of the early Zionist leaders:

They reasoned that since every nation had its land, its language, its customs and its culture, normalcy required a state. But in truth, our history shows that having a state is the greatest abnormalcy for us, because it poses dangers, spiritual dangers, to the Jewish people . . . The Zionists, who were not religious, didn't know how the Jews lived in exile or how they were dealt with. They had these alien concepts which stemmed from the nationalistic awakenings in the Balkan states and elsewhere in the 1880s. Also, they believed that they had been assimilated in the various states, and they didn't like it when in some places they were still considered Jews. So they decided that the only

way was to have a state where we would be on our own and
where nobody would say 'Jew, Jew, Jew!' That, they thought,
would make anti-Semitism disappear.

They went to the various heads of state asking for a country
for the Jews 'to run away from anti-Semitism'. That request,
repeated in several states, served to fuel anti-Semitism. The
anti-Semites in the countries where the Jews, their parents and
grandparents were born began to say: 'You see? The Jews don't
want to live among us'.

He goes on to speak about Theodor Herzl, and wonders whether he
was aware that the Zionist campaign for a Jewish state would
increase anti-Semitism:

But even if he was not aware of this, Herzl had no right to
speak for the Jewish people. Who did he represent?

Chaim Weizmann (1874—1952), bragging about how he
created the state of Israel in his book *Trial and Error*, said that
when he went to the British government and asked for a Jewish
state, it was a miracle that they didn't ask him who he
represented. Because he had no people, he represented
nobody. If they had asked him to produce the people he
represented, he could not have done it, because the mass of the
Jews before World War II, and especially before World War I,
were not Zionists. But in his egotism, Weizmann writes that the
British were intelligent enough to understand that he
represented 'the people to be'.

It is our belief – and our rabbis have already printed this –
that the holocaust was caused, first, by the sin of trying to
establish a Jewish state, and second, by the Zionists'
encouragement of anti-Semitism through their claim that the
Jews did not want to live among the nations.

Zionism feeds anti-Semitism. It likes anti-Semitism,
intensifies it, gives it its ammunition to further its goals.

They come to the United States, they go to France and they
say to the other Jews, 'We are going to save you from anti-
Semitism', when in fact they feed anti-Semitism in order to get
more people to go to their country to replace the *yordim*
[emigrants from Israel].

He recognizes the limited effect of the protests which he and other
American Jews try to make against the current policies of the
American goverment:

We know that any protest we may make here will not get too
far, because the American government is helping Israel not for

the love of Israel but to serve its own interests . . . The superpowers use other nations like pawns in a chess game . . .

Even though we are citizens of the United States and have the greatest respect for it, we, the orthodox Jews, know that no good can come of such struggles for power, especially when they involve arms aid.

2·10 The Voice of the Palestinians

Q Who are
the Palestinians?

When we speak of the Palestinians today, we are thinking of approximately 4 million people who fall into three distinct categories:

1. Palestinians who have been living under Israeli rule in the State of Israel since 1948.

These number	635,000 (approximately)

2. Palestinians who have been living under Israeli military rule in the West Bank and Gaza since 1967.

These number

West Bank	725,000
Gaza Strip	450,000

3. Palestinians of the Dispersion who are distributed as follows

Syria	215,000
Iraq	20,000
Jordan	1,160,800
Lebanon	347,000
Egypt	48,500
Libya	23,000
Kuwait	278,000
South Arabia	127,000
Qater	22,500
United Arab Emirates	34,700
Oman	48,500

There are also probably around 100,000 Palestinians scattered in other parts of the world.

Everett Mendelsohn in a report entitled *A Compassionate Peace* (October 1982), a follow-up of the Quaker Report of 1970, describes the great variety of situations in which these Palestinian communities find themselves:

No single description would fit the experiences of Palestinian communities in different parts of the Arab world. They form different proportions of the populations in their host lands, ranging from 60 per cent in Jordan to below 1 per cent in Iraq, so that the importance of their political and social roles varies. Although the Palestinians share Arabic as a common language and Islam as a common religion (except in Lebanon, where there is a large Christian minority), in the various societies in which they reside they have established very different forms of social and political organisation and have set up different means of receiving or integrating the Palestinian inhabitants. In Jordan many have been able to achieve full citizenship and participate in the affairs of the state (including even cabinet membership), a result of the inclusion of the West Bank in the Kingdom of Jordan after the 1949 armistace agreement. In other countries, however, they remain refugees or, even in the second generation, outsiders. Many live in camps or in city districts or neighborhoods which are effectively separate, and they are often discriminated against. Like other foreign nationals they may engage in business in the Gulf or Arabian states, but a national must be either the senior partner or the business registrant. Palestinians, aware of European history, often compare their present status to that of the Jews in the ghettos of Europe. They have come to fill the role of expatriate professionals, teachers, technicians, and skilled artisans in many societies.

Edward Said speaks of the Palestinians' attachment to the land they have cultivated for centuries, and describes how they have been conscious of their identity throughout the conflicts of the last 100 years:

For any Palestinian there was no doubt that his country had its own character and identity. True, Palestine had been part of the Ottoman Empire until the end of World War I, and true also that in any accepted sense it had not been independent. Its inhabitants referred to themselves as Palestinians, however, and made important distinctions between themselves, the Syrians, the Lebanese, and the Transjordans. Much of what we can call Palestinian self-assertion was articulated in response to the flow of Jewish immigrants into Palestine since the 1880s, as well as to ideological pronouncements made about Palestine by Zionist

organisations. Under the constantly felt sense of foreign
invasion, Palestinian Arabs grew together as a community
during the interwar years. The things that had been taken for
granted – the structure of the society, village and family
identity, customs, cuisine, folklore, dialect, distinctive habits
and history – were adduced as evidence, to Palestinians by
Palestinians, that even as a colony the territory had always been
their homeland, and that they formed a people. Sixty per cent
of the population was in agriculture; the balance was divided
between townspeople and a relatively small nomadic group. All
these people believed themselves to belong in a land called
Palestine, despite their feelings that they were also members of
a large Arab nation; and for all of the twentieth century, they
referred to their country as Filastinuna (our Palestine).

He speaks of how the world is being forced to acknowledge their
existence as a people:

There *is* a Palestinian people, there *is* an Israeli occupation of
Palestinian lands, there *are* Palestinians under Israeli military
occupation, there *are* Palestinians – 650,000 of them – who are
Israeli citizens and who constitute 15 per cent of the population
of Israel, there *is* a large Palestinian population in exile: these
are actualities which the United States and most of the world
have directly or indirectly acknowledged, which Israel too has
acknowledged, if only in the forms of denial, rejection, threats
of war, and punishment. The history of the past forty years has
shown that Palestinians have grown politically, not shrunk,
under the influence of every kind of repression and hardship;
the history of the Jews has shown too that time only increases
attachment to the historically saturated land of Palestine. Short
of complete obliteration, the Palestinians will continue to exist
and they will continue to have their own ideas about who
represents them, where they want to settle, what they want to
do with their national and political future.

John H. Davis answers the charge that the Arab governments used
the Palestinian refugees as a pawn for political purposes:

The fact is that the Palestinian refugee problem has never been
well understood in the Western world. One common belief,
even among responsible persons, is that the refugees have
remained unsettled and unemployed largely because the Arab
Governments have inhibited their settlement or have even held
them as hostages by not allowing them to settle or go to work.
Supposedly, their motivation has been the desire to keep alive

the Palestine issue in the eyes of the world. The evidence is quite to the contrary. Following the upheaval of 1948, virtually all able-bodied male refugees who possessed skills needed in Arab countries, or for that matter, elsewhere, found jobs almost immediately and became self-supporting and have never been dependent on international charity. This group comprised some twenty per cent of the total working force which left their homes in Palestine in 1948-1949; for the most part they were persons from the urban sector of Palestine, their good fortune being that the world needed the skills which they possessed.

In contrast, the farming sector of the refugee population, which comprised about 70 per cent of the total refugee numbers in 1948, did not fare so well. Their problem has been, and is, that as refugees they became surplus farm workers in an era when the world at large, and Arab countries in particular, already had a surplus of people in their rural sectors. In fact, in the Arab countries as a group rural youth is still reaching maturity at a rate per generation more than three times that required to replace the farm parents – a situation that is further aggravated by the fact that the typical rural holding is already too small adequately to support a family of eight to ten persons, or use modern equipment effiiciently. Hence, it was the rural refugees from Palestine who, for the most part, became dependent on international charity. The reason they became dependent was not that they were held as hostages, but that they were unemployable under the competitive employment conditions that then prevailed, and for that matter prevail to this day.

Q Why do many if not most Palestinians feel so bitter towards Israel?

Fawaz Turki, a young Palestinian living in France, expresses the feelings of many young Palestinians in exile in a book called *The Disinherited*, published in 1974:

The deportations, the blowing up of homes, the expropriation of property, the arrogance on the faces of Israeli soldiers walking into Arab coffee shops in Jerusalem to slap the patrons on the face and demand identity cards, and the primitive torture of members of the resistance – all these go on, and to the outside world 'the Arabs' have never had it so good. Look at how our standard of living is better than ever. We earn excellent wages under occupation. We drive cars. We watch television. Our health standards have improved. And they show pictures of our West Bank 'notables', our Uncle Toms and Beni oui oui, as if to attest to this, shaking hands with Israeli military governors. And nobody seems to realize that, during all this, Palestinians called and fought for a secular state and not for a struggle to inflict on Israeli society the same devastation they inflicted on us.

I begin to lose my patience and my sense of rationality. I begin to feel that our lives are not worth living anywhere in this world, anywhere. It is impossible for me to be oblivious of my situation; to be, as it were, happy. Moments of gloom and fury overwhelm my being as I spend restless days in Paris and I see pictures of robust Israelis tilling our land, growing our oranges, inhabiting our cities and towns, co-opting our culture, and talking in their grim stubborn way about how we do not 'exist' and how our country was a 'desert' before they went there. And I gag with anger and mortification.

Edward Said expresses the longings of Palestinians in exile to return to their country, and of those within Israel to have self-government:

Those Palestinians in manifest exile want to return; those in internal exile (inside Israel or under military occupation) want independence and freedom and self-government where they are. A refugee from Galilee or Jaffa who now lives either in Lebanon or in Kuwait thinks primarily in terms of what he lost when he left in 1948 or later; he wants to be put back, or to fight his way back, into Palestine. He wants to return. Conversely, the present Palestinian resident of Gaza, Nazareth or Nablus faces or in some way daily rubs up against an occupying power, its symbols of authority, its basically unchecked domination over him; he wants to see that power removed or, in the case of the Arab Israeli citizen, he no longer wishes to be known and treated negatively as a 'non-Jew'. He wants novelty. One Palestinian wants to move, the other to stay; both want a pretty radical change.

Palestinians have frequently expressed their nationalistic feelings in poetry. **Tawfiq Zayyad,** a Palestinian living in Israel, expressed the conviction that Israel cannot get rid of the Arabs. In a poem called *Baqun* ('We shall remain'), he says that in spite of all the indignities they have to suffer, the Arabs will remain . . .:

. . . Here – we have a past
      a present
      and a future.
Our roots are entrenched

Deep in the earth.
Like twenty impossibles
We shall remain.

Kamal Nasr, a Christian Palestinian poet, was fully committed to the aims and ideals of the Palestine Liberation Organization, and was one of a number of Palestinians murdered in their homes in Beirut by a group of Israeli commandos one night in 1973. This is how he expressed the feelings of the Palestinian refugees:

The refugees are ever kindling
In their camps, in that world of darkness,
The embers of revolt,
Gathering force, for the return,
They have lost their faith in the doctrine of love,
Even here in this land of love and peace
Their stolen rights cry in their hearts,
Inflamed by misery and hunger.
Dismayed by the persistent throng.
The enemy spreads poison and hatred abroad;
'They are Communists', he says, 'Their hopes are false,
Let us kill their hopes to return!'

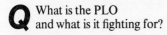 **Q** What is the PLO
and what is it fighting for?

In the eyes of many in the West, the PLO is little more than a terrorist organization, like the Red Brigade, the IRA and the Bader-Meinhof Gang. But however much we may want to condemn its activities as 'terrorism', we must try to listen to what the movement is trying to do and say on behalf of the Palestinian people.

The British Council of Churches Report quotes the following as views which are broadly representative of Palestinian attitudes towards the PLO. A leading Palestininian academic:

The PLO is the aspirations of the people. Anyone who calls himself a Palestinian supports the PLO.

A Palestinian notable:

The Palestinians are a deprived people. The most deprived are the refugees who have no rights. It is from this section that the PLO finds support. Nobody can tell them who represents them. I was not a PLO supporter for nearly ten years. Now I am a member of the PLO.

Everett Mendelsohn describes the position of the PLO in the context of the whole Palestinian movement:

One recent study lists more than twenty Palestinian resistance groups. Among these, Fatah (Palestine National Liberation Movement) is the oldest, largest and most influential. While it is only one of many units of the PLO, it now accounts for 70 per cent of the umbrella group and its leadership has assumed effective control. Fatah's membership runs the spectrum of belief and social orientation in the Palestinian community. It is more conservative than other guerrilla groups and reflects a generally Arab orientation, broadly construed Islamic religious beliefs, and a politically neutralist stance. It contains segments that are Christian and also a strong secular, socialist wing.

Eight guerrila groups now make up the PLO along with Fatah, and Yasir Arafat, the Fatah leader, is Chairman of the PLO executive committee. In the wake of the 1967 war, the PLO filled a vacuum. From the point of view of outsiders, the PLO took on the qualities of a 'government in exile', although in fact it has rejected that political choice. Although known in the media primarily for guerrilla military activities, and terrorism, the PLO has assumed responsibility for many aspects of Palestinian life, especially in refugee communities. It has established a social service system and formed a Palestinian branch of the Red Crescent (headed by a physician, younger brother of Yasir Arafat); it conducts schools and operates an industrial co-operative (SAMED) in Lebanon. The PLO offered a political defence for their resort to terrorism, arguing it 'gives our cause resounding coverage – positive or negative it mattered little'.

Mendelsohn supports the view that the PLO has come to speak with increasing authority for the majority of the Palestinians all over the world:

Israeli leaders have often tended to belittle ideas of Palestinian national identity or to deny the existence of the Palestinians. 'Who are the Palestinians?' Golda Meir asked. Begin called them the 'Arabs of the Land of Israel.' But in the Camp David accords, Begin initialed a document referring to the 'legitimate rights of the Palestinians.' Now, with tacit acknowledgement of the Palestinian people, the focus for discussion has become the Palestine Liberation Organization (PLO) and its role in the political life of the Palestinians. For Israel and for the U.S., the PLO was declared an organisation with which neither power would deal. For most Palestinians it is *the* representative of their nationalist activities, especially in the international arena. The Arab states, across the political spectrum, have declared that the PLO is the 'sole legitimate representative of the Palestinian people'. The Soviet Union and many nations of the Third World accord formal diplomatic status to the PLO, and most Western European nations now maintain some form of unofficial relations with the PLO. At this time it is an illusion to believe that some other group exists that can speak on behalf of the Palestinians without PLO involvement or endorsement. We recognise that there is not always unanimity within the PLO, but it remains the strongest group by far among the Palestinians . . .

One could easily argue, therefore, that just as the Zionist movement was the national liberation movement of the Jewish people, so the PLO has become the national liberation movement of the Palestinian people. The parallel can be pressed at several points. For example, just as there were different reactions to Zionism amongst Jews, so there are differing reactions to the PLO among Palestinians. Just as some of the Zionist leaders of the 1930s and 1940s acted harshly towards some Jewish settlers, so the PLO leadership has on occasions acted harshly towards its own people. The Jewish National Fund earlier in the century has been paralleled by the Palestinian National Fund. If the Palestinians have found it hard, if not impossible to recognize the existence of the state of Israel, this simply reflects the refusal of many Zionists to acknowledge the existence of a Palestinian people. The PLO can thus be seen as in many respects the mirror-image of the Zionist movement.

In order to understand the philosophy and activities of the PLO, it is important to recognize several very distinct stages through which it has developed:

1. In January 1964 the PLO was set up by Arab leaders at a summit conference of the Arab League, with the aim of 'Organizing the Palestinian people to enable them to carry out their role of liberating their homeland and determining their destiny'. During this early period the movement was largely under the control of President Nasser and other Arab governments, and groups of *fedayeen* (freedom fighters) began to make raids into Israel from the surrounding Arab countries.

2. Before 1967 the Palestinians were very reliant on the Arab states. But because of the failure of the 1967 war and the disastrous defeat of the Arab armies, a more grass-roots Palestinian leadership emerged in the PLO with a determination that Palestinians should be masters of their own destiny. Thus in 1968 Yasser Arafat, who had worked as an engineer in the Gulf before joining the *fedayeen* in southern Lebanon, was elected Chairman of the PLO. The leadership of the movement was from now on in the hands of those who had been actively involved in fighting for the cause, and were prepared to take the fight into Israel itself.

After a significant battle in which a large number of Palestinians resisted an Israeli raid on the town of Karakeh inside Jordan, many young Palestinians joined the movement and committed themselves to fight with the *fedayeen*.

During this period the PLO was strongly influenced by the revolutionary ideas that had brought Algeria to independence from the French. Although it has been moving away from this emphasis on armed struggle since 1974, it has never totally renounced it.

3. In 1970 the PLO began to define its goal as the creation of 'the Democratic State of Palestine'. Instead of speaking in terms of 'driving all Jews into the sea', it encouraged Palestinians to work and to fight for a democratic state in Palestine in which Jews and Arabs would have equal rights.

Everett Mendelsohn describes some of the changes in the PLO which took place between 1973 and 1974:

As early as November 1973, Eric Rouleau, veteran Middle East correspondent for Le Monde, described new attitudes among the PLO leadership. Fatah leaders told him that they needed time 'to prepare the grass-roots psychologically for recognising a state whose destruction they have pledged for over a quarter of a century.'

The twelfth meeting of the PNC [Palestinian National Council] in June 1974 saw the first signs of an official reformulation. A resolution, still couched in the language of self-determination for the whole land, spoke also of establishing an 'independent combatant national authority over every part of Palestinian territory that is liberated'. A variety of statements and resolutions by Palestinian leaders continued for several years to present a mosaic of ambiguous views. The concept of a democratic secular state in all of Palestine was dropped, however, and instead 'an independent Palestinian state' became the stated goal. Said Hammami, the PLO representative in London, noted in 1975 that 'the Palestinian Arabs must recognize the fact that there is an Israeli people and this people has a right to live in peace in what they consider to be their own country.' [Said Hammami was later assassinated by an Iraqi-sponsored squad.] About this same time, Dr Issam Sartawi, an independent among the PLO leadership, began discussions with Israeli moderate Zionists initially under the aegis of former French premier Pierre Mendes France and later with the aid of Austrian prime minister Bruno Kreisky. These contacts continue today despite criticism from some Palestinian 'rejectionists' – those who reject any dealings with Israel . . .

David Hirst explains the significance of this development:

The Jew-as-Zionist was still the enemy, of course, and against him and all he stood for *Fatah* would pursue its 'Revolution Till Victory'. Complete liberation was still the aim. And complete liberation still meant 'liquidating the Zionist aggressor-state – politically, militarily, socially and ideologically'. There was no question of accepting some kind of mini-state to be set up in such territories as Israel, under a general settlement, might be induced to evacuate; together, the West Bank and Gaza represented no more than 23 per cent of original Palestine; it would, the *Fatah* theorist said, be a mere puppet – Israel's Bantustan. Only through complete liberation could the Palestinians fulfil their inalienable right to return; only thus could they assure themselves, as a people, of a free and decent life. But it was no longer a call for a literal and absolute justice, a restoration, pure and simple, of the *status quo ante*. If it did not acknowledge the Zionist *fait accompli* itself, it acknowledged the fundamental consequence of it, a physical Jewish presence in Palestine. It was a great leap forward in their thinking; a few years ago even 'discussing this proposal would have been considered as a complete sell-out or high treason'. It happened 'because people who fight can afford to be more tolerant'. The 'Palestine of tomorrow' was to be 'a progressive, democratic, non-sectarian Palestine in which Christian, Moslem and Jew will worship, live peacefully and enjoy equal rights.'

4. In 1974 the PLO was recognized at the Summit Conference of the Arab League at Rabat in Morocco as 'the sole legitimate representative' of the Palestinian people.

Everett Mendelsohn:

This further institutionalization and legitimization of the Palestinian movement reflected several sets of interests. It strengthened the hand of the PLO at the international level, sanctioning the PLO to speak for the Palestinians and to assert greater control over all segments of the movement. It was this latter which was of particular interest to the Arab oil states that are large financial supporters of the PLO and that wanted to assure a responsible Palestinian movement. The Arab states, having achieved a new self-confidence based on wealth from oil and what they conceived to be a positive military performance in the 1973 war, asserted what one observer described as a 'metaphysical right' to the West Bank and Gaza. This Arab support for the PLO has been interpreted as sanctioning a conservative and largely non-revolutionary nationalism for the PLO.

In November 1974 the UN General Assembly recognized the PLO as the representative of the Palestinians, and gave it observer status. It was then that **Yasser Arafat**, as Chairman of the PLO, made his famous speech in which he said:

I have come bearing an olive branch and a freedom fighter's gun. Do not let the olive branch fall from my hand.

5. In 1977 the PLO announced its willingness to accept a Palestinian state on *any part* of Palestine from which the Israelis were willing to withdraw.

Yasser Arafat has often made statements of this kind:

We are ready to live in any part of Palestine from which the Israelis withdraw, or which will be liberated.

For the Palestinians, the PLO is their homeland and their future; it is the government-in-exile, the state. All we need is a piece of land.

Everett Mendelsohn:

What does the PLO believe? Yasir Arafat, the PLO leader, suggested the pattern of policy change through which his organisation has gone. In an interview with the New York Times, May 8, 1980, he is quoted: 'We are the only victims who have offered two solutions; in 1967 we suggested a democratic secular state, but people said we wanted to demolish Israel so we offered another solution. We said that we have the right to establish our independent state in any land from which the Israelis withdraw or we have liberated.' This has become the familiar formula that Arafat and much of the rest of the PLO has used in recent years. In his discussions primarily with Western political leaders and the Western press, Arafat has repeated this formulation. He has consistently refused to give details on its final borders, but he generally has limited his view of a Palestinian state to the currently occupied West Bank and Gaza Strip, 20 per cent of the former land of Palestine. In addition, he has accepted the concept of security provisions, including joint superpower guarantees, demilitarized zones, and

United Nations peacekeeping forces within the Palestinian states. These issues, including careful consideration of security concerns, have been discussed in greater detail by Palestinians regarded as close to the PLO.

He explains Arafat's attitude to the question of recognition of Israel by the Palestinians:

Arafat in recent years has defended PLO discussions with progressive elements, including Zionists in Israel, and has expressed increasing confidence in political means to achieve a just settlement while not ruling out continued guerrilla warfare. On the key question of recognition of Israel he has remained unequivocal, claiming that it represents his political 'trump card' (see *The New York Times*, August 17, 1981), which he will not yet give up. Critics of the PLO can and do point to the Palestine National Covenant, written in 1964 and amended in 1968, which declared the original UN partition of 1947 illegal (Article 19) and called for the liberation of Palestine and the elimination of the Zionist presence in Palestine (Article 15).

6. The Civil War in Jordan in September 1970 was sparked off by the determination of the Jordanian government not to allow the PLO in Jordan to become a state within the state. After being driven out of Jordan, many of the Palestinian fighters settled in camps in Lebanon, where they soon began to threaten the delicate balance between the Christian and Muslim communities. This was one of the major factors which led to the Civil War in Lebanon (1975-76).

Although the Israeli invasion of Lebanon in the summer of 1982 virtually destroyed the PLO as a fighting force, the PLO felt they acquitted themselves well in fighting against the superior weapons of the Israeli army, navy and air force. Through their withdrawal from Beirut they believe they won a moral victory which is helping them to continue their struggle through diplomatic means.

7. It is difficult to predict the future of the PLO. Everything will depend on

  ● the response of Palestinians and of Arab countries to the idea of an autonomous Palestinian entity on the West Bank and in Gaza – perhaps in association with Jordan

  ● the willingness of Israel to accept such a Palestinian entity

  ● the amount of influence and pressure which the world powers (and especially the USA) can bring to bear on Israel and the Palestinians.

Edward Said describes the role played by the PLO until now in helping Palestinians to discover a political identity; he also spells out his understanding of 'the Palestinian mission' as 'a mission of peace'. His views probably reflect the feelings of the majority of Palestinians.

It is not too much to say that the PLO made being a Palestinian not only a possible thing (given the community's catastrophic fragmentation) but a meaningful thing for every Palestinian, no matter where his place of residence, no matter what his final ideological commitment. It has been the PLO's genius to turn the Palestinian from a passive into a participating political being . . .

As far as I am concerned, the Palestinian mission is a mission of peace. I am sure that this is true for the vast majority of our people. We are not just a population of exiles seeking restitution and national self-determination; we have recreated ourselves as a people out of the destruction of our national existence, and our national organization, the Palestine Liberation Organization has symbolized both the loneliness of our vision and the wonderful power of our faith in it . . . In the end the Palestinian mission comes down to individuals – whether it be a leader like Yasser Arafat, or a poet like Samih al Qassem, or any one of thousands of dedicated men and women in Lebanon, Gaza, Nazareth, or Detroit – who by standing before the world and before Zionism can ask the question, are you going to eradicate me to make way for someone else, and if so what right do you have to do so? Why is it right for a Jew born in Chicago to immigrate to Israel, whereas a Palestinian born in Jaffa is a refugee? The real strength of the Palestinian is just this insistence on the human being *as a detail* – the detail likely to be swept away in order for a grandiose project to be realized. The Palestinian therefore stands on a small plot of land stubbornly called Palestine, or an idea of peace based neither on a project for transforming people into nonpeople nor on a geopolitical fantasy about the balance of power, but on a vision of the future accommodating both the peoples with authentic claims to Palestine, not just the Jews.

2·11 Some Conclusions

1. The early leaders of the Zionist movement, like Theodor Herzl and Chaim Weizmann, worked for the creation of a Jewish homeland in Palestine as a solution to the problem of anti-Semitism in Europe. In spite of all they said to the contrary in public, their ultimate goal was the setting up of some kind of Jewish state in Palestine.

2. When Jewish immigrants first started to settle in Palestine in the 1880s, the Jews numbered only about 5 per cent of the total population, and were living in a limited number of centres. It was inevitable that the steady influx of Jewish immigrants would sooner or later lead to friction and to conflict. When the Arabs realized that the Jews might eventually outnumber them and gain control of the country, they naturally did all they could to prevent this happening.

3. The Zionist dream of a Jewish state would never have been fulfilled, and could never have been fulfilled by purely peaceful means. Since the aims of the Jewish leadership were so totally incompatible with the Arabs' desire for self-determination, the struggle between the two communities was bound to lead to violence. When the Arabs resorted to violence, it was in order to protect their interests and avoid being submerged by the immigrant community. When Jews resorted to violence it was to establish themselves as an independent community in a hostile environment.

4. The promises made by the British government during World War I to the Jews, in the Balfour Declaration, and to the Arabs, e.g. in the Hussein-McMahon correspondence, appear to us now to have been contradictory and incompatible. The British government was at best totally unrealistic, and at worst simply dishonest in thinking that a Jewish homeland could be established in Palestine without in any way harming the interests of the Arabs in Palestine. The Arabs had special reason to feel bitter and resentful at the way Britain and the other western powers represented at the Peace Conference at Versailles in 1919 broke all the promises they had made, and instead of granting the Arabs independence, established their own authority throughout the Middle East.

5. In dealing with the problem of the Middle East, the western powers were influenced partly by self-interest, and partly by strong pressure from western Jews. Many governments, especially that of the USA, are still subject to strong pressure from Jewish voters.

6. The problem of the Middle East today is basically the problem of the Palestinians. They believe they have a stronger claim to a homeland in Palestine than the Jews ever did earlier in this century.

3

THE LAND BEFORE AND AFTER JESUS CHRIST

❝ In the last resort this study drives us to one point: the person of a Jew, Jesus of Nazareth, who proclaimed the acceptable year of the Lord only to die accursed on a cross and so to pollute the land, and by that act and its consequences to shatter the geographic dimension of the religion of his fathers. Like everything else, the land also in the New Testament drives us to ponder the mystery of Jesus, the Christ, who by his cross and resurrection broke not only the bonds of death for early Christians but also the bonds of the land. ❞

W.D. Davies

How is the Christian to understand the divine promise that the land would belong to Abraham and his descendants 'as an everlasting possession'? What is he to make of the predictions in the prophets of a return of Jewish exiles to the land? What difference did the coming of Jesus make to Jewish ideas about the land?

Part 3 is a study of the theme of the land through the Old and New Testaments.

3·1 The Promise of the Land

Why was it that Abraham left his ancestral home in Ur of the Chaldees (near the town of Basra in southern Iraq) to settle in a foreign country? The book of Genesis gives us the answer:

> The Lord had said to Abram, 'Leave your country, your people and your father's household and go to the land I will show you.
> I will make you into a great nation
>   and I will bless you;
> I will make your name great,
>   and you will be a blessing.
> I will bless those who bless you,
>   and whoever curses you I will curse;
> and all peoples on earth
>   will be blessed through you.'
> Genesis 12:1–3

Soon after he entered the land, the promise concerning the land was made even more specific:

> To your descendants I give this land, from the river of Egypt to the great river, the Euphrates . . .
> Genesis 15:18

> I am God Almighty; walk before me and be blameless. I will confirm my covenant between me and you . . . The whole land of Canaan, where you are now an alien, I will give as an everlasting possession to you and your descendants after you; I will be their God.
> Genesis 17:1, 8

Abraham was then commanded to practise circumcision as the sign that he accepted the terms of this 'everlasting covenant':

> As for you, you must keep my covenant, you and your descendants after you for the generations to come. This is my covenant with you and your descendants after you, the covenant you are to keep: Every male among you shall be circumcised. You are to undergo circumcision, and it will be the sign of the covenant between me and you . . . My covenant in your flesh is to be an everlasting covenant.
> Genesis 17:9–11, 13

The covenant was therefore a kind of 'package deal', which included four basic promises – with no conditions attached:

- 'I will give you *the land* as an everlasting possession.'

- 'I will greatly increase your numbers . . . and I will make you into *a great nation*.'

- 'I will make an *everlasting covenant to be your God* and the God of your descendants.'

- 'I will bless those who bless you, and *all people on earth will be blessed through you.*'

These were incredible promises to make an to old man without children, who had just entered the land as a foreigner. The rest of the book of Genesis describes how God began to fulfil his side of the covenant – and in particular the promises about the land and the nation.

The Land

Abraham continued his semi-nomadic way of life in the hill-country of Palestine, moving his tents between Shechem, Bethel and Hebron. On one occasion he left the land because of famine, and went down to Egypt, no doubt assuming that God could no longer fulfil his promise to give him a permanent foothold in the land. But he soon found himself telling half-truths to protect his wife, and caused Pharaoh such embarrassment that he was sent back to where he had come from.

Abraham didn't actually own any piece of land until his wife Sarah died many years later. And it's strange that one whole chapter of Genesis is devoted to Abraham's negotiations for the purchase of the cave in Hebron where he buried his wife. But these details begin to make sense when we see that this marked the very first stage of the fulfilment of God's promises. Abraham didn't assume that God's promise about the land gave him the right to steal it from its current owners. And he wasn't interested in accepting the cave as a gift. He insisted on buying the land, paying its full value and making a legal contract in the presence of witnesses. Parts of the chapter even sound as if they are taken straight from a written contract:

> So Ephron's field in Machpelah near Mamre – both the field and the cave in it, and all the trees within the borders of the field – was legally made over to Abraham as his property in the presence of all the Hittites who had come to the gate of the city.
> Genesis 23:17–18

When Abraham's son, Isaac, was tempted to go to Egypt – once again because of famine – he was told by God to stay in the land, and given an assurance that the covenant promise extended also to him:

> Do not go down to Egypt; live in the land where I tell you to

live. Stay in this land for a while, and I will be with you and will bless you. For to you and your descendants I will give all these lands and will confirm the oath I swore to your father Abraham. I will make your descendants as numerous as the stars in the sky and will give them all these lands, and through your offspring all nations on earth will be blessed.
Genesis 26:2–4

Similarly, when Isaac's son, Jacob, was leaving the country to find a wife among his relatives in Padan Aram, he received a vivid confirmation of the promises in his dream at Bethel:

I am the Lord, the God of your father Abraham and the God of Isaac. I will give you and your descendants the land on which you are lying. Your descendants will be like the dust of the earth, and you will spread out to the west and to the east, to the north and to the south. All peoples on earth will be blessed through you and your offspring. I am with you and will watch over you wherever you go, and I will bring you back to this land. I will not leave you until I have done what I have promised you.
Genesis 28:13–15

God therefore assured Abraham's son and grandson that he fully intended to fulfil his promise about the land.

The Nation

For many years Abraham and Sarah must have wondered how this part of the promise could possibly be fulfilled, since they were getting on in years and still had no children. Abraham soon came to the conclusion that, according to custom, his servant Eliezer would have to become his legal heir. But God had other plans:

Then the word of the Lord came to him; 'This man will not be your heir, but a son coming from your own body will be your heir.' He took him outside and said, 'Look up at the heavens and count the stars – if indeed you can count them.' Then he said to him, 'So shall your offspring be.'
Abram believed the Lord, and he credited it to him as righteousness.
Genesis 15:4–6

It was one thing, however, for Abraham to believe God's promise; it was very much harder for him to wait patiently while Sarah grew older and older. Eventually they felt they must take matters into their own hands. So following an accepted custom, they planned for Abraham to have a child by Hagar, Sarah's Egyptian maid, in order to continue the family line. But the arrival of Ishmael only created friction within the family.

In the end, after receiving a further confirmation of the divine promise from three mysterious visitors, Abraham and Sarah finally had a son of their own, whom they called Isaac.

If Abraham now felt more confident of God's ability to fulfil his promise, he must have been thrown into utter confusion some years later when he was called by God to offer his son Isaac as a sacrifice. It must have seemed as if God was mocking Abraham. But this harrowing experience was intended as a test of Abraham's faith. When he proved that he was willing to obey the divine call, he received a further confirmation that the covenant would be fulfilled:

> I swear by myself, declares the Lord, that because you have done this and have not withheld your son, your only son, I will surely bless you and make your descendants as numerous as the stars in the sky and as the sand on the seashore. Your descendants will take possession of the cities of their enemies, and through your offspring all nations on earth will be blessed, because you have obeyed me.
> Genesis 22:16–18

The 'Title Deeds' of the Land

The terms of the covenant promise seem to leave no room for doubt about the divine right of the Jews to possess the land for all time: 'I will give you the land as an everlasting possession.' But when we see the promise about the land in the context of the whole covenant, we can hardly separate it from the other three promises:

> I will make you into a great nation
> I will . . . be your God
> All people on earth will be blessed through you

We cannot have the promise about the land without everything else that goes with it.

3·2 The Conquest of the Land

At the end of the book of Genesis we are left wondering how God is going to fulfil the promise about the land. All the twelve sons of Jacob (i.e. Israel) have gone to settle in Egypt, partly because of yet another famine, and partly because one of the sons, Joseph, is virtually prime minister of Egypt. It looks as if they have left the land and gone to settle in Egypt for good.

Earlier in the book, however, we are given a hint of how God will eventually bring the children of Israel back to the land. When God is reassuring Abraham about the covenant promise, he says:

> Know for certain that your descendants will be strangers in a country not their own, and they will be enslaved and ill-treated four hundred years. But I will punish the nation they serve as slaves, and afterwards they will come out with great possessions . . . In the fourth generation your descendants will come back here, for the sin of the Amorites has not yet reached its full measure.
>
> Genesis 15:13–14, 16

The return to the land began with the dramatic exodus from slavery in Egypt under the leadership of Moses, and was completed through the conquest of the land under his successor, Joshua.

The average Israeli today probably has little difficulty in appreciating the biblical account of the conquest of the land. He can hardly fail to notice the similarities and the differences between the conquest of the land under Joshua and the settlement of Jews in the land since the 1880s. It's not surprising that cabinet ministers in Israel should quote from the Old Testament to support Israel's claim to the West Bank, or that the Israeli government should make the book of Joshua compulsory reading in all schools.

But what if you happen to be an Arab Christian, and find that you are identified in the minds of Israelis with the ancient Canaanites and all the other tribes which Joshua defeated in the thirteenth century BC? How are you likely to think about the book which seems to give the Jews a divine right to take away your land in the twentieth century AD?

And what are we to make of the biblical account which says that God not only condoned the conquest and all that went with it, but actually commanded it? Can we take the easy way out and say that God couldn't possibly have done such a thing, and that the Jews invented this explanation *after* the event to justify their occupation of the land?

If we cannot hope to solve this thorny problem in a few pages, we can at least make certain observations to help us to see it in perspective:

1. Only a few cities were completely destroyed. We therefore need to be careful not to exaggerate the extent of the destruction. An archaeologist, **Alan Millard**, makes the point in the following way:

> The Bible's accounts of Israel's entry into Canaan record the actual destruction of only a few cities. Throughout, they emphasize that Israel drove out the former inhabitants and took

over (inherited) their property. A desolate land with its towns in ruins would be of little benefit to the Israelites, just emerging from 40 years of semi-nomad life. What *had* to be destroyed were the pagan shrines of the Canaanites with their cultic paraphernalia.

Jericho was a special case. The city was an offering to God, a 'firstfruit' of the conquest. Ai and Hazor were also sacked. But again they were exceptional cases, perhaps as focal points of opposition.

2. Even if the Old Testament writers don't seem to have been quite as sensitive to the problem as we are (or think we are) today, they do offer some substantial reasons to explain why the land was given to the children of Israel in this way. These reasons are contained in four important themes which are repeated in many different forms:

● **The land is a gift from God.** The land is described with almost monotonous regularity as 'the land which the Lord your God is giving you' or 'the land the Lord your God is giving you as an inheritance' or 'the land which the Lord your God has given you'.

These expressions are repeated so often that it's easy to miss the point. The land did not belong to the Israelites and their ancestors since the beginning of time. They could not claim that they had owned it from time immemorial. It came to them at this particular time as a gift from God. They had done nothing to deserve it, and they had not acquired it through their own cleverness or skill in war. God had said very clearly and simply:

> ... the land is mine and you are but aliens and my tenants.
> Leviticus 25:23

Since this is how the land came to them, it must always be seen as something given by God – an undeserved, unsolicited gift. It is a sign of the incredible generosity of God.

● **God has given the land to fulfil his promise to Abraham.** In giving the land to the children of Israel under Joshua, God is simply fulfilling the promise he made centuries before to Abraham. He therefore encourages the people to enter the land in the following words:

> See, I have given you this land. Go in and take possession of the land that the Lord swore he would give to your fathers, to Abraham, Isaac and Jacob, and to their descendants after them.
> Deuteronomy 1:8

This means that the conquest of the land should not be seen as an end in itself. It is merely one stage in the unfolding of God's plan for history, which is to lead to blessing for *all* the nations of the earth.

● The conquest of the land was **God's way of judging the inhabitants of the land.** The earlier promise given to Abraham indicates that the other tribes occupying the land at that time had already come under the judgement of God, but that the judgement was being postponed until a future date:

> In the fourth generation your descendants will come back here,
> for the sin of the Amorites has not yet reached its full measure.
> Genesis 15:16

Many passages in the Old Testament law describe the social customs and religious practices of the inhabitants of the land as 'abominations' or 'detestable things'; and archaeologists have confirmed this picture of a corrupt society and a degraded religion. The people are urged not to follow these detestable practices, since it was because of them that the previous inhabitants had been turned out of the land:

> Do not defile yourselves in any of these ways, because this is
> how the nations that I am going to drive out before you became
> defiled. Even the land was defiled; so I punished it for its sin,
> and the land vomited out its inhabitants . . . The native-born
> and the aliens living among you must not do any of these
> detestable things, for all these things were done by the people
> who lived in the land before you, and the land became defiled.
> Leviticus 18:24–27

If we are inclined to think that God showed special favouritism in his dealings with the children of Israel, we should notice that God warned his people that if they were disobedient, he would judge them just as severely and in exactly the same way as he judged those other nations before them:

> And if you defile the land, it will vomit you out as it vomited out
> the nations that were before you.
> Leviticus 18:28

If God used the children of Israel as his instrument of judgement on the inhabitants of the land, the time would come when they would experience the same kind of judgement if they disobeyed the covenant.

● The gift of the land and God's judgement on its previous inhabitants are closely linked with **an appeal to obey God's law.** While God commands the people to destroy all vestiges of Canaanite religion, he is at the same time urging them to obey the new law revealed through Moses. If they are to follow this new way, they must make a clean break with the religious practices of their neighbours:

> Keep my requirements and do not follow any of the detestable customs that were practised before you came and do not defile yourselves with them. I am the Lord your God . . .
> Be holy because I, the Lord your God, am holy.
>   Leviticus 18:30, 19:2

> When you enter the land the Lord your God is giving you, do not learn to imitate the detestable ways of the nations there. Let no-one be found among you who sacrifices his son or daughter in the fire, who practises divination or sorcery, interprets omens, engages in witchcraft, or casts spells, or who is a medium or spiritualist or who consults the dead. Anyone who does these things is detestable to the Lord, and because of these detestable practices the Lord your God will drive out those nations before you. You must be blameless before the Lord your God.
>   The nations you will dispossess listen to those who practise sorcery or divination. But as for you, the Lord your God has not permitted you to do so. The Lord your God will raise up for you a prophet like me from among your own brothers. You must listen to him.
>   Deuteronomy 18:9–15

All these four themes – the land as a gift, the land and the covenant, judgement, and obedience – are brought together in Moses' exhortations to the people before they enter the Promised Land:

> If you ever forget the Lord your God and follow other gods and worship and bow down to them, I testify against you today that you will surely be destroyed. Like the nations the Lord destroyed before you, so you will be destroyed for not obeying the Lord your God. Hear, O Israel. . .
>   After the Lord your God has driven them out before you, do not say to yourself, 'The Lord has brought me here to take possession of this land because of my righteousness.' No, it is on account of the wickedness of these nations that the Lord is going to drive them out before you. It is not because of your righteousness or your integrity that you are going in to take possession of their land; but on account of the wickedness of these nations, the Lord your God will drive them out before you, to accomplish what he swore to your fathers, to Abraham, Isaac and Jacob. Understand, then, that it is not because of your righteousness that the Lord your God is giving you this

good land to possess, for you are a stiff-necked people.
Deuteronomy 8:19; 9:1, 4–6

The Conquest and the Covenant

The person who takes the biblical account of the conquest seriously
will not find it easy to conclude that the Jews were simply using their
God and their religion to justify the occupation of the land. Given
the incredibly low level to which religion had sunk in the land at the
time, God's revelation of a new way had to be combined with a clear
repudiation of the old ways. His revelation of himself had to be
gradual, and he had to deal with one particular people over a period
of many centuries.

When seen in this light, the conquest of the land was one stage in
the unfolding of God's plan for history – an unpleasant but vital
stage, and one that was not to be repeated. This plan was to include
not only the land and the nation, but also the covenant relationship
between God and his people, and the blessing which was to come to
all people on earth.

3·3 Exile from the Land

If the land was a gift which carried with it an obligation to obey the
law of God, it followed naturally that when this obligation was not
honoured, the gift could be taken away. The children of Israel were
not to assume that they could live in the land for ever regardless of
the way they lived. It was perfectly possible for them to forfeit the
right to live in the land.

This sanction was made very clear by Moses in his explanation
of the Law before the children of Israel entered the land:

> After you have had children and grandchildren and have lived
> in the land a long time – if you then become corrupt and make
> any kind of idol, doing evil in the eyes of the Lord your God
> and provoking him to anger, I call heaven and earth as
> witnesses against you this day that you will quickly perish from
> the land that you are crossing the Jordan to possess . . . The
> Lord will scatter you among the peoples, and only a few of you
> will survive among the nations to which the Lord will drive you.
> Deuteronomy 4:25–27

This same warning was repeated at the dedication of Solomon's
temple:

> If you or your sons turn away from me and do not observe the
> commands and decrees I have given you and go off to serve
> other gods and worship them, then I will cut off Israel from the

land I have given them and will reject this temple I have
consecrated for my Name.
1 Kings 9:6–7

The Exile of Israel

The subsequent history of the nation proved that these warnings
were no idle threats. This was the fate of the northern kingdom of
Israel when its capital Samaria was captured in 721 BC:

> The king of Assyria invaded the entire land, marched against
> Samaria and laid siege to it for three years. In the ninth year of
> Hoshea, the king of Assyria captured Samaria and deported the
> Israelites to Assyria. He settled them in Halah, in Gozan on the
> Habor River and in the towns of the Medes. All this took place
> because the Israelites had sinned against the Lord their God,
> who had brought them out of Egypt from under the power of
> Pharaoh king of Egypt. They worshipped other gods and
> followed the practices of the nations the Lord had driven out
> before them, as well as the practices which the kings of Israel
> had introduced . . . So the Lord was very angry with Israel and
> removed them from his presence.
> 2 Kings 17:5–8, 18

The Exile of Judah

A hundred years later, when the Babylonian army was threatening
the southern kingdom of Judah, the prophet Jeremiah tried to warn
the people of the disaster which was approaching:

> The Lord said, 'It is because they have forsaken my law, which
> I set before them; they have not obeyed me or followed my law.
> Instead, they have followed the stubbornness of their hearts;
> they have followed the Baals, as their fathers taught them.'
> Therefore, this is what the Lord Almighty, the God of Israel,
> says: 'See, I will make this people eat bitter food and drink
> poisoned water. I will scatter them among nations that neither
> they nor their fathers have known, and I will pursue them with
> the sword until I have destroyed them'.
> Jeremiah 9:13–16

God's judgement on the *people* (here described as 'my house', and
'my inheritance') will also involve judgement on the *land*:

> I will forsake my house,
>   abandon my inheritance;
> I will give the one I love
>   into the hands of her enemies.
> My inheritance has become to me
>   like a lion in the forest.

> She roars at me;
>> therefore I hate her.
> Has not my inheritance become to me
>> like a speckled bird of prey
>> that other birds of prey surround and attack?
> Go and gather all the wild beasts;
>> bring them to devour.
> Many shepherds will ruin my vineyard
>> and trample down my field;
> they will turn my pleasant field
>> into a desolate wasteland.
> It will be made a wasteland,
>> parched and desolate before me;
> the whole land will be laid waste
>> because there is no-one who cares.
>> Jeremiah 12:7–11

This message of doom began to be fulfilled in 597 BC, when Nebuchadnezzar of Babylon captured Jerusalem, despoiled the temple and deported the cream of the population:

> Nebuchadnezzar removed all the treasures from the temple of the Lord and from the royal palace, and took away all the gold articles that Solomon king of Israel had made for the temple of the Lord. He carried into exile all Jerusalem: all the officers and fighting men, and all the craftsmen and artisans – a total of ten thousand. Only the poorest people of the land were left . . . It was because of the Lord's anger that all this happened to Jerusalem and Judah, and in the end he thrust them from his presence.
>> 2 Kings 24:13–14; 20

The king's uncle, Zedekiah, was installed by the Babylonians as a puppet king; but when he tried to lead an insurrection some years later (586 BC), Jerusalem was largely destroyed, and the land was depopulated even further:

> On the seventh day of the fifth month, in the nineteenth year of Nebuchadnezzar king of Babylon, Nebuzaradan commander of the imperial guard, an official of the king of Babylon, came to Jerusalem. He set fire to the temple of the Lord, the royal palace and all the houses of Jerusalem. Every important building he burned down. The whole Babylonian army, under the commander of the imperial guard, broke down the walls around Jerusalem. Nebuzaradan the commander of the guard carried into exile the people who remained in the city, along

with the rest of the populace and those who had gone over to
the king of Babylon. But the commander left behind some of
the poorest of the land to work the vineyards and fields . . . So
Judah went into captivity away from her land.

2 Kings 25:8–12, 21

Israel had already gone into captivity away from her land 135 years
before – and never returned. Now it was Judah's turn to go into
exile.

The Exile and the Covenant

It may be hard for us today to appreciate what a catastrophe the
exile was to the people of Judah. All their leaders were banished
from the land. The king was deported and stripped of all his powers.
The temple was in ruins and the priests were no longer able to offer
the sacrifices. It must have seemed as if God had broken every
promise he had ever made to Abraham and to David.

We can feel something of the despair and bitterness of the
people in exile in a foreign land in this well-known psalm:

By the rivers of Babylon we sat and wept
    when we remembered Zion.
There on the poplars
    we hung our harps,
for there our captors asked us for songs,
    our tormentors demanded songs of joy;
they said, 'Sing us one of the songs of Zion!'
How can we sing the songs of the Lord
    while in a foreign land?

Psalm 137:1–4

During the exile the people had plenty of time to look again at their
scriptures to find out why they had got themselves into this situation.
Those who understood the Law and the prophets must have realized
that God hadn't broken his covenant with his people. He was simply
applying the sanctions which had been written into the covenant
long ago. The gift of the land was *conditional*, and their continued
possession of the land depended on their loyalty and obedience to
the God who had given it to them.

3.4 The Return to the Land

One reason why the Jews survived the exile was that their Babylonian captors kept them together as a community instead of scatter-
ing them in different places as the Assyrians had done with the
Israelites. Another reason was that their prophets were able to

interpret all that had happened and give them hope for the future.

This hope would have been based partly on promises in the Mosaic law that if the people returned to God in genuine repentance, he would restore them to their land:

> When all these blessings and curses I have set before you come upon you and you take them to heart wherever the Lord your God disperses you among the nations, and when you and your children return to the Lord your God and obey him with all your heart and with all your soul . . . then the Lord your God will restore your fortunes and have compassion on you and gather you again from all the nations where he scattered you. Even if you have been banished to the most distant land under the heavens, from there the Lord your God will gather you and bring you back. He will bring you to the land that belonged to your fathers, and you will take possession of it.
>
> Deuteronomy 30:1–5

How then did the prophets build on this promise? What kind of hopes did they hold out to the Jewish exiles?

Isaiah

The prophecies in the first part of Isaiah (chapters 1–39) were delivered more than 100 years before the exile and spoke of the great judgement to come and the restoration which would follow. Whether the rest of the book (chapters 40–46) was written by the same writer or by a later writer during the exile, it speaks even more clearly of the deliverance of the people after submitting to God's judgement:

> Comfort, comfort my people, says your God.
> Speak tenderly to Jerusalem,
>   and proclaim to her
> that her hard service has been completed,
>   that her sin has been paid for,
> that she has received from the Lord's hand
>   double for all her sins.
>
> A voice of one calling:
> 'In the desert prepare
>   the way for the Lord;
> make straight in the wilderness
>   a highway for our God.
> Every valley shall be raised up,
>   every mountain and hill made low;
> the rough ground shall become level,
>   the rugged places a plain.

And the glory of the Lord will be revealed,
and all mankind together will see it.
For the mouth of the Lord has spoken.'

You who bring good tidings to Zion,
go up on a high mountain.
You who bring good tidings to Jerusalem,
lift up your voice with a shout,
lift it up, do not be afraid;
say to the towns of Judah,
'Here is your God!'
See, the Sovereign Lord comes with power
and his arm rules for him.
Isaiah 40: 1–5, 9–10

Jeremiah

Unlike Isaiah, who had spoken about events which to him were in the distant future, Jeremiah lived through the Babylonian invasion in 597 BC and the destruction of Jerusalem in 586 BC, and remained with those who were left behind in Jerusalem. He prophesied that the exile would last for a limited period:

This is what the Lord says: 'When seventy years are completed for Babylon, I will come to you and fulfil my gracious promise to bring you back to this place . . . Then you will call upon me and come and pray to me, and I will listen to you. You will seek me and find me when you seek me with all your heart. I will be found by you,' declares the Lord 'and will bring you back from captivity. I will gather you from all the nations and places where I have banished you,' declares the Lord, 'and will bring you back to the place from which I carried you into exile.'
Jeremiah 29:10–14 (compare 16:14–15)

Ezekiel

Ezekiel must have been in his mid-twenties when he witnessed the surrender of Jerusalem to the Babylonian army and was taken into exile in Babylon. His first prophecies were about the glory of God and the inevitability of judgement on the sinful people of Judah. Then sometime after hearing of the final destruction of Jerusalem in 586 BC, he began to look forward to the restoration of the nation to the land.

The word of the Lord came to me . . .
Therefore say: 'This is what the Sovereign Lord says: Although I sent them far away among the nations and scattered them among the countries, yet for a little while I have been a sanctuary for them in the countries where they have gone.'

> 'This is what the Sovereign Lords says: I will gather you
> from the nations and bring you back from the countries where
> you have been scattered and I will give you back the land of
> Israel again. They will return to it and remove all its vile images
> and detestable idols . . .
> Ezekiel 11:16–18

The Fulfilment of these Prophecies

When King Cyrus of Persia captured Babylon in 539 BC, his policy
was to repatriate the different groups of exiles in the country. The
edict allowing the Jews to return to Jerusalem is recorded in 2
Chronicles and Ezra, and it is significant that they speak of this
return as a fulfilment of the prophecies of Jeremiah:

> In the first year of Cyrus king of Persia, in order to fulfil the
> word of the Lord spoken by Jeremiah, the Lord moved the
> heart of Cyrus king of Persia to make a proclamation
> throughout his realm and put it in writing: 'This is what Cyrus
> king of Persia says: "The Lord, the God in heaven, has given
> me all the kingdoms of the earth and he has appointed me to
> build a temple for him at Jerusalem in Judah. Anyone of his
> people among you – may the Lord his God be with him, and let
> him go up."'
> 2 Chronicles 36: 22–23, Ezra 1:1–3

The exiles who returned to Judah and Jerusalem settled in the places
which their parents and grandparents had left when they were taken
into exile. Ezra gives a list of all those who returned at this time 'each
to his own town':

> Now these are the people of the province who came up from
> the captivity of the exiles, whom Nebuchadnezzar king of
> Babylon had taken captive to Babylon (they returned to
> Jerusalem and Judah, each to his own town . . .)
> Ezra 2:1; (compare 1 Chronicles 9:2)

At every stage this was a peaceful return. There is no suggestion
either in the prophecies or in the historical accounts that there was
any fighting involved in the resettling of the exiles in their own land.
This is the kind of idyllic picture which Isaiah paints:

> Only the redeemed will walk there,
>   and the ransomed of the Lord will return.
> They will enter Zion with singing;
>   everlasting joy will crown their heads.
> Gladness and joy will overtake them,

and sorrow and sighing will flee away.
Isaiah 35:9–10

Anything less like the conquest under Joshua is hard to imagine!

Popular Ideas about the Land

As Judaism developed in the centuries after the exile, the Jews came to believe that there was an inseparable connection between the people of Israel and the land. Since the land had been given to them by God as an everlasting possession, it was *here* that he wanted them to live, and it was *here* that they had the ideal opportunity to live in total obedience to the law of God. It was as if there were a kind of 'umbilical cord' between Israel and the land.

This is why they always expressed a strong desire to possess soil in the land, and, if they lived away from the land, to make pilgrimage to it, and if possible to die in the land. It also explains why they always considered it vital that the land should be under their own control. The greatest threat to their existence as a nation living under the law of God came from having to live under an alien, occupying power. In a recent study W.D. Davies has summed up their attitude: 'They could only dwell securely in the promised land when it was not occupied territory.'

Another development during this period was that the Jews began to attach special significance to the city of Jerusalem and to the temple. This was because they summed up everything that the land meant for them.

When they became discouraged and depressed about their situation as a nation in the land, some started to dream dreams and to hope that God would one day intervene in an obviously supernatural way to vindicate his people. This led to the development of a new kind of writing called 'Apocalyptic', which generally described visions and dreams using many strange symbols. These writers tried to explain why the powers of evil were frustrating the fulfilment of God's promises, and looked forward to the time when God would establish his kingdom in the land for all the world to see. This kind of writing was particularly popular between 200 BC and AD 100, when the Jews were under the power of the Seleucids and the Romans.

The Scholars' Interpretation of the Land

Some Jewish writers continued to interpret everything the Old Testament said about the land in a very *literal* way; but at the same time they developed a *spiritual* interpretation of the land.

For example, Philo, the Jewish philosopher-theologian who died in Alexandria in AD 50, held firmly to traditional Jewish hopes for the land, but also gave a symbolic interpretation to passages in the Old Testament about the land. Thus in a discussion of Genesis 15:7–8, he begins with the literal meaning of the promised land, and then goes on to interpret the land as a symbol of 'fruitful wisdom':

> What is the meaning of the words, 'I am the Lord God who led thee out of the land of the Chaldeans to give thee this land to inherit?' The literal meaning is clear. That which must be rendered as the deeper meaning is as follows. The 'land of the Chaldeans' is symbolically mathematical theory, of which astronomy is a part. And in this (field) the Chaldeans labour not unsuccessfully or slothfully. Thus He honours the wise man with two gifts. For one thing He takes away from Chaldean doctrine, which in addition to being difficult to seize and grasp, is the cause of great evils and impiety in attributing to that which is created the powers of the Creator, and persuades men to honour and worship the works of the world instead of the Creator of the world. And again, He grants him fruitful wisdom which he symbolically calls 'land' . . .

Their Own yet Not Their Own

The Jews after the exile were therefore no more than a small remnant of the southern kingdom of Judah, and an even smaller remnant of the twelve tribes which had occupied the land under Joshua. They had a limited amount of territory around Jerusalem which was only a fraction of the land ruled by David and Solomon. They had no king; and although at times they had some degree of independence, they lived constantly under the shadow of foreign powers. They could take comfort from the fact that they were in the land; but they could hardly ever feel that they were masters in their own land.

3·5 The Land and the Hopes of Israel

Was this the glorious future that the prophets had spoken of? Was this all that God had in store for his people – that they should live in a small section of their own land and under the control of foreigners? God had fulfilled his promise about the return to the land. But what about all the other things that went with it – like the spiritual renewal of the nation?

Could it be that the promise of a return was to be fulfilled *again* – but this time not in another return of exiles to the land, but rather as part of the fulfilment of *all* the promises contained within the Abrahamic covenant and *all* the hopes of Israel? Our task now is to go back to the prophets and see how the theme of the land is woven into everything else that they said about the future.

Isaiah

Isaiah's description of the restoration of the people speaks of much more than a mere return to the land:

> The desert and the parched land will be glad;
>   the wilderness will rejoice and blossom. . .
> Stengthen the feeble hands,
>   steady the knees that give way;
> say to those with fearful hearts, 'Be strong, do not fear;
>   your God will come, he will come with vengeance;
>   with divine retribution he will come to save you.'
> Then will the eyes of the blind be opened
>   and the ears of the deaf unstopped.
> Then will the lame leap like a deer,
>   and the tongue of the dumb shout for joy.
> Water will gush forth in the wilderness
>   and streams in the desert . . .
> And a highway will be there;
>   it will be called the Way of Holiness.
> The unclean will not journey on it;
>   it will be for those who walk in that Way;
>   wicked fools will not go about on it . . .
>   Isaiah 35:1, 3–6, 8

Jeremiah

Jeremiah links the return to the land with several other important prophetic themes – a promise of national security, the knowledge of God, repentance, and the covenant relationship between God and his people:

> This is what the Lord, the God of Israel, says: 'Like these good figs, I regard as good the exiles from Judah, whom I sent away from this place to the land of the Babylonians. My eyes will watch over them for their good, and I will bring them back to this land. I will build them up and not tear them down; I will plant them and not uproot them. I will give them a heart to know me, that I am the Lord. They will be my people, and I will be their God, for they will return to me with all their heart.'
>   Jeremiah 24: 5–7

Ezekiel

Chapters 36 and 37 are a favourite hunting ground for students of prophecy. Here we find that the prophecy of a return to the land is just one of many different themes concerning what God is going to do for his people:

- I will gather you from all the countries and bring you

back into your own land   36:24; 37:12,14,21

● I will sprinkle clean water on you, and . . . I will cleanse you from all your impurities.   36:25,29,33; 37:23

● I will give you a new heart and put a new spirit in you . . . I will give you a heart of flesh   36:26

● I will put my Spirit in you and move you to follow my decrees and be careful to keep my laws   36:27; 37:14,24

● You will live in the land I gave your forefathers   36:28; 37:25

● You will be my people, and I will be your God   36:28; 37:23,27

● I will call for the grain and make it plentiful . . . the desolate land will be cultivated   36:29,34

● Then the nations . . . will know that I the Lord have rebuilt what was destroyed   36:36; 37:28

● I will make their people (the house of Israel) as numerous as sheep   36:37; 37:26

● Then you, my people will know that I am the Lord   37:13–14; 36:38

● I will make them one nation in the land   37:22

● There will be one king over all of them . . . my servant David will be king over them . . . for ever   37:22,24,25

● They will all have one shepherd   37:24

● I will make a covenant of peace with them . . . an everlasting covenant   37:26

● I will put my sanctuary among them for ever . . . my dwelling-place will be with them   37:26,27

The remaining chapters of the book (38 – 40) are also important because they have much to say about Jerusalem and the land, and because many of these themes are taken up and developed in the New Testament.

Chapters 38 and 39 consist of prophecies against Gog, a nation in the far north, which we are told will one day join with many other nations to attack the land of Israel. Chapters 40 to 48 consist of a series of visions, which are introduced in the following words:

In the twenty-fifth year of our exile, at the beginning of the year, on the tenth of the month, in the fourteenth year after the fall of the city – on that very day the hand of the Lord was upon me and he took me there. In visions of God he took me to the land of Israel and set me on a very high mountain, on whose south side were some buildings that looked like a city.

Ezekiel 40:1–2

In his vision Ezekiel sees a plan of the whole temple area and describes the temple ritual. At one stage he sees the glory of God filling the temple (43:1–9), and later sees a river flowing from the temple down to the Dead Sea (47:1–12). We are then given the boundaries of the land (47:13–23):

> These are the boundaries by which you are to divide the land for an inheritance among the twelve tribes of Israel, with two portions for Joseph. You are to divide it equally among them. Because I swore with uplifted hand to give it to your forefathers, this land will become your inheritance.
>
> Ezekiel 47:13–14

The final chapter explains how the land is to be divided between the tribes:

> 'This is the land you are to allot as an inheritance to the tribes of Israel, and these will be their portions,' declares the Sovereign Lord.
>
> Ezekiel 48:29

The book ends with the words:

> And the name of the city from that time on will be: THE LORD IS THERE.
>
> Ezekiel 48:35

Zechariah

Zechariah lived in the period immediately following the return from exile, and his prophecies date from around 520—518 BC. He looks forward to yet another return of exiles 'from the countries of the east and the west':

> And the word of the Lord Almighty came to me. This is what the Lord Almighty says: 'I am very jealous for Zion; I am burning with jealousy for her.'
>
> This is what the Lord says: 'I will return to Zion and dwell in Jerusalem. Then Jerusalem will be called the City of Truth, and the mountain of the Lord Almighty will be called The Holy Mountain.'
>
> This is what the Lord Almighty says: 'Once again men and women of ripe old age will sit in the streets of Jerusalem, each with cane in hand because of his age. The city streets will be filled with boys and girls playing there.'
>
> This is what the Lord Almighty says: 'It may seem marvellous to the remnant of this people at that time, but will it seem marvellous to me?' declares the Lord Almighty.
>
> This is what the Lord Almighty says: 'I will save my people

from the countries of the east and the west. I will bring them
back to live in Jerusalem; they will be my people, and I will be
faithful and righteous to them as their God.'
Zechariah 8:1–8

Another passage speaks of the return of exiles of the northern
kingdom of Israel (referred to here as 'the house of Joseph' and 'the
Ephraimites') and exiles of the southern kingdom of Judah:

I will strengthen the house of Judah
    and save the house of Joseph.
I will restore them because I have compassion on them.
They will be as though
    I had not rejected them,
for I am the Lord their God
    and I will answer them.
The Ephraimites will become like mighty men,
    and their hearts will be glad as with wine . . .
I will signal for them
    and gather them in.
Surely I will redeem them;
    they will be as numerous as before.
Though I scatter them among the peoples,
    yet in distant lands they will remember me.
They and their children will survive,
    and they will return.
I will bring them back from Egypt
    and gather them from Assyria.
I will bring them to Gilead and Lebanon,
    and there will not be room enough for them.
Zechariah 10:6–10

Hope for the Nation

Here indeed was a glorious future to look forward to!

The prophets were speaking of the time when God would fulfil
the promises he had made to Abraham. Their message was simply
- that the people would live in *the land* for ever
- that they would become a *great nation*
- that God would be *their God*
- that through them *all people on earth* would be blessed.

Would these promises ever be fulfilled? If so, when and how?

3·6 *The Birth of the Messiah*

Luke's account of the birth of Jesus contains many important clues
about who he was and what he was going to do for his people – all of

them related to promises and hopes in the Old Testament.

The Annunciation to Mary

The words of the angel announcing the birth of Jesus contain a very clear echo of the original promise concerning the line of David:

The Annunciation to Mary

You will be with child and give birth to a son, and you are to give him the name Jesus. He will be great and will be called the son of the Most High. The Lord God will give him *the throne of his father David*, and *he will reign over the house of Jacob for ever*; *his kingdom will never end*.

Luke 1:31–33

The Promise to David

The Lord declares to you that the Lord himself will establish a house for you: When your days are over and you rest with your fathers, I will raise up your off-spring to succeed you, who will come from your own body, and I will establish his kingdom. He is the one who will build a house for my Name, and *I will establish the throne of his kingdom for ever*. I will be his father, and he shall be my son . . . Your house and *your kingdom shall endure for ever* before me; *your throne shall be established for ever*.

2 Samuel 7:11–14,16

Whereas David was told that his kingdom would last for ever through an unbroken line of *his descendants*, Mary is told that *Jesus himself* will reign for ever. He is to reign over 'the house of Jacob' – which means the whole house of Israel. His kingdom will not be limited to 'the house of Judah', as was the kingdom of all David's descendants who ruled in Jerusalem after Solomon; he will reign over the whole nation, united into one.

The Song of Mary

In her song of praise to God (the Magnificat), Mary speaks of the 'great things' that God has done for her personally and relates them to the fulfilment of what God had promised to Abraham:

My soul praises the Lord
  and my spirit rejoices in God my Saviour,
for he has been mindful
  of the humble state of his servant.
From now on all generations will call me blessed,
  for the Mighty One has done great things for me – holy is his name.

He has helped his servant Israel,
  remembering to be merciful
to Abraham and his descendants for ever,
  even as he said to our fathers.
    Luke 1:46–49, 54–55

The Song of Zechariah

Soon after the birth of John the Baptist, his father Zechariah connects all that is happening with the promises given to the prophets and the covenant with Abraham:

Praise be to the Lord, the God of Israel,
  because he has come and has redeemed his people.
He has raised up a horn of salvation for us
  in the house of his servant David
(as he said through his holy prophets of long ago),
  salvation from our enemies
  and from the hand of all who hate us –
to show mercy to our fathers
  and to remember his holy covenant,
the oath he swore to our father Abraham:
to rescue us from the hand of our enemies,
  and to enable us to serve him without fear
in holiness and righteousness
  before him all our days.
    Luke 1:68–75

The first part of the song defines salvation as '*salvation from our enemies*'; the second part defines salvation in terms of '*the forgiveness of their sins*'

And you, my child, will be called a prophet of the Most High;
  for you will go on before the Lord to prepare the way for
him,
to give his people the knowledge of salvation
  through the forgiveness of their sins,
because of the tender mercy of our God,
  by which the rising sun will come to us from heaven
to shine on those living in darkness
  and in the shadow of death,
  to guide our feet into the path of peace.
    Luke 1:76–79

The Song of Simeon

One person who recognized the significance of the birth of Jesus was the aged Simeon, who was present when Joseph and Mary brought Jesus to be presented in the temple on the fortieth day after his birth:

> Now there was a man in Jerusalem called Simeon, who was
> righteous and devout. He was waiting for the consolation of
> Israel, and the Holy Spirit was upon him. It had been revealed
> to him by the Holy Spirit that he would not die before he had
> seen the Lord's Christ.
> Luke 2:25–26

When he took Jesus in his arms he praised God with the words:

> Sovereign Lord, as you have promised,
>   you now dismiss your servant in peace.
> for my eyes have seen your salvation,
>   which you have prepared in the sight of all people,
> a light for revelation to the Gentiles
>   and for glory to your people Israel.
> Luke 2:29–32

Simeon clearly understood that Jesus was to be 'the Lord's Christ',
the one who would bring about 'the consolation of Israel' (or 'the
restoration of Israel'). He also believed that the consolation or
restoration of Israel was about to take place in the person of Jesus.

Anna the Prophetess

Another person who recognized the identity of Jesus was Anna:

> There was also a prophetess, Anna . . . She never left the
> Temple but worshipped night and day, fasting and praying.
> Coming up to them at that very moment, she gave thanks to
> God and spoke about the child to all who were looking forward
> to the redemption of Jerusalem.
> Luke 2:36–38

There must have been a circle of people known to Anna who were
looking forward to 'the redemption of Jerusalem', or 'the liberation
of Jerusalem'.

Anna's message to them after seeing Jesus was that *he* was the
one who would have a vital role to play in the fulfilment of their
hopes.

If Simeon and Anna, like the vast majority of their fellow-Jews in
the first century thought of 'the consolation of Israel' and 'the
redemption of Jerusalem' as historical events which would one day
take place in the city of Jerusalem and the land of Palestine, they
now believed that the restoration of Israel and the liberation of
Jerusalem *had already begun to take place* through the birth of Jesus
the Messiah.

3·7 The Messiah and the Land

Jesus had very little to say specifically about the land – in fact, there is only one clear and obvious reference to the land in his teaching. This is all the more surprising when we see his message against the background of typical Jewish hopes and expectations of the first century AD.

Since promises about the land, however, were only one aspect of the covenant made with Abraham, we need to look for any clues which show how Jesus thought about the fulfilment of that covenant. And since predictions of a return to the land were interwoven with everything else that the prophets said about the future, we have to take note of anything which indicates how Jesus understood the fulfilment of the hopes and longings of the people of Israel.

'The Meek ... will Inherit the Earth'

The Sermon on the Mount begins with these eight well-known sayings describing the characteristics and the blessings of those who belong to the kingdom of God.

> Blessed are the poor in spirit,
>   for theirs is the kingdom of heaven.
> Blessed are those who mourn,
>   for they will be comforted.
> Blessed are the meek,
>   for they will inherit the earth.
> Blessed are those who hunger and thirst for righteousness,
>   for they will be filled.
> Blessed are the merciful,
>   for they will be shown mercy.
> Blessed are the pure in heart,
>   for they will see God.
> Blessed are the peacemakers,
>   for they will be called sons of God.
> Blessed are those who are persecuted because of righteousness,
>   for theirs is the kingdom of heaven.
> Matthew 5:3–10

It isn't too difficult to understand what it means to be comforted, to be filled, to be shown mercy, to see God and to be called sons of God. But what does it mean to 'inherit the earth'? The Greek word translated 'earth' (*gen*) can also mean 'land'; and the Hebrew word which lies behind this Greek word is *'erets*, the word that is used throughout the Old Testament for 'the land'. The *Kittel Theological Dictionary of the New Testament* suggests that the word 'land' is used here in the eschatological sense to mean 'the land of promise', and comments:

> The kingdom which Psalm 37:11 promises to the *'anawin*, 'the poor', is Palestine perfected in the Messianic glory.

Jesus is therefore saying that 'the meek will inherit *the land*', and the expression is taken straight from Psalm 37, which contains no fewer than seven references to 'the land' or 'the inheritance':

> *Dwell in the land* and enjoy safe pasture.
> Those who hope in the Lord will *inherit the land*.
> . . . but the meek will *inherit the land* . . .
> The blameless . . . *their inheritance* will endure for ever.
> Those the Lord blesses will *inherit the land* . . .
> The righteous will *inherit the land* . . .
> *He will exalt you to possess the land* . . .
> Psalm 37:3,9,11,18,22,29,34

The Psalmist was obviously thinking of the land of Palestine, 'the land which the Lord has given you as an inheritance.' On the lips of Jesus, however, the land now begins to take on a new meaning: those who will inherit and possess the land and dwell securely in it for ever are the poor in spirit of any nation who mourn and are meek.

Abraham had been promised that the land would belong to his descendants for ever; but now Jesus gives his description of who those descendants are.

Abraham had been promised that he would be the ancestor of a great nation; now Jesus spells out his understanding of who are the true people of God.

Abraham had been promised that there would be a special relationship between God and his descendants; Jesus now describes the kind of people who will be called sons of God, and will see God.

Abraham had been promised that through his descendants all peoples on earth would be blessed; now Jesus extends God's blessing to anyone who is poor in spirit and hungers and thirsts for righteousness.

'Freedom for the Prisoners'

At the very beginning of his public ministry Jesus read some words from Isaiah in a service in the synagogue at Nazareth, and claimed that they had been fulfilled in himself:

> The scroll of the prophet Isaiah was handed to him. Unrolling it, he found the place where it is written:
>   'The Spirit of the Lord is on me,

> because he has anointed me
> to preach good news to the poor.
> He has sent me to proclaim freedom for the prisoners
> and recovery of sight for the blind,
> to release the oppressed,
> to proclaim the year of the Lord's favour.'
> Then he rolled up the scroll, gave it back to the attendant and
> sat down. The eyes of everyone in the synagogue were fastened
> on him, and he said to them, 'Today this scripture is fulfilled in
> your hearing.'
> Luke 4:17-21

In their original context in Isaiah 61:1-2 the words he quoted were referring to 'the prisoners' and 'the oppressed' among the people of Judah in exile in a foreign country. He knew as well as his audience that Isaiah's prophecy of a return to the land had been fulfilled in the return of the exiles from Babylon. But here he stands up before a Jewish congregation and makes the astonishing claim, 'Today this scripture is fulfilled in your hearing'.

In the mind of Jesus, therefore, the prisoners, the blind and the oppressed were the people sitting in the same synagogue and walking the streets of Nazareth. Using Old Testament language about leading exiles back to the land from a foreign country he claimed that he had been appointed and commissioned by God to meet their deepest needs.

'Good News is Preached to the Poor'

When John the Baptist was in prison, he sent some of his disciples to ask Jesus the question, 'Are you the one who was to come, or should we expect someone else?' In his reply Jesus used expressions from Isaiah chapters 35 and 61 to describe what he believed he had been called to do, and thus to explain who he was:

> At that very time Jesus cured many who had diseases, sicknesses and evil spirits, and gave sight to many who were blind. So he replied to the messengers: 'Go back and report to John what you have seen and heard, *The blind receive sight, the lame walk,* those who have leprosy are cured, *the deaf hear*, the dead are raised, and *the good news is preached to the poor*.'
> Luke 7:21-22

> Then will *the eyes of the blind be opened* and *the ears of the deaf unstopped.*
> Then will *the lame leap* like deer, and the tongue of the dumb shout for joy.
> Isaiah 35:5-6
> The Spirit of the Sovereign Lord is on me,
> because the Lord has anointed me *to preach good news to the poor.*
> Isaiah 61:1

We have already seen in section 3·5 that Isaiah 35 is a poetic description of the return of exiles to the land. It speaks of 'the redeemed' who will return and 'enter Zion with singing'. Jesus is therefore once again taking poetic imagery from an Old Testament passage about the return of Jewish exiles from Babylon, and using it to describe what he is doing in his public ministry.

A New Testament scholar, **R.T. France**, makes this comment on the significance of Jesus using the Old Testament in this way: 'The inevitable conclusion seems to be that Jesus presented his ministry as the fulfilment of the whole future hope of the Old Testament, the day of the Lord and the coming of the Messiah. Even where the original reference seems to be focussed on a political restoration of God's people (especially true in Isaiah 35) Jesus can find the fulfilment in his own ministry.'

'Many will Come from the East and the West'

Jesus was astonished at the faith of the Roman centurion who believed that Jesus could heal his servant who was sick at home simply by saying the word, and without having to go to him. This is what he said to those who were following him at the time. His words contain a clear echo of Isaiah 43 and Psalm 107:

I tell you the truth, I have not found anyone in Israel with such great faith. I say to you that many will come *from the east and the west*, and will take their places at the feast with Abraham, Isaac and Jacob in the kingdom of heaven. But the subjects of the kingdom will be thrown outside, into the darkness where there will be weeping and gnashing of teeth
Matthew 8:10–12

I will bring your children *from the east* and gather you *from the west*.
I will say to the north, 'Give them up!'
   and to the south, 'Do not hold them back.'
Bring my sons from afar
   and my daughters from the ends of the earth – everyone who is called by my name . . .
Isaiah 43:5–7
Let the redeemed of the Lord say this . . .
those he gathered from the lands,
   from east and west, from north and south.
Psalm 107:2–3

Here again, therefore, Jesus takes expressions which, in their original context, speak of the ingathering of Jewish exiles *to the land*, and uses them to speak of the future ingathering of people from all over the world *into the kingdom of God*. He even goes further and no doubt shocks many of his Jewish hearers when he warns that many Jews will be excluded from the kingdom.

R.T. France concludes: 'It seems, therefore, that, far from looking for some future regathering of the Jewish people to Palestine, Jesus actually took Old Testament passages which originally had that connotation, and applied them instead to the ingathering of the Christian community from all nations, even in one case, to the exclusion of some Jews!'

These ideas are reflected in another saying of Jesus recorded by John:

> I have other sheep that are not of this sheep pen. I must bring them also. They too will listen to my voice, and there will be one flock and one shepherd.
> John 10:16

They are also expressed even more explicitly by John in his comment on what the high priest said about the death of Jesus:

> He did not say this on his own, but as high priest that year he prophesied that Jesus would die for the Jewish nation, and not only for that nation but also for the scattered children of God, to bring them together and make them one.
> John 11:51–52

It wasn't that Jesus was simply 'spiritualizing' Old Testament prophecies, and thereby leaving open the possibility that they might one day be interpreted literally. Rather, according to him, the gathering of believers into the kingdom of God was the true fulfilment of these prophecies.

Some Christian writers have pointed out that the prophets predicted the return of the exiles from *all* countries – from north, south, east and west. Moreover, they say, some of the prophets (notably Zechariah) specifically predicted that exiles of the northern kingdom of Israel would return to the land as well as exiles from the southern kingdom of Judah. They go on to ask: has anything happened in history which fits this description – *except* the recent return of Jews to the land?

The question at first sight seems unanswerable; it sounds a convincing 'knock-down' argument. But if the Christian is to interpret Old Testament prophecy in the light of the teaching of Jesus, the question simply doesn't arise. Why? Because in the perspective of Jesus, the ingathering of the exiles – from the north, south, east and west – takes place when men of all races are gathered into the kingdom of God. This is the true, the real, the intended fulfilment of the prophecy.

3·8 The Messiah and Jerusalem

Jerusalem had figured prominently in the prophetic hopes concerning the future of Israel. In the teaching of Jesus, however, the main significance of Jerusalem was that it was the place where he would die and rise again, and that it would soon be destroyed as a judgement from God.

Predictions of the Passion

When Jesus predicted his suffering, death and resurrection in Jerusalem, he spoke of them as the fulfilment of prophecy:

> We are going up to Jerusalem, and everything that is written by the prophets about the Son of Man will be fulfilled. He will be turned over to the Gentiles. They will mock him, insult him, spit on him, flog him and kill him. On the third day he will rise again.
> Luke 18:31–33, compare Mark 8:31

It is widely accepted that when Jesus spoke of his resurrection as being 'on the third day', he was using the words Hosea 6:1–2. In their original context, these verses express the hope of a national restoration, i.e. the resurrection of the people of Israel:

> Come, let us return to the Lord.
>> He has torn us to pieces
>>> but he will heal us;
>> he has injured us
>>> but he will bind up our wounds.
> After two days he will revive us;
>> on the third day he will restore us,
>> that we may live in his presence.
> Hosea 6:1–2

These hopes and aspirations for the nation were hardly fulfilled in the centuries following the prophet's lifetime. So what did Jesus mean when he made such a deliberate reference to these hopes and said that he would be raised from the dead 'on the third day'? The answer suggested by R.T. France is that 'Jesus could only apply Hosea's words to himself if he saw himself as in some way the heir to Israel's hopes.' He goes on to quote this significant sentence from C.H. Dodd's book *According to the Scriptures*: 'The resurrection of Christ *is* the resurrection of Israel of which the prophets spoke.'

Jesus is therefore claiming that in some way *he himself* is a representative of the whole people of Israel, and that the promised restoration of the nation is going to take place in and *through him*.

Predictions of the Fall of Jerusalem

Mark, Luke and Matthew all record sayings of Jesus about the end of the age, which were spoken in Jerusalem during the last week of his life.

● The thirteenth chapter in Mark begins with a prediction of the destruction of the temple:

> As he was leaving the temple, one of his disciples said to him, 'Look Teacher! What massive stones! What magnificent buildings!' 'Do you see all these great buildings?' replied Jesus. 'Not one stone here will be left on another; every one will be thrown down.' As Jesus was sitting on the Mount of Olives opposite the temple, Peter, James, John and Andrew asked him privately, 'Tell us, when will these things happen? And what will be the sign that they are all about to be fulfilled?'
> Mark 13:1–4

In his answer to these questions Jesus speaks of false prophets, wars, earthquakes and famines which are to be 'the beginning of birth pains'; and warns his disciples to expect persecution from civil and religious authorities, and even from their own families. He then speaks about the time when the temple will be desecrated, using expressions borrowed from the book of Daniel (9:27;11:31;12:11):

> When you see the abomination that causes desolation standing where it does not belong – let the reader understand – then let those who are in Judea flee to the mountains. Let no-one on the roof of his house go down or enter the house to take anything out. Let no-one in the field go back to get his cloak. How dreadful it will be in those days for pregnant women and nursing mothers! Pray that this will not take place in winter, because those will be days of distress unequalled from the beginning, when God created the world, until now – and never to be equalled again. If the Lord had not cut short those days, no one would survive. But for the sake of the elect, whom he has chosen, he has shortened them. At that time, if anyone says to you, 'Look, here is the Christ!' or, 'Look, there he is!' do not believe it. For false Christs and false prophets will appear and perform signs and miracles to deceive the elect – if that were possible. So be on your guard; I have told you everything ahead of time.
> Mark 13:14–23

The next two verses speak about cosmic disturbances:

> But in those days, following that distress,
> 'the sun will be darkened,

and the moon will not give its light;
the stars will fall from the sky,
and the heavenly bodies will be shaken.'

These words have generally been interpreted as referring to disturbances in the universe which will occur at the end of the world. It is
quite possible, however, that they should be taken very closely with
the previous verses to refer to the fall of Jerusalem. (The reasons for
this interpretation of verses 24–27 are explained in detail in R.T.
France's book *Jesus and the Old Testament*. See especially pages
227–39.) The main reason for this interpretation is that the quotation
is taken straight from a prophecy of Isaiah about the fall of Babylon,
Isaiah 13:10. If Isaiah could speak of cosmic disturbances
accompanying the fall of *Babylon* (which took place in 539 BC), it is
perfectly understandable that Jesus could use the same kind of
poetic language to describe the fall of *Jerusalem*. We don't have to
think in terms of literal disturbances in the cosmos at the end of the
world.

If this is a possible interpretation, it means that Jesus wanted his
Jewish hearers to understand that God was going to punish the holy
city of Jerusalem in the same way as he had punished the pagan city
of Babylon. If they understood the point of the quotation, they
would no doubt have been shocked and deeply offended at the comparison.

The following verse speaks about the coming of the Son of man:

At that time men will see the Son of Man coming in clouds with
great power and glory.
Mark 13:26

Here again we have a saying which has generally been interpreted as
referring to the second coming of Jesus Christ at the end of the
world, but which could *also* be speaking about events in the near
future. The picture of the coming of the Son of man on the clouds is
almost certainly taken from one of Daniel's visions in the Old Testament:

In my vision at night I looked, and there before me was one like
a son of man, coming with the clouds of heaven. He
approached the Ancient of Days and was led into his presence.
He was given authority, glory and sovereign power; all peoples,
nations and men of every language worshipped him. His
dominion is an everlasting dominion that will not pass away,
and his kingdom is one that will never be destroyed.
Daniel 7:13–14

Since this passage (like many others in Daniel) is about the kingdom
of God, it is natural to connect it with another important saying in

Mark's Gospel about the coming of the kingdom of God:

> I tell you the truth, some who are standing here will not taste
> death before they see the kingdom of God come with power.
> Mark 9:1

If there was a connection in Jesus' mind between the coming of the
kingdom of God 'with power' (Mark 9:1) and the coming of the Son
of man 'with great power' (Mark 13:26), when were they to happen?
The answer must be that since Jesus said the kingdom would come
while many of his hearers were still alive, the coming of the Son of
man would also take place during this period. We can hardly avoid
making a connection between the words 'the present generation will
live to *see* it all' (Mark 13:20) and the words 'then they will *see* the
coming of the Son of man . . .' (Mark 13:26)

What then could the coming of the kingdom of God and the
coming of the Son of man mean at this particular time? The
'coming' described in Daniel's vision is a coming to God; the Son of
man is presented before God and receives authority, glory and
sovereign power. The resurrection and ascension fit this description
perfectly, since it was supremely through these events that Jesus was
vindicated by God, raised to glory and established in his kingdom.
And if the fall of Jerusalem is linked with this sequence of events, it
is because it was one more event by which Jesus was vindicated
before men.

Jesus is saying that in the years to come it will become clear
through all that happens that God has vindicated him openly. Men
will 'see' with the eyes of faith that the Son of man has entered into
his eternal kingdom and that the kingdom of God has come among
men.

This interpretation of the coming of the Son of man does not
rule out the traditional interpretation of these words, which relates
them to the second coming. It simply means that the *primary*
reference in the words about the coming of the Son of man is to his
public vindication in the near future.

The next verse speaks about something closely related to the
coming of the Son of man:

> And he will send his angels and gather his elect from the four
> winds, from the ends of the earth to the ends of the heavens.
> Mark 13:27

The Greek word translated as 'angels' is *aggelous*, which is the
common word for 'messengers'. It would therefore be perfectly
legitimate to translate the sentence 'he will send *his messengers* and

gather his elect...' This saying echoes several Old Testament passages which speak of the gathering of exiles; and in Matthew's version of the same saying, the 'trumpet call' comes from a verse in Isaiah which describes the return of exiles from Assyria and Egypt:

And he will send his angels and gather his elect from the four winds, *from the ends of the earth to the ends of heaven.* Mark 13:27	Even if you have been banished to *the most distant land under the heavens*, from there the Lord your God will gather you and bring you back. Deuteronomy 30:4 'Come! Come! Flee from the land of the north,' declares the Lord. 'Come, O Zion! Escape, you who live in the Daughter of Babylon!' Zechariah 2:6–7
And he will send his angels ... with *a loud trumpet call*, and they will gather his elect from the four winds, from one end of the heavens to the other. Matthew 24:31	And in that day *a great trumpet* will sound. Those who were perishing in Assyria and those who were exiled in Egypt will come and worship the Lord on the holy mountain in Jerusalem. Isaiah 27:13

Thus when we compare the words of Jesus with the Old Testament sources from which some of their ideas and expressions are taken, it appears that once again the primary reference in Jesus' words is not to the end of the world, but to an event in history. He has already said that 'the gospel must first be preached to all nations' (Mark 13:10). Now he is saying the same thing, but this time using a poetic image from the Old Testament: God will soon send out his messengers to all nations to gather all his chosen people into the kingdom.

The remaining verses of this part of Mark 13 underline the point that everything Jesus has predicted up till now will happen in the near future:

Now learn this lesson from the fig tree: As soon as its twigs get tender and its leaves come out, you know that summer is near. Even so, when you see these things happening, you know that it is near, right at the door. I tell you the truth, this generation will

certainly not pass away until all these things have happened.
Heaven and earth will pass away, but my words will never pass
away.
Mark 13:28–31

When we reach Mark 13:32 however, there can be no doubt that
Jesus is speaking about events in the more distant future. The time is
described as 'that day or hour', and it is generally agreed that the
reference is to the second coming of Jesus Christ and the end of the
world:

No one knows about that day or hour, not even the angels in
heaven, nor the Son, but only the Father. Be on guard! Be
alert! You do not know when that time will come.
Mark 13:32–33

What then does Mark's version of the discourse about the end of the
age contribute to our understanding of how Jesus thought about
Jerusalem and its future? At the very least, we can draw three conclusions:

● Apart from predicting the fall of Jerusalem and the destruction of the temple, Jesus was silent about the future of the land.

● Jesus spoke of the fall of Jerusalem and the destruction of the
temple as an act of divine judgement on the Jewish people for their
unbelief.

● Jesus spoke of the events in the coming years (including the
resurrection, the ascension and the fall of Jerusalem) as a sequence
of events by which God would vindicate the Son of man and bring in
the kingdom of God.

This is Luke's version of the part of the discourse which deals with
the future of Jerusalem:

When you see Jerusalem surrounded by armies, you will know
that its *desolation* is near. Then let those who are in Judea flee to
the mountains, let those in the city get out, and let those in the
country not enter the city. For this is the time of *punishment* in
fulfilment of all that has been written. How dreadful it will be in
those days for pregnant women and nursing mothers! There
will be *great distress in the land* and *wrath against this people*.
They will *fall by the sword* and will be taken as prisoners to all
the nations. Jerusalem will be trampled on by the Gentiles until
the times of the Gentiles are fulfilled. There will be *signs in the
sun, moon and stars*. On the earth, nations will be in anguish and
perplexity at the roaring and tossing of the sea. Men will faint
from terror, apprehensive of what is coming on the world, for
the heavenly bodies will be shaken. At that time they will see

the Son of man coming in a cloud with power and great glory.
When these things begin to take place, stand up and lift up your
heads, because your redemption is drawing near.'
Luke 21:20–28

There are at least four sayings in this version which are not found
either in Mark or in Matthew:

1. There are several very clear (and presumably deliberate) echoes
of Isaiah's prophecy concerning the fall of Babylon (Isaiah 13):

Luke 21	Isaiah 13
. . . its *desolation* is near. (20)	. . . to make the land *desolate* (9)
. . . the time of punishment . . . (22)	. . . I will *punish* the world . . .(11)
. . . *wrath* against this people. (23)	. . . *wrath* and fierce *anger* (9)
	. . . the *wrath* of the Lord . . . his burning *anger* (13)
They will *fall by the sword* (24)	. . . all who are caught will *fall by the sword* . . . (15)

2. 'This is the time of punishment in fulfilment of all that has been
written' (Luke 21:22). Jesus here emphasizes what is implied in his
use of the quotation from Isaiah: the fall of Jerusalem is to be seen as
an act of divine judgement on the city and the people. Moreover,
these events are to be seen as the fulfilment of '*all* that has been
written' – i.e. presumably *all* that has been written about Jerusalem.

3. 'When these things begin to take place, stand up and lift up your
heads, because your redemption is drawing near' (Luke 21:28). We
have already seen the word 'redemption' in the birth narratives, and
noticed that Anna the prophetess spoke about Jesus to all who were
looking forward to 'the redemption of Jerusalem' (Luke 2:38). The
word occurs again in Luke 24:21 where the two disciples express
their hopes that Jesus was 'the one who was going to redeem Israel'.
If the quotation about cosmic disturbances is a poetic way of
speaking about the fall of Jerusalem (Luke 21:25–26), and if the
words about the coming of the Son of man with power and great
glory speak of his vindication through his death, resurrection and
ascension and through the coming judgement of Jerusalem, then the
redemption which Jesus speaks about here is not primarily something which will be achieved at the end of the world. It must be no
different from the 'redemption of Jerusalem' (Luke 2:38), 'the consolation of Israel' (Luke 2:25) and the 'redemption of Israel' (Luke
24:21). In Luke's thinking, this process of redemption was set in

motion the moment Jesus was born. And this saying of Jesus speaks of the redemption being completed in the near future.

4. 'Jerusalem will be trampled on by the Gentiles until the times of the Gentiles are fulfilled' (Luke 21:24). Other translations of this verse read: 'Jerusalem will be trampled down by foreigners until their day has run its course' (New English Bible). 'The heathen will trample over Jerusalem until their time is up' (Today's English Version).

This verse is often interpreted as a prediction that Jerusalem would be under the domination of non-Jews *until* the times of the Gentiles were fulfilled, but *after* that time, it would again come under Jewish rule. Many popular books on prophecy not only insist that Jesus was clearly predicting the eventual return of Jerusalem to Jewish rule; they also conclude that the return of Jerusalem to Jewish rule must be regarded as an important sign pointing forward to 'the last days'. They therefore attach great importance to the recapture of the Old City of Jerusalem by the Israelis in the war of June 1967.

The main problem with this interpretation is that it reads ideas into the text which can hardly be found in the text itself.

Some sentences using the word 'until' *do* imply something about the more distant future. If I say 'I will go on discussing this question with you *until* I have convinced you', the obvious implication is that when I have convinced you, I will stop talking! But there are equally many sentences in which it makes nonsense to try to draw implications about what will happen after the time referred to. For example, when God promised Jacob, 'I will not leave you *until* I have done what I have promised you' (Genesis 28:15), he could hardly mean that he would be with Jacob until he had fulfilled his promise, but that *after* that time he would leave him!

Even if Jesus does imply that Jerusalem will one day be returned to the Jews, the main thrust of what he is saying concerns the destruction of Jerusalem in the near future rather than events in the more distant future. He is more concerned to warn his hearers about what will happen before some of them die, than to predict what will happen in the dim and distant future.

So when Jesus said that Jerusalem would be trampled on by the Gentiles until the times of the Gentiles were fulfilled, he *may* have wanted his disciples to draw the conclusion that Jerusalem would one day *cease to be* trampled on by the Gentiles. But this was not the main point he wanted them to grasp. He said nothing at all about what would follow the times of the Gentiles, and didn't give any clue about the significance of Jerusalem coming once again under Jewish rule.

Luke's version of the discourse therefore points to the same conclusions as the discourse in Mark: that Jesus was silent about the future of the land; that the fall of Jerusalem was to be an act of divine judgement; and that through all the events of the coming years God was going to bring in his kingdom.

How then did Jesus understand the significance of Jerusalem for his ministry as the Messiah? It was in Jerusalem that his death and resurrection would fulfil 'all that is written by the prophets about the Son of Man'. And before long the holy city of Jerusalem would be attacked and destroyed, simply because its people had failed to recognize 'the time of God's coming' in the person of the Messiah.

Like Isaiah, Jeremiah and Ezekiel centuries before, Jesus spoke of God's judgement on the people and the land. But unlike them, he did *not* tell them that if they repented in their exile, God would restore them to their land. Was this because he assumed that the same pattern of exile and return would be repeated all over again, and that a return in the twentieth century would play just as vital a part in God's plan for the world as the return in the sixth century BC? The alternative is to understand that when the majority of the Jewish people refused to accept Jesus as their Messiah, God could no longer deal with them on exactly the same basis as he had done before. God's plan for the Jewish people was entering a completely new phase.

3·9 The Redemption of Israel

Once again we're indebted to Luke, this time for his vivid account of two significant meetings between the risen Jesus and his disciples. When Jesus appears to the two disciples on the road to Emmaus they don't recognize him at first, and start describing the events of the past week in Jerusalem leading up to his death. They express the extreme disappointment, even disillusionment, that they have experienced:

> He was a prophet, powerful in word and deed before God and all the people. The chief priests and our rulers handed him over to be sentenced to death, and they crucified him; but *we had hoped that he was the one who was going to redeem Israel*. And what is more, it is the third day since all this took place. In addition, some of our women amazed us. They went to the tomb early this morning but didn't find his body. They came and told us that they had seen a vision of angels, who said he was alive. Then some of our companions went to the tomb and found it just as the women had said, but him they did not see.
>
> Luke 24:19–24

Jesus, however, doesn't seem to show a great deal of sympathy for their hopes for the nation of Israel. Instead he rebukes them for their dullness and slowness to understand the prophets:

> 'How foolish you are, and how slow of heart to believe all that the prophets have spoken! Did not *the Christ* have to suffer these things and then enter his glory?' And beginning with Moses and all the Prophets, he explained to them what was said in all the Scriptures concerning *himself*.
> Luke 24:25–27

One of the surprising things about this conversation is that Jesus appears to ignore the subject that they are really interested in – namely, the redemption of Israel. He simply speaks of himself as 'the Christ' (i.e. the Messiah, God's anointed agent), and goes on to say why it was necessary for him to suffer and die. He then explains everything in the Scriptures concerning *himself* – not Israel.

Was Jesus thinking only of himself? Was he deaf to what the two men were saying? Was he talking at cross purposes with them? No! He wanted them to understand that *all* that the prophets had said about *Israel* and its redemption had been fulfilled in *himself*. It wasn't that he was disinterested in their hopes for the nation. Rather he was trying to tell them that he *had* accomplished the redemption of Israel – although not in the way they had expected. The redemption of Israel had already been carried out through the suffering, death and resurrection of the Christ.

The Kingdom of Israel and the Kingdom of God

In his summary of the appearances of Jesus during the forty days between the resurrection and the ascension, Luke says that he was teaching the disciples 'about the kingdom of God' (Acts 1:3). When he spoke about the coming of the Holy Spirit, they still found it difficult to see the connection between Jesus' concept of the kingdom of God and their own ideas of the kingdom of God:

> On one occasion, while he was eating with them, he gave them this command: 'Do not leave Jerusalem, but wait for the gift my Father promised, which you have heard me speak about. For John baptised with water, but in a few days you will be baptised with the Holy Spirit.' So when they met together, they asked him, 'Lord, are you at this time going to restore the kingdom to Israel?
> Acts 1:4–6

The disciples seem to have had a kind of mental block. Even if they accepted and believed all Jesus' teaching about the kingdom of God, they still held on to their Jewish hopes for the future of the nation of Israel. They were looking forward to the establishment of an independent Jewish state, no longer under Roman control. And they assumed that since this was a vital part of the establishment of the kingdom of God on earth, the resurrection of Jesus provided the unique opportunity for this next stage in the unfolding of God's plan.

This, however, was Jesus' reply:

> (7) It is not for you to know the times or dates the Father has set by his own authority. (8) But you will receive power when the Holy Spirit comes on you; and you will be my witnesses in Jerusalem, and in all Judea and Samaria, and to the ends of the earth.
>
> Acts 1:7–8

There are two possible interpretations of Jesus' answer, and the crucial question we need to decide is: what is the connection of thought between verse 7 and verse 8?

According to the first interpretation, we need to separate verses 7 and 8, because there is no vital connection between them. Jesus was not challenging the disciples' *idea* of a restored Jewish state, but only correcting their ideas about the *time* when it would come into being. Jesus was saying in effect: 'A restored, independent Jewish state is certainly part of God's plan for the coming of the kingdom; but it will not come into being now and it is not for you to know when it will be established.' Those who accept this interpretation often go on to claim that we in our day *do know* something about 'dates and times', since we have witnessed the establishment of an independent Jewish state in Palestine.

According to the second interpretation, verses 7 and 8 need to be taken very closely together, because both of them are answering the disciples' question. Jesus was not only trying to correct the disciples' idea about the *timing* of these events (verse 7), he was also trying to correct the *idea* that was implied in the question (verse 8). He wanted them to put on one side the idea of the kingdom which they had inherited from their Jewish background, and to accept a completely new idea of the kingdom of God. It was to be a kingdom which would include anyone from Jerusalem, Judea, Samaria and from the ends of the earth who would believe the testimony of the apostles.

It was therefore as if he was saying, 'I want you to put out of your minds once and for all the idea that the establishment of a sovereign Jewish state has any special significance in the establishment of the kindgom of God. I want you to see the kingdom of God in a different light – as a kingdom which is spiritual and therefore has nothing to do with any territorial kingdom; a kingdom which is international and has no connection with any national kingdom.'

If the context doesn't suggest which of these two interpretations is more convincing, we need to look at the writings of the apostles to see if there is anything to suggest that *after* this meeting they continued to look forward to a restored Jewish state in the land.

3·10 The Land in the Kingdom of God

Given the political situation in first-century Palestine, the writers of the New Testament had every reason to hope for a national restoration for the Jewish people. But did they in fact do so? There is nothing whatsoever to suggest that they held onto these hopes. On the contrary, we find a great deal of evidence which indicates that they grasped the new concept of the kingdom of God which Jesus had tried to teach them. This means that our ideas of how they understood the meaning of the land need not be based simply on an argument from silence.

Peter

The testimony of Peter is of special value, because he was the first of the disciples to realize that there was a significant difference between his own typically Jewish idea of the 'Messiah' and Jesus' understanding of what the Messiah must be and do.

In the following passage from his first epistle, written about thirty years after the death of Jesus, he uses the familiar Old Testament word 'inheritance' and gives it a new meaning:

> Praise be to the God and Father of our Lord Jesus Christ! In his great mercy he has given us new birth into a living hope through the resurrection of Jesus Christ from the dead, and into *an inheritance* that can never perish, spoil or fade – kept in heaven for you, who through faith are shielded by God's power until the coming of the salvation that is ready to be revealed in the last time.
> 1 Peter 1:3–5

A first-century Jew would inevitably have associated the word 'inheritance' with the land, because this is one of the main ways in which the word is used all through the Old Testament. For example:

> He brought his people out like a flock . . .
>   . . . brought them to the border of *his holy land*,
>   to the hill country his right hand had taken.
>
> He drove out nations before them
>   and allotted their lands to them as *an inheritance*;

he settled the tribes of Israel in their homes.
Psalm 78: 52,54–55

We can be sure that this is the background of the word 'inheritance' in Peter's mind, because he goes on to make an implied contrast between the inheritance of the land and the inheritance of the Christian believer: the land *could* perish, or be spoiled, whereas the spiritual inheritance of the believer *cannot* perish or be spoiled in any way, because it is kept in heaven for all who believe.

In the following chapter we find a similar example of the bold way in which Peter reinterprets Old Testament themes: he takes titles which were reserved exclusively for the Jews and applies them to *all* who believe in Christ – whether Jew or Gentile:

You are a chosen people, a royal priesthood, a holy nation, a people belonging to God, that you may declare the praises of him who called you out of darkness into his wonderful light. Once you were not a people, but now you are the people of God; once you had not received mercy, but now you have received mercy.
1 Peter 2:9–10

The Acts of the Apostles

One could make out a good case for saying that the book of Acts was intended by Luke to be (among other things) a counterpart to the book of Joshua in the Old Testament. Whereas Joshua describes the gradual conquest of the land beginning from Jericho, Acts describes the gradual spread of the Christian church beginning from Jerusalem.

The book of Joshua begins with God's command to enter and conquer the land: 'go in and take possession of the land the Lord your God is giving you for your own . . .' (Joshua 1:11). The book of Acts begins with the command of the risen Jesus to his disciples to start a different kind of conquest: 'you will be my witnesses in Jerusalem, and in all Judea and Samaria, and to the ends of the earth' (Acts 1:8).

Joshua and the tribes were to possess their allotted inheritance by killing its inhabitants 'with the edge of the sword'. In Acts, however, Paul speaks of the word of God as the weapon by which Christians are to occupy their inheritance: 'Now I commit you to God and to the word of his grace, which can build you up and give you an inheritance among all those who are sanctified' (Acts 20:32).

The book of Joshua describes the different stages by which the land was conquered – beginning with the capture of Jericho and Ai, then going on with the campaigns in the south and the north. The book of Acts describes how the gospel was first preached in

Jerusalem, in Samaria, and then in Caesarea to the first Gentile; from Antioch the message was taken by Paul into Asia Minor, then to Greece, and finally to Rome.

Both Joshua and Acts describe the many difficulties which had to be faced and overcome; and the story in Acts of Ananias and Sapphira and their deception over the sale of their land (Acts 5:1–11) is an exact parallel to the story in Joshua of Achan, whose theft and lying held up the advance of the whole army (Joshua 7). In Joshua we find repeated several times in different forms a formula which describes times of peace and consolidation after times of fighting: 'then the land had rest from war . . .' (Joshua 11:23; see also 14:15; 21:44; 23:1). We find something similar in Acts with sentences like 'then the church . . . enjoyed a time of peace. It was strengthened; and . . . grew in numbers' (Acts 9:31). 'So the word of God spread' (Acts 6:7; see also 2:47; 12:24; 13:49; 19:20).

If Luke and the early Christian church thought in terms of conquest, they were thinking of the conquest not of the land but of the whole world. The only sword that would be used for this conquest was the sword of the word of God which would enable those who believed it to possess the inheritance that God had promised them. The gospel of Jesus was not only for the people in the land, but for all nations of the world.

Paul

The subject of the land is conspicuous by its absence in the letters of Paul. He seems to show no interest in the land in the purposes of God. Even in a passage in Romans where he lists several of the privileges of the Jewish people he makes no mention of the land:

> I speak the truth in Christ – I am not lying, my conscience
> confirms it in the Holy Spirit – I have great sorrow and
> unceasing anguish in my heart. For I could wish that I myself
> were cursed and cut off from Christ for the sake of my brothers,
> those of my own race, the people of Israel. Theirs is the
> adoption as sons; theirs the divine glory, the covenants, the
> receiving of the law, the temple worship and the promises.
> Theirs are the patriarchs, and from them is traced the human
> ancestry of Christ, who is God over all, for ever praised! Amen.
> Romans 9:1–5

The promise of the land was included in the 'covenants', and the prophecies about the land must have been included in 'the promises' which he refers to here. But it can hardly be an accident that, whereas the land figured prominently in the thinking of orthodox Jews at the time, Paul does not include the land in his list. Although he writes in Romans 11 of the glorious future that they can look forward to as a people, there is no suggestion that it is associated with the land.

The reason for this silence must be that Paul believed that Jesus was the fulfilment of *all* the divine promises. In one of his earliest letters, he describes *all* Christians, both Jews and Gentiles, as 'Abraham's seed' and therefore inheritors of the promise given to Abraham:

> You are all sons of God through faith in Christ Jesus, for all of you who were baptised into Christ have been clothed with Christ. There is neither Jew nor Greek, slave nor free, male nor female, for you are all one in Christ Jesus. If you belong to Christ, then you are Abraham's seed, and heirs according to the promise.
> Galatians 3:26–29

Christians have no difficulty in believing that the promises concerning Abraham's descendants, about the covenant relationship between God and his people, and about the blessing for all people on earth have been fulfilled in and through Christ. But what about the promise concerning the land? Does it have to be put in a category of its own? Can we say that the other three aspects of the covenant have been fulfilled in a *spiritual* way in Christ, while the promise about the land must be interpreted *literally* – and that the land therefore belongs by a God-given right to Abraham's physical descendants for all time?

If Paul thought in these terms, it's very strange that he doesn't add any kind of qualification concerning the land. If this is what he really meant, one might have expected him to say: 'You are the heirs of the promise given to Abraham – *except* that part of the promise which refers to the land, which applies only to the Jews who are the physical descendants of Abraham.' It is difficult to see how he could say that *all* believers are the seed of Abraham and therefore inheritors of the promise, but at the same time believe that one aspect of the promise does *not* apply to all believers.

Later in the same letter he gives an allegorical interpretation to the story of Sarah and Hagar, and draws a distinction between the actual city of Jerusalem and 'the heavenly Jerusalem':

> These things may be taken figuratively, for the women represent two covenants. One covenant is from Mount Sinai and bears children who are to be slaves: This is Hagar. Now Hagar stands for Mount Sinai in Arabia and corresponds to the present city of Jerusalem, because she is in slavery with her children. But the Jerusalem that is above is free, and she is our mother.
> Galatians 4:24–26

This kind of 'spiritualizing' of the Old Testament was not strange or new for orthodox Jews. What *is* significant, however, is that Paul should describe 'the present city of Jerusalem' as being 'in slavery with her children'. Presumably it wasn't just because Jerusalem was under Roman occupation that he could speak of the city in these terms; it must have been because the vast majority of the Jewish people had rejected their promised Messiah:

> ... the Jews ... killed the Lord Jesus and the prophets and also
> drove us out. They displease God and are hostile to all men in
> their effort to keep us from speaking to the Gentiles so that
> they may be saved. In this way they always heap up their sins to
> the limit. The wrath of God has come upon them at last.
> 1 Thessalonians 2:14–16

If Paul had lived to see Jerusalem regaining its freedom and coming under Jewish rule in 135 or 1967, he would no doubt have *continued* to think of Jerusalem as being in slavery with all her children. Political freedom for the Jewish people had little or nothing to do with the kingdom of God in the thinking of Paul.

At the end of Galatians Paul gives another striking example of how the coming of Christ has transformed his Jewish attitudes. He takes the name 'Israel' and applies it to those of all races who have come to recognize Jesus as God's Messiah:

> May I never boast except in the cross of our Lord Jesus Christ,
> through which the world has been crucified to me and I to the
> world. Neither circumcision nor uncircumcision means
> anything, what counts is a new creation. Peace and mercy to all
> who follow this rule, even to *the Israel of God.*
> Galatians 6:14–16

If the translation '*even* to the Israel of God' is correct, it would seem that for Paul the name 'Israel' is no longer the exclusive possession of the physical descendants of Abraham, Isaac and Jacob. 'The Israel of God' embraces all who have taken up their cross to follow in the footsteps of the crucified Messiah.

It is possible, however, that the sentence can be translated '*and* to the Israel of God' (New English Bible). In this case 'the Israel of God' must be those among the Jewish people who believe in Christ and therefore 'follow this rule' that Paul had laid down. In view of all that he has already said in the same letter, he could hardly still be thinking of the whole Jewish people as 'the Israel of God'.

The Letter to the Hebrews

This letter was written by an unknown author to Christians from a Jewish background. The writer takes up one theme after another from the Old Testament and shows how its full meaning has been revealed in and through Jesus – in his birth, life, death, resurrection and ascension.

In chapter 4 he takes the theme of the land, which he describes as 'that rest' or 'God's rest':

> Therefore, since the promise of entering *his rest* still stands, let us be careful that none of you be found to have fallen short of it. For we also have had the gospel preached to us, just as they did; but the message they heard was of no value to them, because those who heard did not combine it with faith. Now we who have believed enter *that rest* . . .
> Hebrews 4:1–3

In chapter 10 he speaks of Jesus as the fulfilment of the sacrificial system in the temple:

> Day after day every priest stands and performs his religious duties; again and again he offers the same sacrifices, which can never take away sins. But when this priest (Jesus) had offered for all time one sacrifice for sins, he sat down at the right hand of God.
> Hebrews 10:11–12

In chapter 11 he speaks of Abraham living in the promised land, but looking forward to 'a better country – a heavenly one':

> By faith he (Abraham) made his home in the promised land like a stranger in a foreign country; he lived in tents, as did Isaac and Jacob, who were heirs with him of the same promise. For he was looking forward to the city with foundations, whose architect and builder is God. . . . People who say such things show that they are looking for a country of their own . . . They were longing for *a better country – a heavenly one*. Therefore God is not ashamed to be called their God, for he has prepared a city for them.
> Hebrews 11:9–10, 14, 16

At the climax of the letter in chaper 12 the writer draws a contrast between the literal Mt Sinai where Moses received the Law, and 'Mount Zion . . . the heavenly Jerusalem':

> You have not come to a mountain that can be touched and that is burning with fire; to darkness, gloom and storm; to a trumpet blast or to such a voice speaking words . . . But you have come to *Mount Zion, to the heavenly Jerusalem, the city of the living God*. You have come to thousands upon thousands of angels in joyful assembly, to the church of the first-born, whose names are

> written in heaven. You have come to God, the judge of all men,
> to the spirits of righteous men made perfect, to Jesus the
> mediator of a new covenant, and to the sprinkled blood that
> speaks a better word than the blood of Abel . . .
>
> Therefore, since we are receiving a kingdom that cannot be
> shaken, let us be thankful, and so worship God acceptably with
> reverence and awe, for our God is a consuming fire.
> Hebrews 12:18–19, 22–24, 28–29

Most if not all Christians would believe that the temple and its
sacrifices have been fulfilled once and for all in Jesus. When we have
seen their deeper meaning fulfilled in the person of Jesus, we no
longer expect or want to see a purely literal fulfilment. A literal fulfilment of such promises would seem rather like lighting a candle
when the sun is shining; it's not longer necessary! But if this is true
for the temple and its sacrifices, why can't it also be true for the
land? Why make it an exception, and insist that unlike other themes,
everything associated with the land must be interpreted literally?

It is perfectly understandable that Jews should believe that the
establishment of Israel holds out a hope of survival for the Jewish
people in a hostile world in the twentieth century. And Christians
may or may not accept the ideals of Zionism. But if we understand
how the writer of the letter to the Hebrews thought about the land,
how can we believe that the establishment of a Jewish state in the
land is the fulfilment of Old Testament hopes and aspirations for the
land? Now that the Messiah has come, we cannot possibly go back!

3·11 The Final Fulfilment of the Covenant and the Hopes of Israel

There is one book in the New Testament more than any other which
describes the hopes of a Jewish Christian about the final fulfilment of
the covenant God made with Abraham and of all the hopes of Israel
– the book of Revelation. It does this by describing a series of visions
of past, present and future realities.

If we can assume that John the disciple was the author of both
the Gospel according to John and the book of Revelation, we have
the opportunity to see how one writer develops Old Testament
themes about the land and Jerusalem in two books which are very
different in character from each other. Moreover, the book of
Revelation is specially important because so much Christian
teaching about prophecy (for example, about the millennium) is
based on this book.

The following are two examples of how John takes up themes

concerning the land and Jerusalem and gives them a Christian interpretation:

The glory of the Lord filling the temple

Ezekiel's visions of the temple in the new Jerusalem form part of 'the visions of God' which he describes to the exiles in Babylon (see section 3·5). In one of these visions he sees the glory of God returning to the new temple:

> Then the man brought me to the gate facing east, and I saw the *glory of the God of Israel* coming from the east. His voice was like the roar of rushing waters, and the land was radiant with his *glory.* . . The *glory of the Lord* entered the temple through the gate facing east. Then the Spirit lifted me up and brought me into the inner court, and the *glory of the Lord* filled the temple.
> Ezekiel 43:1–5

John in his Gospel records a saying of Jesus in which he claimed indirectly to be the fulfilment of all that the temple stood for:

> Then the Jews demanded of him, 'What miraculous sign can you show us to prove your authority to do all this?'
>
> Jesus answered them, 'Destroy this temple, and I will raise it again in three days.'
>
> The Jews replied, 'It has taken forty-six years to build this temple, and you are going to raise it in three days?' But the temple he had spoken of was his body.
> John 2:18–21

Once John had seen Jesus in this light, it was only natural that he should speak of seeing the glory of God – not in a restored temple in Jerusalem, but in the face of Jesus:

> The Word became flesh and lived for a while among us. We have seen his glory, the glory of the one and only Son, who came from the Father, full of grace and truth.
> John 1:14

When we come to the book of Revelation, we find that John has developed Ezekiel's vision of the new Jerusalem and the new temple into a picture of the final consummation of God's plans for the universe:

> Then I saw a new heaven and a new earth, for the first heaven and the first earth had passed away, and there was no longer any sea. I saw the Holy City, the new Jerusalem, coming down out of heaven from God, prepared as a bride beautifully dressed for her husband. And I heard a loud voice from the

throne saying, 'Now the dwelling of God is with men, and he
will live with them. They will be his people, and God himself
will be with them and be their God.'

I did not see a temple in the city, because the Lord God
Almighty and the Lamb are its temple.
Revelation 21:1–3, 22

In his Gospel, therefore, John relates Ezekiel's vision of the new
temple to the *first* coming of Jesus Christ: Jesus himself is the new
temple and the glory of God is revealed through him. In Revelation,
he relates it to the *second* coming of Christ: he sees 'a new heaven
and a new earth', when this world as we know it ('the first earth') has
passed away. The words from the throne indicate that what he is
seeing in the vision is the final and complete fulfilment of the
covenant promise made to Abraham: 'Now the dwelling of God is
with men, and he will live with them. *They will be his people, and God
himself will be with them and be their God.*'

The river of living water

This picture is found in three different prophets: Ezekiel, Zechariah
and Joel. It occurs first of all in Ezekiel, where it is part of his vision
of the new temple (see section 3·5):

The man brought me back to the entrance to the temple, and I
saw water coming out from under the threshold of the temple
towards the east (for the temple faced east). The water was
coming down from under the south side of the temple, south of
the altar. He then brought me out through the north gate and
led me round the outside to the outer gate facing east, and the
water was flowing from the south side.

As the man went eastward with a measuring line in his
hand, he measured off a thousand cubits and then led me
through water that was ankle-deep . . . He measured off
another thousand, but now it was a river that I could not cross,
because the water had risen and was deep enough to swim in –
a river that no one could cross . . .

Then he led me back to the bank of the river. When I
arrived there, I saw a great number of trees on each side of the
river. He said to me, 'This water flows towards the eastern
region and goes down into the Arabah, where it enters the Sea.
When it empties into the Sea, the water there becomes fresh.
Swarms of living creatures will live wherever the river flows . . .
Fruit trees of all kinds will grow on both banks of the river.
Their leaves will not wither, nor will their fruit fail. Every
month they will bear, because the water from the sanctuary

flows to them. Their fruit will serve for food and their leaves for healing.'
Ezekiel 47:1–3, 5–9, 12

It seems that the prophets felt free to borrow pictures and images from each other – and even sometimes to adapt them. Thus when Zechariah takes up the same picture, he speaks of water flowing *both* to the east *and* to the west:

On that day living water will flow out from Jerusalem, half to the eastern sea and half to the western sea, in summer and in winter. The Lord will be king over the whole earth.
Zechariah 14:8–9

Joel at a later date uses the image as part of his picture of the prosperity of the new age when God will establish his people in the land:

In that day the mountains will drip new wine,
and the hills will flow with milk;
all the ravines of Judah will run with water.
A fountain will flow out of the Lord's house
and will water the valley of acacias.
Judah will be inhabited for ever
and Jerusalem through all generations.
Joel 3:18, 20

When this same picture is used by Jesus, the streams of living water flow not from the temple, but from every individual who believes in him *or* (according to another possible interpretation) from Jesus himself. The words 'streams of living water will flow from within him' in John 7:38 must be taken from these visions in the prophets, since there is no other saying resembling it anywhere else in the Old Testament:

On the last and greatest day of the Feast, Jesus stood and said in a loud voice, 'If a man is thirsty, let him come to me and drink. Whoever believes in me, as the Scripture has said, streams of living water will flow from within him.' By this he meant the Spirit, whom those who believed in him were later to receive. Up to that time the Spirit had not been given, since Jesus had not yet been glorified.
John 7:37–39

The same theme appears once again in John's vision of 'a new heaven and a new earth'. Here the city from which the water is flowing is 'the Holy City, the new Jerusalem coming down out of heaven from God . . .':

> Then the angel showed me the river of the water of life, as clear
> as crystal, flowing from the throne of God and of the Lamb
> down the middle of the great street of the city. On each side of
> the river stood the tree of life, bearing twelve crops of fruit,
> yielding its fruit every month. And the leaves of the tree are for
> the healing of the nations.
> Revelation 22:1–2

The apostle John therefore sees the prophetic vision of the river of
living water as being fulfilled in two ways: firstly, in Jesus' giving of
the spirit to the believer or in the experience of the believer who is
filled with the Spirit and is therefore able to bring life to others, and
secondly in the new heaven and new earth. If these were the
thoughts that were going through John's mind when he read the
visions in Ezekiel, Zechariah and Joel, it's hard to imagine that he
could *also* be looking forward to the time when a brilliant irrigation
scheme would be devised to bring water from Jerusalem across the
desert of Judea and down to the Dead Sea!

Christians generally believe that the New Testament writers give
us an authoritative interpretation of the Old Testament – or rather,
the normative interpretation of the Old Testament. This means, for
example, that if we want to know what the sacrificial system in the
temple was all about, we look to the writings of the apostles. Since
the risen Jesus 'opened their minds so they could understand the
Scriptures' (Luke 24:45), we can look to their writings to find out
how Jesus interpreted the Old Testament.

The Christian today does not have the liberty to interpret the
Old Testament in any way that appeals to him. Everything in the Old
Testament has to be read through the eyes of the apostles. It is they
who, so to speak, give us the right spectacles for a genuinely
Christian reading of the Old Testament.

Therefore if I as a Christian in the twentieth century find that
certain details in books like Ezekiel appear to fit certain situations in
the Middle East today, I must resist the temptation to draw direct
connections with these contemporary events. The reason is that
since the apostle John has given me *his* interpretation of Ezekiel's
versions, I ought to recognize that this is *the normative interpretation*
of these visions, and dare not say that his is only *one possible
interpretation*. I do not have the liberty to work out from Ezekiel 38
the scenario for a Russian invasion of Palestine in the 1980s; *or* to
draw a plan of Ezekiel's temple from chapters 40–47 and expect that
it will one day be built in Jerusalem; *or* to draw a map of Palestine
according to Ezekiel's division of the land in chapter 48 and expect
that this will one day be the territory occupied by the state of Israel.
I don't have this liberty simply because this is not how the apostle

John interpreted these visions.

What about the millennium?

Some Christians may well be asking at this point: why has there been no discussion of the millennium? If you're discussing the book of Revelation, how can you possibly avoid taking the bull by the horns and entering into the controversy about what is the millennium and when it will take place?

The omission has been deliberate – for two reasons.

Firstly, I personally believe that the whole controversy about the millennium has forced the interpretation of prophecy into a kind of strait-jacket. The categories for interpreting prophecy have all been fixed, and the positions have all been frozen: you are either a pre-millennialist, or a post-millennialist, or an a-millennialist. Prophecy is all about the future, and the interpretation of prophecy is concerned with working out a kind of blue-print, a time-table which describes the sequence of events leading up to and following the millennial reign of Christ.

I suspect that it is largely because Christian interpretation of prophecy in evangelical churches has been forced into these categories that it has *either* proved to be incapable of helping Christians to get to grips with the actual realities of the Middle East in the twentieth century, *or* has given answers which result in a political bias which is totally one-sided.

Secondly, there are many sincere Christians who are concerned about how to relate the Bible to what's happening in the Middle East, but are blissfully ignorant of all the technicalities of the millennial controversy – or else are completely sickened by the intensity of this particular kind of doctrinal controversy.

For these two reasons, I did not think it would be helpful or edifying to raise a banner for one particular school of prophecy, or to quote well-known champions of other schools and attempt to refute them. This doesn't mean that I'm totally ignorant of the issues raised by the millennial controversy or that I've deliberately ignored the teaching of Dispensationalism. Readers who are familiar with all the arguments of the different schools may very quickly be able to attach a label to the position that I have taken. But those who have not been, or don't want to be, initiated into these mysteries may have the advantage of being able to judge the argument on its own merits, without being prejudiced by having it all neatly labelled with the slogans of one particular school.

What I have tried to do therefore is to by-pass the whole controversy about the millennium, in the hope that we may be able to see what the Bible has to say about the land from a different perspective and in a new light.

'Come, Lord Jesus'

Instead of ending on a note of controversy we should notice how our study of the land in the Bible has now brought us full circle: what John has described in his visions is simply the final and complete fulfilment of the covenant which God made with Abraham:

● the promise of *the land* has now given way to the promise of 'a new heaven and a new earth' (Revelation 21:1)

● *the nation* which God promised would become great and numerous has now become 'the 144,000 from all the tribes of Israel' (Revelation 7:4)

● the promise of *a special relationship between God and his people* is fulfilled because now 'the dwelling of God is with men, and he will live with them. They will be his people, and God himself will be with them and be their God.' (Revelation 21:3)

● the promise of *blessing for all peoples on earth* will finally be fulfilled in the 'great multitude that no-one could count, from every nation, tribe, people and language, standing before the throne and in front of the Lamb' (Revelation 7:9)

With this hope before him, it's no wonder that John should end the book with a prayer and a blessing:

Come, Lord Jesus.
The grace of the Lord Jesus be with God's people. Amen.

3·12 Some Conclusions

1. The original promise about the land belonging to Abraham and his descendants 'as an everlasting possession' was part of the whole covenant with Abraham, which also included a promise about the nation, about the covenant relationship between God and his people, and about the blessing which would come to all people on earth.

2. The promise about the land began to be fulfilled through Abraham's legal purchase of land, and found further fulfilment in the conquest of the land under Joshua.

3. Continued possession of the land was conditional on obedience. Since the land was a gift from God, he could easily withdraw the people's right to live in the land for a time if they did not fulfil the terms of the covenant. The northern kingdom of Israel was taken into exile in Assyria in 721 BC, and as far as we know, never returned to the land. The cream of the southern kingdom of Judah was taken into exile in Babylon in 597 and 586 BC.

4. Prophecies about a return to the land were primarily concerned with the Jews who were exiles in Babylon. 2 Chronicles and Ezra described the return of exiles from Babylon to Jerusalem from 539 BC onwards as the fulfilment of the prophecies of Jeremiah.

5. Promises about the land and the predictions about a return to the land should not be separated from other promises and predictions in the Old Testament and must be interpreted according to the same principles. The prophets looked forward to the complete political and spiritual restoration of the nation in the land, a restoration through which God's purposes for the nation and for the world would be fulfilled.

6. The birth of Jesus is described as the fulfilment of the promise made to Abraham and of the hopes expressed by the prophets.

7. In the teaching of Jesus, the theme of the kingdom of God takes the place of the theme of the land and everything else associated with it in the Old Testament. He used language from the Old Testament about the ingathering of the exiles and the redemption or restoration of the nation of Israel to describe his own ministry.

8. Apart from predicting the destruction of Jerusalem (which took place in AD 70), Jesus was silent about the future of the land.

9. Jesus claimed that through his life, death and resurrection he had accomplished 'the redemption of Israel'.

10. In contrast to Jewish writers who developed both literal and spiritual interpretations of the land side by side, the New Testament writers showed no interest in a literal interpretation. Since they were silent about the future of the land and at the same time interpreted the concept of the land in the light of Jesus and his kingdom, they must have believed that this was the only possible interpretation of the significance of the land for the Christian, whether Jew or Gentile. Once the New Testament writers had seen the significance of the land and the nation in the context of the kingdom of God which had come into being in Jesus of Nazareth, they ceased to look forward to a literal fulfilment of Old Testament prophecies of a return to the land and a restored Jewish state. The one and only fulfilment of all the promises and prophecies was already there before their eyes in the person of Jesus. The way they interpreted the Old Testament must be the norm for the Christian interpretation of the Old Testament today.

4

IS THERE ANY WORD FROM THE LORD?

❝ Jeremiah was put into a vaulted cell in a dungeon, where he remained a long time. Then King Zedekiah sent for him and had him brought to the palace, where he asked him privately, *'Is there any word from the Lord?'* **❞**
Jeremiah 37:16–17

Many people today believe that the return of Jews to the land and the establishment of the state of Israel are to be seen as the fulfilment of promises and prophecies in the Old Testament. But is this the only way of using the Bible to interpret all that we have witnessed in the land?

Part 4 explores other themes from the Old and New Testaments which may shed light on some of the questions concerning the land today.

4·1 The Passion for Truth

The more one reads about the conflict over the land, the easier it is to become as cynical as Pilate and ask 'What is truth?' Each side accuses the other of deliberately concealing or distorting the truth.

The Sunday Times of 19 June 1977 carried a detailed report on the use of torture on Arab prisoners in Israel. The Israeli embassy in London rejected this report in the following terms:

> Allegations of this nature have been repeatedly put out by Arab propaganda sources in recent years and proved to be totally unfounded in the light of detailed and documented investigation.

Walter Barker, the General Secretary of the Church's Ministry Among the Jews, wrote a critical review of a recent book, *Palestine Comes First* by Lucas Grollenberg, a Dutch Dominican priest:

> The writer claims to give an account of what really happened as opposed to the Zionist propaganda view supposedly accepted uncritically by the Christian and the West. One of the intriguing facets of this bitter controversy is how convinced both sides are that the other's propaganda is the most successful! The historical survey, while having every sympathy with Arab hopes, aspirations and needs, lacks any sensitivity to the Jewish point of view . . .
>
> It is essential that if Christians from the West write or speak about this tragic controversy they should do so with balance. This is obviously lacking here, so as a Christian contribution it is a poor one.

Lance Lambert, a Jewish Christian writer who identifies very strongly with Israel, repeats the common Israeli argument about 'continuing lies and propaganda' which have kept the Arab refugee problem alive:

> Whereas every one of the non-Arab countries that received a flood of refugees did their best to settle the new arrivals, the strenuous efforts of the Arab countries has been to prevent or limit such resettlement. The reason for this callousness is simple and is avowedly political. If the Arab refugees were to find new jobs and homes in Syria, Lebanon, Jordan and Egypt, they might too easily settle down and lose their sense of Palestinian identity and yearning for their old homes, which has been kept alive through continuing lies and propaganda. For this reason alone the Arab Governments have denounced and thwarted all

international attempts to resettle the refugees away from Israel's borders.

Allegations of Arab distortions are matched by similar accusations against the Jews.

George Antonius, a Palestinian historian, writing in 1938 in *The Arab Awakening*:

Zionist propaganda is active, highly organized and widespread; the world Press, at any rate in the democracies of the West, is largely amenable to it; it commands many of the available channels for the dissemination of news, and more particularly those of the English-speaking world. Arab propaganda is, in comparison, primitive and infinitely less successful: the Arabs have little of the skill, polyglottic ubiquity or financial resources which made Jewish propaganda effective. The result is, that for a score of years or so, the world has been looking at Palestine mainly through Zionist spectacles and has unconsciously acquired the habit of reasoning of Zionist premises.

William Zuckerman, a Jew, writing in *The Jewish Newsletter* in 1958:

The terrifyingly gruesome power of modern propaganda to take over men's minds and lives, to manipulate their emotions and turn them into animals, is to my mind nowhere expressed more clearly than in the Zionist propaganda about Arab refugees put out over the last ten years. This propaganda has literally succeeded in changing black into white, lies into truth and serious social injustice into an act of justice, praised by thousands. This propaganda has turned capable men with more than average understanding into dupes and fools who believe everything that they are told; it has made friendly and gentle men and women with a strong sense of compassion into harsh fanatics, without any feeling for anyone other than their own people.

General Carl von Horn, the Swedish Commander of the United Nations Truce Supervisory Organization (UNTSO) in Palestine from 1951 to 1963, was very critical about Israeli reporting of events during this period:

The highly skilled Israeli Information Service and the entire press combined to manufacture a warped, distorted version which was disseminated with professional expertise through every available channel to their own people and their sympathisers and supporters in America and the rest of the world. Never in all my life had I believed the truth could be so cynically, expertly bent.

David Hirst gives two examples of what he believes to be deliberate mis-information put out by Israeli government ministers about the Palestinians. **Levi Eshkol**:

> What are the Palestinians? When I came here there were 250,000 non-Jews, mainly Arabs and bedouins.

An Israeli minister of education urged that Israeli youth should be given this information about Palestinian Arabs:

> It is important that our youth should know that when we returned to this country we did not find any other nation here and certainly no nation which had lived here for hundreds of years. Such Arabs as we did find here arrived only a few decades before us in the 1830s and 1840s as refugees from the oppression of Muhammad Ali in Egypt.

What would the Old Testament prophets have to say about a situation of this kind?

'Truth is nowhere to be found'

In his confession on behalf of the people, *Isaiah* realizes that truth and justice go together, so that when there is no truth, there can be no justice:

> For our offences are many in your sight,
>   and our sins testify against us.
> Our offences are ever with us,
>   and we acknowledge our iniquities:
> rebellion and treachery against the Lord,
>   turning our backs on our God,
> fomenting oppression and revolt,
>   uttering lies our hearts have conceived.
> So justice is driven back,
>   and righteousness stands at a distance;
> truth has stumbled in the streets,
>   honesty cannot enter,
> Truth is nowhere to be found,
>   and whoever shuns evil becomes a prey.
> Isaiah 59:12–15

Amos describes the reaction of the majority to anyone who dared to speak the truth and expose what was wrong:

> You hate the one who reproves in court,
>   and despise him who tells the truth.
> Amos 5:10

Jeremiah speaks of God in his wrath having to reject a whole generation of the people because 'truth has perished':

> This is the nation that has not obeyed the Lord its God or responded to correction. Truth has perished; it has vanished from their lips. Cut off your hair and throw it away; take up a lament on the barren heights, for the Lord has rejected and abandoned this generation that is under his wrath.
> Jeremiah 7:28–29

> 'Friend deceives friend,
>   and no-one speaks the truth.
> They have taught their tongues to lie;
>   they weary themselves with sinning.
> You live in the midst of deception;
>   in their deceit they refuse to acknowledge me,'
> declares the Lord.
> Jeremiah 9:5–6

Zechariah, however, looks forward to a better future, and in his vision of the restored Jerusalem, the city is called 'The City of Truth':

> This is what the Lord says: 'I will return to Zion and dwell in Jerusalem. Then Jerusalem will be called The City of Truth, and the mountain of the Lord Almighty will be called The Holy Mountain.'
> Zechariah 8:3

> This is what the Lord Almighty says: 'Just as I had determined to bring disaster upon you and showed no pity when your fathers angered me,' says the Lord Almighty, 'so now I have determined to do good again to Jerusalem and Judah. Do not be afraid. These are the things you are to do: Speak the truth to each other, and render true and sound judgement in your courts; do not plot evil against your neighbour, and do not love to swear falsely. I hate all this,' declares the Lord.
> Zechariah 8:14–17

What would it mean in practical terms for Christians and Jews to demonstrate this kind of prophetic passion for truth in all their thinking about the land?

The writers of the 1970 Quaker Report entitled *The Search for Peace in the Middle East* explain how their report arose out of a concern to find 'the most complete truth we could understand'.

> Out of our own concern, and with the urging of both Jews and Arabs, a group of Quakers began in 1968 the exploration of possible approaches to peace in the Middle East. As we

listened to people in many walks of life, and to high officials in Jordan, Israel, Lebanon, the United Arab Republic, at the UN, and in various world capitals, we were drawn into an effort to record the viewpoints we encountered and to make some attempt at assessing the possibilities of finding a solution . . .

Having listened long and carefully to the many viewpoints of the interested parties, we believe we have a reasonably clear understanding of those viewpoints and how they developed. We have tried to hear all of the assorted and contradictory voices as the cries of real people overcome by real fears and frustrations – and explainable hatreds. We are convinced that no solution to the conflict can be found until it is possible for the outer world and the antagonists themselves, to hear – really hear – what the divergent voices are trying to say. No one truly interested in eventual peace in the Middle East can dismiss any of these voices as manifestations of depersonalized evil or demonic unreason . . .

We have had this manuscript reviewed in detail by many Jews and Arabs, including high Israeli, Lebanese, Jordanian and United Arab Republic officials and by scholarly experts of varied nationalities. Acting on their advice, we have made many changes, while writing more than a dozen drafts, to correct mistakes of fact and to eliminate phrases and nuances deemed unfair or unsound by either side. We must assume that defects will still be found in the document. But, more important, we must accept the fact that on some issues we have had to declare ourselves in ways that put us clearly, with respect to a given point, on one side or the other.

We have tried simply to follow the best light we could find toward the most complete truth we could understand.

General Carl von Horn writes about the difficult task faced by the United Nations Truce Supervisory Organization (UNTSO) in trying to remain neutral and objective in the conflict. His comments underline the need for knowing the truth – the whole truth about what has happened and is still happening:

Our *raison d'être* as peacekeepers was objectivity and impartiality. Yet these very qualities were exactly those which led to hostility. It was understandable; time and time again in the course of frank discussions with Israeli officers and officials, I had heard them openly repudiate the idea of objectivity. Their flat statement 'You are either for or against us', explained why – having dared to be entirely objective – I had now been branded as irrevocably 'against'. I had seen it happen many times before from my predecessors down to the ordinary observer on the frontiers who, in the course of his duty, had incurred Arab or Israeli hostility simply because his *impartial* version had been *very* different from theirs. Even nastier was an Israeli tendency immediately to brand objectivity as anti-Semitic; a convenient label which could be smeared on to any UN soldier whose impartial report did not weigh down in favour of the Israelis.

We had from time to time incurred a certain degree of animosity in our dealings with the Arabs, but never in the same implacable and frenetic way. The Arab could be difficult, intolerant, indeed often impossible; but their code of behaviour was on an infinitely higher and more civilized level. I think that we all came to this conclusion in the UNTSO, which was strange, because there was hardly a man among us who had not originally arrived in the Holy Land without the most positive and sympathetic attitude towards the Israelis and their ambitions for their country.

Never in my life have I encountered a nation with such an infinite talent for turning goodwill into disillusion and so often disgust. It seemed as though the state were possessed of some demon with a capacity to turn potential friends into enemies. I am certain that I shall be bitterly attacked for setting down my impressions so frankly, but unfortunately they are the truth. All of us who went to Israel knew very little about Arabs, but a great deal about the Jews and their appalling sufferings in the Second World War. I have never been – and I am not – anti-Semitic; I have always numbered Jews among some of my closest friends since boyhood. I have good friends in Israel, wonderful families who stood by me and welcomed me into their homes during the height of the boycott. Many of our personnel, too, had close friends in the new state long before they came out to Jerusalem, and I would think that seldom before have the members of any organization – and this was a truly international one – started off with such a fund of goodwill towards a state which had emerged at the cost of such dreadful suffering.

What went wrong? I always had a talk with staff members who were leaving the Mission. Invariably it was the same story. Nearly all of them had arrived with the honest intention to help both parties to the Armistice Agreement, but with a conscious sympathy for the people of 'poor little Israel'. Yet after two or three years in daily contact with officials, soldiers and private individuals on both sides, there had been a remarkable change in their attitude. I found it sad but very significant that when I asked them what their most negative experiences had been during their service with UNTSO the reply was almost invariably: 'The consistent cheating and deception of the Israelis'.

Denys Baly comments on a different kind of untruthfulness: the unwillingness of the Arabs to hear the truth about themselves:

The blindness of the Arab leaders and of the people is a fact – an ugly undeniable fact. There have been those who have grown rich by the sufferings of their countrymen and those who have been content to flee to lands where they could live in greater security and then pour scorn on the foreign nations for not giving that help which they themselves were not prepared to give. It cannot be denied, even by the most fervent admirer of the Arabs, that they have done nothing like as much to help their own people as the Jews have done to help theirs, nor can it be denied that their politicians have often callously used the misery of the refugees as a means to an end; that the very existence of the refugees is partly the result of Arab misunderstanding of the situation; that the Arabs have from time to time encouraged violence and hatred and have again and again refused to face self-evident facts; and that they have been far too ready to blame their unhappiness on anyone but themselves. One meets many of the Arab people who in private conversation are ready to admit these things and are deeply troubled about them. It is true, as we found with the Jews, that reasons can be found to explain these weaknesses, but reasons do not make black white, nor do they convert weakness into strength.

He also suggests what a prophetic passion for truth might do to the whole Christian church:

Repentance is not merely an act; it is an attitude of mind. It is a passion for the truth, an urgent desire to know the worst as well as the best, a readiness to begin again in a new way, a constantly proceeding examination of one's way of life, and with it all an ever remade decision to put right what is wrong. . .

What is needed there [in the Middle East] almost more than anything else is a ruthless intellectual honesty which will break every barrier of emotionalism, sentiment, tradition and nationality, so that at the last people will be found able to question their own motives and behaviour. Hardly anywhere does it exist, and neither Islam nor the type of Judaism which is found in Israel encourage it . . . Only if the Christian Church can regain this passion for truth, whatever it may cost, will they begin to see it as a way of life.

A passion for truth among evangelical Christians might mean, at the very least, a willingness to listen seriously to other interpretations of prophecy than the ones they hold so strongly. **Graham Hoskins**, in an article entitled *Christian Attitudes to the Middle East Problem*, has commented on some evangelical reactions to the book *Furnace of the Lord* by Elizabeth Elliot:

Elizabeth Elliot, widow of the missionary Jim Elliot, and author of well-known books about the murder of her husband by Auca Indians and their subsequent conversion, had already proved herself one of the great Christians of the twentieth century. In 1967, after the Six Day War, she visited Jerusalem. She had no background knowledge of the Middle East and arrived with a slight bias to the dispensationalist view. However, she examined the situation with an open mind. Her book has been called impartial and is indeed very fair to the Jews, but it has a slight but very definite inclination to the Arab point of view. Moreover she takes a completely different approach from that of the dispensationalists. It seems clear that attempts have been made to suppress the book. I was told while on a stay in Israel last year by people at St. George's Hostel in Jerusalem that Mrs. Elliot had great difficulty in getting the book published because it was considered much too pro-Arab. Apparently no Christian publisher would publish it and she ended up having to get a secular publisher, Doubleday, to publish it. Hodder and Stoughton published it in Great Britain but Christian bookshops seem to have avoided it and the British edition went out of print after only three years. I was informed that Christian bookshops in Australia do not hold copies and it has to be ordered direct from America.

Mrs. Elliot does write some things which would have caused great displeasure among Israel's supporters: 'I saw things which the Ministry of Tourism would just as soon I hadn't seen: hillsides which for centuries had been cultivated and terraced by Arabs, turned into desert since 1948. The Israelis had neither knowledge nor inclination to preserve the olive trees and I saw hundreds of acres of crumbling terraces, dried vines, dying trees. It would be impossible to cultivate these terraces by machine, and in modern Israel economically unsound to cultivate them in the ancient way.' . . .

Mrs. Elliot also discovered the Palestine problem, and this discovery evidently turned her sympathies towards the Arab cause. . . . It is deplorable that her book was not given a fair hearing, a situation that Mrs. Elliot herself hints at in her Acknowledgements.

4·2 The Demands of the Law

Is it too naive to suggest that when so many are urging us to see what the *Prophets* say about the land, we ought to start by considering what the *Law* might have to say on the subject? The books of the *torah* which contain the divine promise to Abraham about the land also contain the divine Law revealed to Moses.

Many Christians and Jews appeal to the *torah* because it contains the title deeds of the land. But they contain much more than that on subjects which concern the land. So if we may use some words of Paul in a different context, we may have to ask: 'Tell me, you who want to be under the law (i.e. the *torah*), are you not aware of what the law says?' (Galatians 4:21).

'Thou shalt . . . thou shalt not . . .'

There are three commandments in particular which may need to be spelt out, since we are concerned with rights to ownership of the land and all the violence committed by those who in recent years have claimed it as their own:

> You shall not murder . . .
> You shall not steal . . .
> You shall not covet your neighbour's house. You shall not
> covet your neighbour's wife, or his manservant or maidservant,
> his ox or donkey, or anything that belongs to your neighbour.
> Exodus 20:13, 15, 17

In the Mosaic Law murder is clearly distinguished from manslaughter, and the penalty for murder leaves no doubt about the seriousness of this crime:

> Anyone who strikes a man and kills him shall surely be put to
> death. However, if he does not do it intentionally, but God lets
> it happen, he is to flee to a place I will designate. But if a man
> schemes and kills another man deliberately, take him away
> from my altar and put him to death.
> Exodus 21:12–14

One particular form of stealing – stealing land – is strongly condemned:

> Do not move your neighbour's boundary stone set up by your

predecessors in the inheritance you receive in the land the Lord
your God is giving you to possess.
Deuteronomy 19:14

Cursed is the man who moves his neighbour's boundary stone.
Deuteronomy 27:17

The significance of the Old Testament law in our discussion
becomes all the more apparent when we see the confusing variety of
standards by which people have approached the question of the
land. By the standards of nineteenth century western imperialism,
there was nothing strange or wrong in the idea of immigrants from
Europe settling in Palestine, or of the western powers dividing up the
defeated Ottoman Empire among themselves and establishing their
own authority. Athough the great powers today have rejected such
attitudes, it's obvious that their policies are still determined largely
by expediency and national self-interest.

The United Nations is based on the assumption that there now
exists an internationally-accepted code of practice. Member nations
have declared their support for principles like 'self-determination'
and 'the inadmissability of the acquisition of territory by war'. Over
the question of the Middle East, however, the UN seems to have had
little moral authority in practice – except in the acceptance of its
Partition Plan in 1947. The cynic could be forgiven for saying that
the UN merely represents the collective self-interest of all its
members (especially the most powerful ones), and that it can all too
easily be exploited by particular groups of nations for their own
ends.

Amidst such confusion, therefore, the Old Testament law should
point – at least for the Jew and the Christian – to a higher moral
standard. It should encourage us to consider the question of the land
in the light of a law which is higher than the demands of national
self-interest or the moral consensus of the international community.

Chaim Weizmann, speaking to a UN committee of enquiry in
1947, recognized his willingness as a Jew to be judged by the Law of
Moses, but admitted that his people were not keeping that Law:

> In all humbleness, *thou shalt not kill* has been ingrained in us
> since Mount Sinai. It was inconceivable ten years ago that Jews
> should break this commandment. Unfortunately, they are
> breaking it today, and nobody deplores it more than the vast
> majority of the Jews. I hang my head in shame when I have to
> speak of this fact before you.

'Do not oppress an alien'

Since the Israelites had so recently come out of slavery in Egypt, they were expected to remember what it was like to be aliens who are vulnerable and powerless in a foreign land. When they entered the promised land and established themselves as a nation, they were therefore told not to oppress any aliens living in their midst:

> Do not ill-treat an alien or oppress him, for you were aliens in Egypt.
> Exodus 22:21

> Do not oppress an alien; you yourselves know how it feels to be aliens, because you were aliens in Egypt. (. . . ye know the heart of a stranger. Authorized Version)
> Exodus 23:9

If as Chaim Weizmann said, 'the Jewish problem revolves fundamentally round the homelessness of the Jewish people', one might have expected that the Jews of all people in the twentieth century would 'know the heart of a stranger'.

How has it happened, therefore, that the Jews in Israel, after returning to their land and creating a Jewish state in order to escape from oppression elsewhere, have found themselves in a position of having to take harsh measures to deal with the aliens in their midst? In spite of what the constitution says about equal rights for all communities and all religions, the Arabs, who are living in their own land, often have good reason to complain that they are not treated as native-born Israeli Jews.

Chaim Weizmann, in his autobiography, *Trial and Error*, 1949:

> I am certain the world will judge the Jewish state by how it will treat the Arabs.

Simha Flapan, an Israeli historian, writing in *Zionism and the Palestinians*, one of the most extensive studies on the attitudes of Zionists to the Palestinians (1979), describes Weizmann's attitude towards the Palestinians all through his life:

> Weizmann's attitude towards the Palestinians was the gravest error of his political leadership, more serious than any other because Weizmann did not deviate from his attitude for even a brief period. His disdain for the Palestinians orginated not only in the fact that lacking previous contact with them, he was influenced by his British advisers. From the very beginning, he approached the Palestinians with a prejudice that blinded him to the most obvious facts.
>
> He must have known of the existence of the Palestinian people and their opposition to Zionist colonisation, because as early as 1891, his major spiritual mentor and close associate,

Ahad Ha'am, had warned of major Arab resistance to Jewish immigration and settlement. Ahad Ha'am had no solution to the problem, but urged that at least it be taken seriously. To lessen the conflict, he suggested prudent behaviour, just treatment and respect for Arab customs and culture. Weizmann followed Ahad Ha'am's guidance in his relations with all Arabs except the Palestinians; with regard to them he listened to Aaron Aaronsohn, who viewed the Palestinians as backward, treacherous and corrupt.

He sums up the effects of Weizmann's 'non-recognition of the Palestinians':

Weizmann was sincere in his desire for a just solution to the conflict with the Palestinians. But his non-recognition of the Palestinians as a national entity could not but lead to a policy of injustice . . .

Unfortunately, Weizmann's legacy in this most vital aspect of Jewish-Arab relations has had a more lasting impact than any other. The Palestinians were never regarded as an *integral* part of the country for whom long-term plans had to be made, either in the Mandatory period or since the establishment of the state. This explains why the Palestinian problem has remained at the heart of the Israeli-Arab conflict until the present day . . .

Non-recognition of the Palestinians remains until the present the basic tenet of Israel's policy-makers who, like the Zionist leadership before 1948, nurture the illusion that the Palestinian national problem disappeared with the creation of the state of Jordan, leaving only the residual humanitarian problem of the refugees to be solved.

The war of 1948 was deemed to have vindicated the policy of non-recognition of the Palestinians; on the surface, the Palestinian people, dispersed as refugees all over the Middle East, had ceased to exist, and only the conflict between Israel and the Arab states remained unresolved.

Nearly 30 years had to pass before it became clear that the 1948 war did not liquidate the *national* problem of the Palestinians, but only aggravated and complicated it, changing some of its aspects and adding new ones, coming to resemble the problem of the Jews dispersed throughout the world, which the Zionist movement proposed to solve by 'ingathering of the exiles'.

David Ben-Gurion spelt out very clearly how he understood the status of the Arabs in a Jewish state:

> Israel is the country of the Jews and only of the Jews. Every Arab who lives there has the same rights as any minority citizen in any country of that world, but we must admit the fact that he lives in a Jewish country.

Golda Meir went to the extent of denying the existence of the Palestinian people:

> It was not as though there was a Palestinian people in Palestine considering itself as a Palestinian people and we came and threw them out and took their country away from them. They did not exist.

Samuel Katz dismisses claims about the existence of the Palestinian Arabs as a people:

> There was never a 'Palestinian Arab' nation. To the Arab people as a whole, no such entity as Palestine existed. To those of them who lived in its neighbourhood, its lands were a suitable object for plunder and destruction. Those few who lived within its bounds may have had an affinity for their village (and made war on the next village), for their clan (which fought for the right of local tax-gathering) or even for their own town. They were not conscious of any relationship to a land, and even the townsmen would have heard of its existence as a land, if they heard of it at all, only from such Jews as they might meet . . .
> The feeling of so many nineteenth century visitors that the country had been waiting for the return of its lawful inhabitants was made the more significant by the shallowness of the Arab imprint on the country . . .

Menachem Begin:

> In our country there is only room for Jews.

Dr Nahum Goldmann, a leader in the Zionist movement from the 1940s, recognized the vital importance of the Arab problem for the Jewish state; this is what he wrote in his autobiography in 1970:

> One of the great oversights in the history of Zionism is that when the Jewish homeland in Palestine was founded, sufficient attention was not paid to relations with the Arabs. Of course, there were always a few Zionist speakers and thinkers who stressed them . . . And the ideological and political leaders of

the Zionist movement always emphasized – sincerely and earnestly, it seems to me – that the Jewish national home must be established in peace and harmony with the Arabs. Unfortunately these convictions remained in the realm of theory and were not carried over, to any great extent, into actual Zionist practice. Even Theodor Herzl's brilliantly simple formulation of the Jewish question as basically a transportation problem of 'moving people without a home into a land without a people' is tinged with disquieting blindness to the Arab claim to Palestine. Palestine was not a land without people even in Herzl's time; it was inhabited by hundreds of thousands of Arabs, who in the course of events, could sooner or later have achieved independent statehood, either alone or as a unit with a larger Arab context.

W. Brunn, a Jew, writing in 1919, points out the irony of the situation in which many Jews in Palestine have given the Arabs the same kind of treatment from which they themselves suffered in Europe:

> We who are suffering persecutions throughout the world and who claim all human rights for ourselves are going to Palestine reversing the roles.

4·3 Pointing the Prophetic Finger

Most of the popular books on prophecy assume that since the return of Jews to the land and the establishment of the State of Israel are so obviously the fulfilment of prophecy, there's no need to enter into the rights and wrongs of all that has been done. God predicted it all long ago, and now it has happened – so it must be the will of God! Since this is the way that God planned it and wanted it to happen, there's no need to ask questions about *how* it has happened.

If there is ever any attempt to make moral judgement, it usually takes the form of wholehearted support of the idea of a Jewish state and most of its policies and actions. If anyone is singled out for condemnation, it's usually the Arabs who have dared to oppose the Jews. An extract from a full-page advertisement in *The New York Times* (1976) reads:

> Because the Jewish people are the people of prophecy, they are the people of the land.
>
> And we, knowing him who made the promise, totally support the people of and the land of Israel in their God-given, God-promised, God-ordained right to exist.
>
> Any person or group of nations opposed to this right isn't just fighting Israel. But God and time itself.

Another problem that we face in any discussion concerning the State of Israel is the fact that anyone who dares to criticize its actions, or to question the very idea of the State of Israel, can very easily be accused of anti-Semitism.

Every one of us is sensitive to criticism, however mild or strong, and whoever it comes from. And Jews have special reason to be sensitive to criticism, knowing what has motivated so much criticism in the past, and what it has led to. But there is a real danger that this sensitivity can sometimes make it difficult for the Jew to listen to *any* criticism of the State of Israel.

A statement from the Ecumenical Theological Fraternity in Israel rightly challenges the resolution of the UN which describes Zionism purely and simply as 'a form of racism'. But in doing so, it comes dangeroulsy close to saying that *any* criticism of Zionism is a form of anti-Semitism:

> It is impossible to present Judaism and Zionism as two entirely different things. There is only a very thin line between anti-Zionism and anti-Semitism or anti-Judaism. Zionism has to be seen as an important and valid expression of a fundamental dimension of Judaism.

When the line is as thin as this, it becomes virtually impossible for an outsider to criticize any action or policy of the State of Israel without being accused of anti-Semitism.

In his book *Israel – America's Key to Survival*, **Mike Evans**, an American Christian writer, quotes a letter he received from a member of the American Arab anti-Discrimination Committee. This is the last paragraph of the letter:

> Perhaps you are now convinced that I must be an anti-Semite, or oblivious to the historical tragedy that befell the Jewish people of Europe forty years ago. Perhaps you wonder why I dare challenge the commonly held Western Christian support for the Israeli state. I dare to challenge this support because I have witnessed the unholy violence that political Zionism has bred in its creating an exclusionist state. I have witnessed the horrifying instant-replay of a tortured people slowly wielding the instruments of torture. I have seen the results of official and unsanctioned displacement of villages, towns and cities of Palestinian families, the uprooting of generations of a proud, simple people, all in the name of my God. I have witnessed the testimony of young Israeli soldiers confessing their moral agony over the orders they must follow to maintain national security among the people whose land they now control by rule of the

gun. I have read in the eyes of mothers – both Israeli Jews and Palestinian Arabs – the pain of unknown futures for their children, reflecting the sickness which military occupation has spread into the souls of all their children.

Evans makes the following comment on the letter:

> The letter reflects a subtle anti-Semitism that is often masked by a profession of Christian love. It overlooks God's special commitment to Israel and the need to stand with the nation He established. We must be careful to avoid this kind of mistake.

Is it possible to learn from the prophets when and where we may have to point the prophetic finger?

'You are the man!'

The Law of Moses very easily became a dead letter if there was no one around who could interpret and apply it both to individuals and to the community. When David arranged for Uriah the Hittite to be killed in battle and then took his wife Bathsheba for himself, it can't have been because he didn't know the commandments 'you shall not murder' and 'you shall not commit adultery'. He simply didn't see his actions in terms of murder and adultery – until the prophet Nathan told the parable about the rich man stealing the poor man's lamb, and then pointed his finger at him with the words 'You are the man!' (2 Samuel 12:1–7).

'Have you murdered a man and seized his property?'

The prophet Elijah made several predictions about the future (for example, concerning the drought, 1 Kings 17:1); but there was more to his ministry than mere prediction.

King Ahab no doubt had many good reasons for trying to obtain possession of the vineyard belonging to Naboth which adjoined his own property. His first attempt to acquire the vineyard was perfectly fair and above-board:

> Let me have your vineyard to use for a vegetable garden, since it is so close to my palace. In exchange I will give you a better vineyard, or, if you prefer, I will pay you whatever it is worth.
> 1 Kings 21:2

The vineyard, however, was worth more to Naboth than its cash value, and he refused to sell it:

> The Lord forbid that I should give you the inheritance of my fathers.
> 1 Kings 21:3

Urged on by Jezebel, his wife, Ahab then resorted to deceit and finally to violence:

> So the elders and nobles who lived in Naboth's city did as Jezebel directed in the letters she had written to them. They proclaimed a fast and seated Naboth in a prominent place among the people. Then two scoundrels came and sat opposite him and brought charges against Naboth before the people, saying, 'Naboth has cursed both God and the king.' So they took him outside the city and stoned him to death. Then they sent word to Jezebel: 'Naboth has been stoned and is dead . . .' When Ahab heard that Naboth was dead, he got up and went down to take possession of Naboth's vineyard.
> 1 Kings 21:11–14, 16

The sequel to the story indicates the seriousness of Ahab's crimes in the eyes of God:

> Then the word of the Lord came to Elijah the Tishbite: 'Go down to meet Ahab king of Israel, who rules in Samaria. He is now in Naboth's vineyard, where he has gone to take possession of it. Say to him, "This is what the Lord says: Have you not murdered a man and seized his property?" Then say to him, "This is what the Lord says: In the place where dogs licked up Naboth's blood, dogs will lick up your blood – yes, yours!"'
> 1 Kings 21:17–19

'Filled . . . with the Spirit of the Lord . . . to declare to Jacob his transgression'

When the prophet Amos started denouncing the crimes of one foreign nation after another, the people of Judah and Israel must have felt confident, if not complacent, since they were innocent of the catalogue of crimes for which their neighbours were going to be punished (Amos 1:1—2:3). But before long they discovered that the severest judgement was reserved for themselves, because of their special relationship with God:

> You only have I chosen
>   of all the families of the earth;
> therefore I will punish you
>   for all your sins.
> Amos 3:2

Making moral judgements was therefore just as much a part of the prophetic ministry as making predictions about the future.

Micah had something to say about the distant future:

> In the last days

the mountain of the Lord's temple will be established
    as chief among the mountains;
it will be raised above the hills,
    and peoples will stream to it.
Micah 4:1

But he also believed he was called to expose the sins of his people:

But as for me, I am filled with power,
    with the Spirit of the Lord,
    and with justice and might,
to declare to Jacob his transgression,
to Israel his sin.
Micah 3:8

Isaiah echoed these same words in declaring the commission that he himself had received from God:

Shout it aloud, do not hold back.
Raise your voice like a trumpet.
Declare to my people their rebellion
    and to the house of Jacob their sins.
Isaiah 58:1

The writings of many Jews, however, amount to an admission that there have been many 'Naboth's vineyards' in Palestine since 1880. **Max Nordau**, a prominent Zionist leader, on hearing for the first time that there was an Arab population in Palestine, ran to Herzl crying:

I did not know that; but then we are committing an injustice.

Moshe Dayan:

Jewish villages were built in the place of Arab villages. You don't even know the names of these Arab villages, and I don't blame you, because these geography books no longer exist. Not only do the books not exist, the Arab villages are not there either. Nahalal (Dayan's own village) arose in the place of Mahlul, Gvat (a kibbutz) in the place of Jibta, Sarid (another kibbutz) in the place of Haneifa, and Kfar-Yehoshua in the place of Tel-Shaman. There is not one single place built in this country that did not have a former Arab population.

Joseph Weitz, writing about a visit to what had once been an Arab village:

I went to visit the village of Mu'ar. Three tractors are completing its destruction. I was surprised; nothing in me moved at the sight of the destruction. No regret and no hate, as though this was the way the world goes. So we want to feel good in this world, and not in some world to come. We simply want to live, and the inhabitants of those mud-houses did not want us to exist here. They not only aspire to dominate us, they also wanted to exterminate us. And what is interesting – this is the opinion of all our boys, from one end to the other.

Nathan Chofshi, a Russian Jew, and contemporary of David Ben-Gurion:

If Rabbi Kaplan (an American Zionist rabbi) really wanted to know what happened, we old Jewish settlers in Palestine who witnessed the flight could tell him how and in what manner we, Jews, forced the Arabs to leave cities and villages. In the last analysis, these are the bare facts which strike our eyes: here was a people who lived on its own land from 1300 years. We came and turned the native Arabs into tragic refugees. And still we dare to slander and malign them, to besmirch their name. Instead of being deeply ashamed of what we did and of trying to undo some of the evil we committed by helping these unfortunate refugees, we justify our terrible acts and even attempt to glorify them.

Chaim Weizmann expressed his willingness for the whole Zionist programme to be judged in the light of the law and the prophets. Speaking to fellow Jews he once said:

If you wish to secure your redemption through means . . . which do not accord with Jewish morality, with Jewish ethics or Jewish history, I say to you that you are worshipping false gods . . . Go and read Isaiah, Jeremiah and Ezekiel, and test that which we do and wish to do in the light of teachings of our greatest prophets and wise men. They knew the nature and character of the Jewish people. Zion will be redeemed through righteousness, and not by any other means.

Rabbi Elmer Berger, for example, an American Jew speaking to a Christian audience in Holland after the end of World War II said he believed that God must be allowed to stand in judgement, through his prophetic word, on *every* nation, including Israel. If critical voices from outside the Jewish community can be easily ignored, it shouldn't be so easy to ignore such voices from *within* which challenge Zionism in the light of the Law and the Prophets.

Measured by any of the rigorous, covenanted criteria of the Prophetic tradition, the state of Israel is not 'the temple of the

Lord'. Those who credit it with such sanctity, in my opinion, perform a disservice to the great, spiritual tradition we share. They do no lasting good, even in the world of realistic politics, to either the state of Israel itself or – more importantly – to the people who live there. And these two considerations, I think are strong motivations in your country. For I believe I understand the particular poignancy with which the people of Holland recall those savage days of nearly three decades ago and I also understand, at least in part, the fundamental orientation of the religious commitment of perhaps a majority of the people of this country. Together with most of the people of the world, I share the tragic memory and I respect the religious commitment. But I earnestly suggest that the religious commitment can best help mankind avoid another holocaust and more tragic memories, not by deifying the present state of Israel, but rather by insisting that the majestic vision of God in Zion must stand in the same rigorous, stern, moral judgement of this Zionist state as you demand this same God stand in judgement of this nation of yours, or as I demand – to the best of my powers – He stand in judgement of my own country.

4.4 The Call for Justice

The Jewish people have been asking the world to give them justice after so many centuries of ill-treatment and oppression. The Palestinians have been doing all they can to draw attention to their plight and to persuade world opinion of the justice of their cause. Both sides are simply demanding justice, and asking the world to recognize their rights.

This passionate concern for justice is another important aspect of the ministry of the prophets.

'Let justice roll on like a river'

This is how the prophet **Amos** denounced social injustices in the northern kingdom of Israel in the eighth century BC:

> You who turn justice into bitterness
>   and cast righteousness to the ground . . .
> You hate the one who reproves in court
>   and despise him who tells the truth.
> You trample on the poor
>   and force him to give you corn.
> Therefore, though you have built stone mansions,
>   you will not live in them;
> though you have planted lush vineyards,
>   you will not drink their wine.

> For I know how many are your offences
>   and how great your sins.
> You oppress the righteous and take bribes
>   and you deprive the poor of justice in the courts.
> Therefore the prudent man keeps quiet in such times,
>   for the times are evil.
> Seek good, not evil,
>   that you may live.
> Then the Lord God Almighty will be with you,
>   just as you say he is.
> Hate evil, love good;
> maintain justice in the courts.
>   Amos 5:7, 10–15
>
> I hate, I despise your religious feasts;
>   I cannot stand your assemblies . . .
> But let justice roll on like a river,
>   righteousness like a never-failing stream!'
>   Amos 5:21, 24

Isaiah condemned his own people, the southern kingdom of Judah, because 'justice is far from us':

> Surely the arm of the Lord is not too short to save,
>   nor his ear too dull to hear.
> But your iniquities have separated
>   you from your God;
> your sins have hidden his face from you,
>   so that he will not hear.
> For your hands are stained with blood,
>   your fingers with guilt.
> Your lips have spoken lies,
>   and your tongue mutters wicked things.
> No-one calls for justice;
>   no-one pleads his case with integrity.
>
> They rely on empty arguments and speak lies;
>   they conceive trouble and give birth to evil . . .
> Their deeds are evil deeds,
>   and acts of violence are in their hands.
> Their feet rush into sin;
>   they are swift to shed innocent blood.
> Their thoughts are evil thoughts;
>   ruin and destruction mark their ways.
> The way of peace they do not know;
>   there is no justice in their paths.

They have turned them into crooked roads;
   no-one who walks in them will know peace.

So justice is far from us,
   and righteousness does not reach us . . .
We look for justice, but find none;
   for deliverance, but it is far away.
   Isaiah 59:1–4, 6–9, 11

Jeremiah addressed strong words to his people who were confident that the existence of the temple in Jerusalem provided a guarantee of their security regardless of the moral condition of society:

Hear the word of the Lord, all you people of Judah who come through these gates to worship the Lord. This is what the Lord Almighty, the God of Israel, says: Reform your ways and your actions, and I will let you live in this place. Do not trust in deceptive words and say, 'This is the temple of the Lord, the temple of the Lord, the temple of the Lord!' If you really change your ways and your actions and deal with each other justly, if you do not oppress the alien, the fatherless or the widow and do not shed innocent blood in this place, and if you do not follow other gods to your own harm, then I will let you live in this place, in the land I gave to your forefathers for ever and ever. But look, you are trusting in deceptive words that are worthless.
   Will you steal and murder, commit adultery and perjury, burn incense to Baal and follow other gods you have not known, and then come and stand before me in this house, which bears my Name, and say, 'We are safe' – safe to do all these detestable things? Has this house, which bears my Name, become a den of robbers to you? But I have been watching! declares the Lord.
   Jeremiah 7:2–11

If we try to apply this aspect of the message of the prophets to the conflict over the land, we may need to begin by listening more carefully to the voices of the Jewish people calling for justice.
   This cry for justice is reflected, for example, in Saul Bellow's report of a conversation with **Professor J.L. Talmon**, the noted Israeli historian. Commenting on the 1973 war Talmon expresses the longing of Jews in Israel to be treated by the same standards of justice which are applied to other nations:

The 1973 war badly damaged their [i.e. Israel's] confidence. The Egyptians crossed the Suez Canal. Suddenly the abyss opened again. France and England abandoned Israel. The UNbloc vote revived the feeling that she 'shall not be reckoned among the nations'. While Israel fought for life, debaters weighed her sins and especially the problem of the Palestinians. In this disorderly century refugees have fled from many countries. In India, in Africa, in Europe, millions of human beings have been put to flight, transported, enslaved, stampeded over borders, left to starve, but only the case of the Palestinians is held permanently open. Where Israel is concerned the world swells with moral consciousness. Moral judgement, a wraith in Europe, becomes a full-blooded giant where Israel and the Palestinians are mentioned. Is this because Israel has assumed the responsibilities of a liberal democracy? Is it for other reasons? What Switzerland is to winter holidays and the Dalmation coast to summer tourists, Israel and the Palestinians are to the West's need for justice – a sort of moral resort area.

The right of Israel to exist, Talmon says, has to be won by special exertions, 'by some special atonement through being better than others'. This is Israel's most persistent torment and paradox.

We will also need to listen to the cry of the Palestinians. The following reports are taken from *The West Bank and the Rule of Law*, a book written by Raja Shehadeh and Jonathan Kuttab, two young Palestinian lawyers from the West Bank, and published in 1980 by the International Commission of Jurists in Geneva:

Witholding Permits to Drill Artesian Wells

In a country where rain water is scanty and cannot be depended upon for farming, drilling of artesian wells is the only means of reclaiming land for agriculture. However, since 1967 only two permits have been given to Palestinians to drill wells for agricultural use. In one of these, the applicant was licensed to drill in a specified area. When the well was dug, it was discovered that only salty water, unsuitable for irrigation, could be found there. These permits are not withheld from Jewish settlers in the West Bank for whom many artesian wells have been dug by the state affiliated water company, Makerot. Settlers utilize these wells along with the water rights which the Custodian of absentee property has acquired and which are put to their use as well.

According to Israeli statistics, in the year 1977/1978 there were 314 Arab owned artesian wells in the West Bank from which were discharged 33 million cubic metres of water. There were 17 wells drilled by the Israeli water company to serve the

Israeli settlements, from which were discharged 14.1 million cubic metres. In other words, 30% of the water was taken from the 17 modern wells constructed to serve the settlers, while the Arabs were denied permits to construct similar wells.

This policy of withholding permits for drilling wells has meant that a large sector of the population who would otherwise be engaged in agriculture began to seek work in Israel as unskilled labourers, with the result that the West Bank has become dependant on Israel even for agricultural products.

Punishment of Families

On suspicion of throwing a stone at an Israeli vehicle, Tariq Shumali, aged 16, was arrested on May 13, 1980. He was beaten so severely that he had to be hospitalized for internal kidney haemorrhage. No other member of the family was charged or suspected of any wrong doing. Nevertheless, his father was jailed, his sister was dismissed from her job as a teacher in a public school, the Shumali house in Beit Sahour, near Bethlehem, was sealed off, and the family was forcefully deported to a deserted refugee camp in Jericho and ordered to make their new home in one of the delapidated mud houses in the desolate conditions of the camp, which had been abandoned since the 1967 war. The intention of the authorities was to make of the Shumalis an example of the treatment that will be inflicted on the whole family of any suspected stone-thrower. They also intended to introduce into the West Bank the method of internal deportation which hitherto had been used only in Gaza. It must be noted here that all this punishment was inflicted on the Shumalis before the accused son had been put on trial and his guilt established.

Punishment of entire towns or villages

The collective punishment of whole towns or villages for the act of a few is not uncommon. Throughout the thirteen years of occupation it has taken many forms, some harsher than others. One case in point, is Hebron.

On May 2 1980 three guerillas attacked a bus carrying Israeli settlers near the Hadassah building in Hebron. There were a number of casualties amongst the Israelis, including some fatal. The authorities retaliated by punishing all 60,000 inhabitants of the city of Hebron. This they did in the following ways:

● They imposed a strict curfew which lasted for over a month. The Israelis were not unaware of the consequences which ensue from the imposition of such a curfew on an

agricultural town. Having been prohibited from attending to
their crops and livestock the Hebronites suffered severe losses.
Similarly economic loss to owners of workshops and glass
factories was severe and students lost many days of study.

● They deported the mayor and qadi of the town.

● Long after the curfew was lifted Hebronites were still
prevented from travelling outside the West Bank as well as
receiving visitors from abroad.

● All telephone lines were disconnected for 45 days.

● Merchants from Hebron were not allowed permits to
export their produce across the bridge to Jordan until the
middle of June 1980, when the ban was lifted.

● The owners of cars bearing Hebron licence plates
continued to be harrassed and delayed at road blocks placed at
the entrances of the city, which were not removed until several
months after the incident. They also received similar treatment
at checkpoints throughout the West Bank.

● All the male inhabitants of the town were made to go
through long hours of questioning and waiting in extreme
weather conditions.

● The inhabitants had to submit to house to house searches.
Eye-witness accounts of these searches by soldiers who took
part in them revealed that in the process food supplies were
destroyed, furniture wrecked and parents were beaten and
humiliated before their children. All this was done pursuant to
specific instructions by their officers.

Measures similar to the above were taken against the
'Dheisheh' refugee camp near Bethlehem, the Jalazoun refugee
camp, the village of Halhoull and other towns and villages.

The La Grange Declaration I drawn up by an ecumenical group of
Christians – evangelical, mainline Protestant, Roman Catholic and
Orthodox, meeting at La Grange, Illinois in 1979 and 1981, outlines
what the prophetic call for justice might mean for *all* the parties in
the conflict:

As believers committed to Christ and his kingdom, we
challenge the popular assumptions about biblical interpretation
and the presuppositions of political loyalty held so widely by
fellow Christians in their attitudes toward the conflict in the
Middle East.

We address this urgent call to the church of Jesus Christ to
hear and heed those voices crying out as bruised reeds for
justice in the land where our Lord walked, taught, was
crucified, and rose from the dead. We have closed our hearts to

these voices and isolated ourselves even from the pleading of fellow Christians who continue to live in that land.

We are anguished by the fact that countless Christians believe that the Bible gives to the modern state of Israel a divine right, divine sanction to the state of Israel's policy of territorial acquisition. We believe such an understanding must be judged in light of the whole of biblical revelation affirming that in the revelation of Jesus Christ God's covenants find their completion. Therefore, we plead for all Christians to construct a vision of peace in the Holy Land which rests on the biblical injunctions to correct oppression and seek justice for all peoples.

Forthrightly, we declare our conviction that in the process of establishing the state of Israel, a deep injustice was done to the Palestinian people. Confiscating their land and driving many into exile and even death. We are further grieved by the ongoing deprivation of basic civil rights to those Arabs who live today in the state of Israel.

Moreover, for 13 years large portions of the Holy Land and its people, including the West Bank of the Jordan River, Gaza, and East Jerusalem, have suffered under foreign military occupation, even as in our Lord's time. Land is seized from its inhabitants. Water for farming is rationed and restricted. Schools and universities are closed by the Israeli military authorities. And 100,000 people have been arrested, in large part for speaking their convictions. Of these, some have been subjected to brutal torture, described by the US Consulate in Jerusalem as 'systematic' and documented beyond any question.

We confess our silence, our indifference, our hardheartedness, and our cowardice, all too often, in the face of these dehumanising realities.

Earnestly, we pray for a new anointing of the Spirit in our hearts, creating us into a more faithful people used to break every yoke of oppression and let the broken victims go free.

We extend our hearts to our Jewish brothers and sisters, common sons and daughters of Abraham. Like us in the United States, their corporate national spirit is being corroded by the weight of their government's reliance on rampant militaristic policies and actions. We would pray for them, and with them, for a vision of security rooted in expanding channels of trust rather than escalating arsenals of armed might.

Historically and today, the state of Israel's territorial ambitions have been justified as security needs. Through the decades, this has instigated a cycle of violence and counterviolence that still continues, engulfing all sides, and leaving none unblemished from the spilling of innocent blood. We pray with the psalmist for every bow to be broken and every spear to be snapped.

Too many of us have been lulled into the shallow hope that peace can be built in the Middle East through the US supply of more weapons, with the continued military occupation of the West Bank, Gaza and East Jerusalem, and while basic human and political rights of the Palestinian people are denied. We call on Christ's followers to repent from their complicity – through either their indifference or their uncritical embrace of US policies – in the continuing cycle of Middle Eastern violence, accelerated by our tax dollars and our government's political decisions.

The Arab people and their land have been plundered for centuries by Western Christendom. We acknowledge and confess a continuing legacy of prejudice evidenced today toward Arab people, both Christian and Muslim.

We repudiate with equal and uncompromising fervour the enduring prejudice toward the Jewish people still present this day in our society and in our churches (those churches include, ironically, many of those churches with staunchly pro-Israel biases, drawn from their versions of biblical interpretation).

Overcoming these divisions and hatreds, we affirm, as God's revelation declares, our common humanity with all.

We believe that any biblical hope for peace and security for all peoples in the Middle East must encompass some form of restitution for past wrongs. Life, peoplehood, and land are all God's gifts. These gifts enjoyed by the Jewish people of Israel have been denied to the Palestinian people. Therefore, we yearn and we call for the building of a peace that includes the clear expression of political self-determination and justice for the Palestinian people. This includes leadership of their own choosing and a sovereign state. Our firm conviction is that through asserting these rights the way can be opened for Israeli people and Palestinian people to find peace and true security in that land.

4·5 Non-Selective Judgement

It's all too easy for us to indulge in what has been called 'selective indignation'. We denounce the crimes of other nations, but are blind to the crimes of our own. We single out one particular community for condemnation, but are silent about the crimes of others.

Thus, for example, a government loudly condemns South Africa for its policy of apartheid, while it gives wholehearted support to another country which practises its own form of apartheid. A politician describes the PLO as a terrorist organization and Yasser Arafat as a murderer of innocent Jewish children; and he quietly forgets about the Irgun and the Haganah, and what Menachem Begin did to the village of Deir Yassin. An Arab journalist describes the involvement of the great powers in the Middle East as 'western imperialism', but cannot admit that Egypt's involvement in the Yemen in the 1960s was a form of eastern imperialism.

How did the Old Testament prophets avoid the snare of selectivity?

'Woe to the Assyrian, the rod of my anger'

It can't have been pleasant for the people of Judah to be told by the prophet Isaiah that God was about to use a foreign power, Assyria, as an instrument of judgement to punish them for their disobedience to the Law:

> The Lord will bring on you and on your people and on the
> house of your father a time unlike any since Ephraim broke
> away from Judah – he will bring the king of Assyria . . .
>   In that day the Lord will use a razor hired from beyond the
> River – the king of Assyria – to shave your head and the hair of
> your legs, and to take off your beards also . . .
> Isaiah 7:17, 20

Before long, however, says Isaiah, the Assyrians themselves will be ready for judgement. For even while being used by God as an instrument of judgement on the people of Judah, they will provoke the judgement of God through their pride and arrogance, and through their excessive violence in war:

> Woe to the Assyrian, the rod of my anger,
>   in whose hand is the club of my wrath!
> I send him against a godless nation,
>   I despatch him against a people who anger me,
> to seize loot and snatch plunder,
>   and to trample them down like mud in the streets.
> But this is not what he intends,
>   this is not what he has in mind;
> his purpose is to destroy,
>   to put an end to many nations.
> 'Are not my commanders all kings?' he says . . .
> Isaiah 10:5–8

When the Lord has finished all his work against Mount Zion

and Jerusalem, he will say, 'I will punish the king of Assyria for the wilful pride of his heart and the haughty look in his eyes.'
For he says:

'By the strength of my hand I have done this,
    and by my wisdom, because I have understanding.
I removed the boundaries of nations,
    I plundered their treasures;
    like a mighty one I subdued their kings . . .'
Isaiah 10:12–13

O my people who live in Zion,
    do not be afraid of the Assyrians,
who beat you with a rod
    and lift up a club against you, as Egypt did.
Very soon my anger against you will end
    and my wrath will be directed to their destructions.
Isaiah 10:24–25

Instead of trying to identify who 'the Assyrians' might stand for in the present scenario in the Middle East, we might notice that this passage provides one more example of the way that the prophets, when they spoke about future events, weren't simply interested in the prediction of events. If all Isaiah had to do was to foretell the invasion of the Assyrians, he could no doubt have sat back with some complacency when he saw his predictions coming true. This is what God predicted – and look! It's happening before our eyes!

But the prophet had a much keener moral sense than this. He realized that being used by God as an instrument of judgement against the people of Judah didn't mean that the Assyrians were exempt from God's judgement. If a listener had asked Isaiah 'is the Assyrian invasion "of God"?' he would certainly have answered that it *was* 'of God' – but that this didn't mean that the Assyrians had *carte blanche* from God to act however they liked.

No individual and no nation is ever immune from judgement just because it is being used by God in a particular way at a particular stage of history. There can never be any exemption from responsibility and accountability before God. Therefore if a Jew or a Christian is convinced that the State of Israel is 'of God' in the sense that it represents the fulfilment of prophecy, this should not mean that the State of Israel can behave as it wishes and assume that its actions are acceptable to God. The crushing of Judah by Assyria was certainly the fulfilment of prophecy; but Assyria had to pay the price at a later stage for over-stepping the mark.

Denys Baly suggests how the 'double judgement' described by Isaiah 10 may have been working itself out in the twentieth century with the Jews and Arabs:

> When we turn to consider what the events of the past forty years have meant to the people of the Middle East themselves, we see the double judgement of which Isaiah spoke. Only those whose enthusiasm for the Arab cause has blinded them to the facts should fail to take account of the tragic weakness of the Arabs. Their complacency, their certainty that they are the people and that wisdom will die with them, their rigidity, their high-sounding words, their inability to combine, the lack of courage of most of them save the Bedouin – these are the weaknesses which have put them at the mercy of Israel. Three things have been given to the Arab world at once: independence, the stimulus of new and exciting ideas and the possibility of quite overwhelming wealth, and with them at the same time has come the necessity of decision. The question is now what they will do with all these gifts. Will those in power use the new wealth for their own aggrandizement or for the benefit of the people? Will Egypt use her position of power for the benefit or the control of the other Arab nations? Will they struggle to overcome their past history in the face of the need for unity? Will the oil-countries consider their riches as something to be kept entirely within their own borders? Are the refugees always to remain a pawn in the game? These are the kind of questions of which the judgment is made, and the presence of Israel is the spur. Had there been no Israel, the questions would have come less sharply and the need for unity have been made less apparent. No one can deny the troubles of the Arabs. The West has not treated them fairly, not even with so much as common courtesy, but that is not now the question for them. Their crisis is now to know whether any of their own number will arise to tell them their own shortcomings, and, bluntly, whether they would rather listen to him or shoot him.

> We must not, however, make the mistake of believing that the chastisement of Arab follies means that Israel is therefore justified. It is the tragedy of Israel that she has found no peace, and no peace is likely to be granted to her for a long time. She has gathered in those who were afraid, and they are afraid still. The security they longed for most earnestly is the thing which is still beyond their reach, the crock of gold at the rainbow's end.

'Why do you make me look on injustice?'

When we read the sickening story of the violence which began with the first clashes between Jews and Arabs, we can understand the complaints which **Habakkuk** addressed to God:

How long, O Lord, must I call for help,
    but you do not listen?
Or cry out to you 'Violence!'
    but you do not save?
Why do you make me look at injustice?
    Why do you tolerate wrong?
Destruction and violence are before me;
    there is strife, and conflict abounds.
Therefore the law is paralysed,
    and justice never prevails.
The wicked hem in the righteous,
    so that justice is perverted.

Habakkuk 1:2–4

O Lord, are you not from everlasting?
    My God, my Holy One, we will not die.
O Lord, you have appointed them to execute judgement;
    O Rock, you have ordained them to punish.
Your eyes are too pure to look on evil;
    you cannot tolerate wrong.
Why then do you tolerate the treacherous?
    Why are you silent while the wicked
    swallow up those more righteous than themselves?

Habakkuk 1:12–13

In his answer, God assures the prophet that he is not turning a blind
eye to injustice, and that the Babylonians will be judged for all the
crimes they are committing:

See, he is puffed up;
    his desires are not upright –
but the righteous will live by his faith –
    indeed, wine betrays him;
he is arrogant and never at rest.
Because he is as greedy as the grave
    and like death is never satisfied,
he gathers to himself all the nations
    and takes captive all the peoples.

Will not all of them taunt him with ridicule and scorn saying,
'Woe to him who piles up stolen goods
    and makes himself wealthy by extortion!
    How long must this go on?'
Will not your debtors suddenly arise?
    Will they not wake up and make you tremble?
    Then you will become their victim.

Because you have plundered many nations,
   the peoples who are left will plunder you.
For you have shed man's blood;
   you have destroyed lands and cities and everyone in them.

Woe to him who builds a city with bloodshed
   and establishes a town by crime!
Has not the Lord Almighty determined
   that the people's labour is only fuel for the fire,
   that the nations exhaust themselves for nothing?
For the earth will be filled with the knowledge of the glory of
   the Lord,
   as the waters cover the sea.

Woe to him who gives drink to his neighbours,
   pouring it from the wineskin till they are drunk
   so that he can gaze on their naked bodies.
You will be filled with shame instead of glory.
   Now it is your turn! Drink and be exposed!
The cup from the Lord's right hand is coming round to you,
   and disgrace will cover your glory.
The violence you have done to Lebanon will overwhelm you,
   and your destruction of animals will terrify you.
For you have shed man's blood;
   you have destroyed lands and cities and everyone in them.
    Habakkuk 2:4–8, 12–17

If the cap fits the Christian churches because of the way they have
'humiliated and disgraced' (Habakkuk 2:15 Today's English Version)
their Jewish neighbours over many centuries, they must wear it . . .

If the cap fits the European governments which have exploited
anti-Semitism in the nineteenth and twentieth centuries, and 'plotted
the ruin of many peoples' (2:10), they must wear it . . .

If the cap fits the western powers which have been 'greedy as the
grave' (2:5) and have 'plundered many nations' (2:8), they must wear
it . . .

If the cap fits the Irgun and the Haganah who have 'shed men's
blood' (2:8, 17) and built 'a city with bloodshed' (2:12) they must
wear it . . .

If the cap fits the fedayeen who have 'shed man's blood' (2:8, 17)
in their desperate attempt to resist Zionism and to win back their
land, they must wear it . . .

If the cap fits the Jewish leadership which built 'a realm by unjust
gain to set its nest on high, to escape the clutches of ruin' (2:9), they
must wear it . . .

If the cap fits any of the Arab countries which are using their oil wealth to make themselves 'wealthy by extortion' (2:6) they must wear it . . .

If the cap fits any of the world powers today which desires to preserve its power and influence in the world, and 'gathers to himself all nations and takes captive all the nations' (2:5) it must wear it . . .

4·6 The Nation among the Nations

In November 1952 the Israeli Knesset adopted a Status Law which defined the status of the World Zionist Organization in relation to the State of Israel. It began by affirming that the state regards itself as the creation of the whole Jewish people, and that its gates are open to all Jews. It includes the following paragraph about the gathering of Jewish exiles:

> The mission of gathering in the exiles, which is the central task of the State of Israel and the Zionist Movement in our days, requires constant efforts by the Jewish people in the Diaspora; the State of Israel, therefore, expects the co-operation of all Jews, as individuals and groups, in building up the State and assisting the immigration to it of the masses of the people, and regards the unity of all sections of Jewry as necessary for this purpose.

Does the Christian have any right to look at the vision of Zionism in the light of the Old Testament? Do we dare to ask how it relates to ideas in the Old Testament about the relationship between the chosen people and other nations?

'Chosen . . . out of all the people on the face of the earth'

At an early stage in the nation's life, Moses attempted to make the children of Israel aware of their identity:

> You are a people holy to the Lord your God. The Lord your God has chosen you out of all the peoples on the face of the earth to be his people, his treasured possession.
> Deuteronomy 7:6

This special calling from God demanded rigid separation from the surrounding nations:

> When the Lord your God brings you into the land you are entering to possess and drives out before you many nations . . . and when the Lord your God has delivered them over to you

and you have defeated them, then you must destroy them
totally. Make no treaty with them, and show them no mercy.
Do not intermarry with them. Do not give your daughters to
their sons or take their daughters for your sons, for they will
turn your sons away from following me to serve other gods, and
the Lord's anger will burn against you and will quickly destroy
you.

Deuteronomy 7:1–4

'Your people shall be my people'

In the time of the Judges, Ruth the Moabitess left her own people
on the east bank of the Jordan and followed Naomi her mother-in-
law with the well-known words 'your people shall be my people'. In
this way a foreigner, a Gentile, became an ancestor of King David.
The book of Ruth was therefore a constant reminder that foreigners
could in certain circumstances be integrated into the life of the
nation and not be rigidly excluded.

'My house shall be called a house of prayer for all nations'

The prophet **Isaiah**, writing in the eighth century BC, looked forward
to the day when people of other nations would benefit from all that
God had done for his people Israel. In the following passage he
speaks of foreigners who 'join themselves' or 'bind themselves' to
Jehovah, the Lord, and come to belong to his people:

This is what the Lord says:

'Maintain justice and do what is right,
for my salvation is close at hand
and my righteousness will soon be revealed . . .'

Let no foreigner who has joined himself to the Lord say,
'The Lord will surely exclude me from his people.'
And let not any eunuch complain,
'I am only a dry tree.'

For this is what the Lord says:
'To the eunuchs who keep my Sabbaths, . . .
who hold fast to my covenant –
to them I will give within my temple and its walls
a memorial and a name
better than sons and daughters;
I will give them an everlasting name
that will not be cut off.
And foreigners who bind themselves to the Lord
to serve him,

to love the name of the Lord,
    and to worship him,
all who keep the Sabbath without desecrating it
    and who hold fast to my covenant –
these I will bring to my holy mountain
    and give them joy in my house of prayer.
Their burnt offerings and sacrifices
    will be accepted on my altar;
for my house will be called
    a house of prayer for all nations.'
The Sovereign Lord declares –
    he who gathers the exiles of Israel:
'I will gather still others to them
    besides those already gathered.'
Isaiah 56:1–8

'A blessing in the midst of the earth'

A whole chapter of Isaiah consists of 'an oracle concerning Egypt'. It speaks of God judging the nation of Egypt, and later restoring it – even to the extent of bringing the nation to acknowledge the God of Israel.

It must have sounded incredible, if not shocking, for Isaiah's listeners to hear that the people of Egypt, who centuries before had been their oppressors, would one day be converted and turn to worship Yahweh their God. It would have sounded as inconceivable for them as for an American Christian audience today to be told that one day the Russian people as a whole would reject communism and embrace Christianity.

The oracle ends with the prophecy that Egypt, Israel and Assyria will one day be united together to become 'a blessing in the midst of the earth':

> In that day there will be a highway from Egypt to Assyria. The Assyrians will go to Egypt and the Egyptians to Assyria. The Egyptians and Assyrians will worship together. In that day Israel will be the third, along with Egypt and Assyria, a blessing on the earth. The Lord Almighty will bless them, saying, 'Blessed be Egypt my people, Assyria my handiwork, and Israel my inheritance.'
> Isaiah 19:23–25

We must leave on one side the intriguing question of if and when this prophecy has been fulfilled: was it in the Camp David Agreements of 1979? Or was it fulfilled in the first few centuries AD when Egypt became in effect a Christian country, and enjoyed close links with the Syriac Church in the area of present-day Syria? The important point for us to notice is that Isaiah puts two *foreign* nations – pagan, godless nations at that – on the same level as Israel! The children of Israel had always thought of themselves as God's chosen people – but now God is calling *Egypt* 'my people!' What would happen to the concept of the chosen people if that ever happened?

'They have mingled the holy race'

After their return from exile in Babylon around the middle of the fifth century BC, Ezra and Nehemiah felt compelled to enforce Moses' prohibition of foreign wives, even to the point of making men put away their foreign wives. Ezra writes:

> After these things had been done, the leaders came to me and said, 'The people of Israel, including the priests and the Levites, have not kept themselves separate from the neighbouring peoples with their detestable practices . . . They have taken some of their daughters as wives for themselves and their sons, and have mingled the holy race with the peoples around them. And the leaders and officials have led the way in this unfaithfulness.'
> Ezra 9:1–2

This is how Ezra wanted them to rectify the situation:

> You have been unfaithful; you have married foreign women, adding to Israel's guilt. Now make confession to the Lord, the God of your fathers, and do his will. Separate yourselves from the peoples around you and from your foreign wives.
> Ezra 10:10–11

Even if Ezra and Nehemiah were aware of the visions of the prophets before them, they found themselves faced with a potentially dangerous situation. They believed they had to take immediate practical steps to ensure the survival of the nation and the purity of its faith.

It isn't relevant for us to ask at this point whether or not they did the right thing in the situation. But it *is* relevant to ask whether Zionism is closer to Ezra's idea of 'the holy race' or to Isaiah's vision of a people which welcomes 'foreigners who join themselves to the Lord'.

One can understand how Theodor Herzl could believe that the creation of a Jewish state would solve the problem of anti-Semitism in Europe. And one can have a strong sympathy for any Israeli who argues the need for Israel on the grounds of expediency – provided he is willing to consider the price that *others* have had to pay.

Although Herzl himself didn't use the Old Testament at all in putting forward his idea of the Jewish state, other more devout, practising Jews weren't slow to relate the Zionist vision to the Old Testament. But it's quite a different matter when we find Christians today who support this way of using the Old Testament.

Can the State of Israel be in any sense – for the Jew or for the Christian – the fulfilment of the promise that through Abraham and his descendants 'all peoples of the earth' would be blessed? Can the Christian agree that '*this* [the Jewish state which we see today] is *that* which was spoken by the prophets [like the visions of Isaiah and Zechariah]'? Could it even be seen as one stage in the fulfilment of these visions?

When seen in the light of the idea of the chosen people as it developed in the Old Testament – from Moses to Ruth, to Isaiah, Zechariah, Ezra and Nehemiah – the modern Jewish state looks more like a step *backwards* than a step *forwards*.

Many Jews have commented on the problem that has been created within Judaism by the existence of Jewish state.

Haim Cohen, a judge of the Supreme Court of Israel:

> The bitter irony of fate has decreed that the same biological and racist arguments extended by the Nazis, and which inspired the inflammatory laws of Nuremberg, serve as the basis for the official definition of Jewishness in the bosom of the State of Israel.

I.F. Stone, an American Jewish journalist, who was decorated by the Irgun in 1948, writing in 1967:

> Israel is creating a kind of moral schizophrenia in World Jewry. In the outside world the welfare of Jewry depends on the maintenance of secular, non-racial pluralistic societies. In Israel, Jewry finds itself defending a society in which mixed marriages cannot be legalized, in which non-Jews have a lesser status than Jews and in which the ideal is racial and exclusionist. Jews must fight elsewhere for their very security and existence – against principles and practices they find themselves defending in Israel. Those from the outside world, even in their moments of greatest enthusiasm amid Israeli accomplishments, feel twinges of claustrophobia, not just geographical but spiritual. Those caught up in prophetic fervor soon begin to feel that the light they hoped to see out of Zion is only that of another narrow nationalism.

He comments on the tension between the universal vision of historic Judaism and the nationalism of the State of Israel:

> It must also be recognized, despite Zionist ideology, that the periods of greatest Jewish accomplishment have been

associated with pluralistic civilization in their time of expansion and tolerance: in the Hellenistic period, in the Arab civilization of North Africa and Spain, and in Western Europe and America. Universal values can only be the fruit of a universal vision; the greatness of the prophets lay in their overcoming of ethnocentricity. A lilliputian nationalism cannot distill truths for all mankind. Here lie the roots of a growing divergence between Jew and Israeli, the former with sense of mission as a witness in the human wilderness, the latter concerned only with his own tribes' welfare.

Rabbi Yosef Becher believes the idea of a Jewish state goes against the principles of Judaism:

> According to our belief, we are not allowed to have a state. The whole concept of a state is foreign to Judaism, which is a faith, a religion. Through the prophets and by the will of the Almighty, the Jews once had a state – the First Temple and the Second Temple – but when they sinned, the Almighty, again through the prophets, declared that they should be disbanded, and from then on the Jews were not allowed to have a state.
>
> The Talmud was made in Babylon. The Code of Laws was made in Europe. Jews were able to take care of their religion better when they were among the nations . . .
>
> The Talmud says that if the Jews are forced to run from one place, there will be other kings who will let them live in their countries. This is how Judaism survived. The rabbis were against a Jewish state because it was not the will of the Almighty. When it is his will, it will happen in a supernatural way – with the coming of the Messiah, when all kinds of miracles will be wrought about which we have no idea. As the Prophet Isaiah says, it will be a time when all nations will pray under one house on the mountain of the Lord where the Temple stood. The Temple will not be made one by man, and at that time no nation will lift up a sword against any people.
>
> We pray for this and wait for it, but until then we must remain among the peoples. It is safer for us. If we have a state, we could bring catastrophe upon ourselves, even if that state is religious and especially if it is irreligious, as the present state of Israel is.

This is how he sums up his hopes for the State of Israel:

> We believe that the state of Israel is a passing occurence, a temporary thing. It is one way that Satan has used to lure Jews away from their faith. We want the state to disappear, but we

want it to disappear in a peaceful way.

We want the state of Israel to disappear in a peaceful way, but we have no way to bring that about except prayer, and we pray for the disappearance of Israel three times a day.

Of course, the Zionists are themselves using violence against the Palestinians. We know they use bombs and kill children and others for no reason whatever, and there is no way to express the way we feel about that, but what can we do? We pray.

Dow Marmur, a Jewish rabbi in London, has recently written a book entitled *Beyond Survival: Reflections on the Future of Judaism.* In a review of the book Bishop Kenneth Cragg summarizes its argument in the following way:

'The mystical bond . . . and the neurotic tangle' (page 93) is a phrase that perhaps best sums up this frank, sensitive and, at times, exasperating, book. Its author is Rabbi of the North Western Reform Synagogue in London. He wants to take Judaism and Jews 'beyond' what he sees as their inordinate pre-occupation with survival. This pre-occupation he finds characteristic of the three main manifestations of Jewry. Traditional Orthodoxy finds survival through a rigorous loyalty to the past. Reform Judaism tends to emphasise present and future, but in his view, accomodates the world and its threat of assimilation too confidently. Zionism achieves a present, and – it hopes – a future security but only at the actual, or potential sacrifice or primary Jewish values.

The book pleads for a coming together of these three, each 'educating' the other in a unifying discipline so that they operate to alert each to dimensions which the others need but which also need them. There is no space here to detail his argument in this triangular connection and how it relates to synagogue and home, to state and family, to the role of the rabbi and of women, to the political and secular order. The author is alive to the problems, probes them honestly and has strenuous intentions for their 'solution'.

Cragg comments on the way Marmur presents his argument in the context of the story in Genesis of Jacob wrestling with the angel:

He sets his whole presentation in the context of Jacob wrestling with the angel at the brook, Jabbok. 'The elimination of the struggle deprives of the blessing.' Only in encouter with the future resolutely can the promise be reached, even if 'wrestling' Jacob is crippled in the process. The 'angel', for Dow Marmur, is 'the guardian angel of Esau', and perhaps, in a wider context, the spirit of the Gentile world. He does not mention the possibility that the struggle was about penitent honesty over Jacob's dubious past and the consequent 'new name' then bestowed. (Perhaps that is Gentile, Christian exegesis. But Jacob's apprehension about meeting Esau surely has to do not only with danger to his present gains but truth about his crooked past? Or does the duplicity at his old father's deathbed matter not?)

At all events, Jacob/Israel is called to perennial conflict. As at Peniel, his 'blessing' can only be had in being disadvantaged. His whole self-awareness is an awareness of actual or impending enmity. He has for ever to calculate in a crisis of survival.

He is a constant hostage to circumstance and can only triumph by struggling with real, feared, or imagined, adversity. This, mirrored in 'wrestling' Jacob, *is* the Jewish dilemma and gives to everything Jewish, whether Orthodoxy, Reform, Zionism, an incessant focus on self-ensuring response to hostility, actual or potential.

Cragg then goes on to express his response as a Christian to the argument of the book:

It is just this stance of Jewishness which Rabbi Marmur wants to exorcise (insofar as it makes 'survival' the be-all-and end-all). Yet it is a stance to which he himself falls constantly victim. And this is where the book might be called exasperating. If only, somehow, Jewry could belong with mankind! But, somehow, tragically it never can. There is, as he sees it, the eternal problem of Anti-Semitism, a problem wholly at the door of the 'Gentile' world. There is persecution. There is the scapegoat 'syndrome' 'necessitating' Jews. There is assimilation, or the threat of it. Since, for example, Oxford, with its culture and openness to Jewry, constitutes a danger of assimilation, 'both, Auschwitz and Oxford, have the same effect on the future of Judaism (page 36). What an utterly desolating stance this is! Surely one of the sharpest needs of Jewish thought is a theology of 'the Gentiles', so that somehow what Marmur himself calls 'this neurotic tangle between Jews and their enemies' can be unravelled, and so ended . . .

There is much else that is perceptive and venturesome in this book. Yet it leaves a mere 'Gentile' reader who cares deeply about Jewry, the synagogue and Israel, and wants to understand 'the mystical bond', still aware that he, too, has only 'wrestled' (at this reconstruction of Peniel) with another occasion of the age-long problem that is 'the neurotic tangle'. When shall we all, Jew and Gentile alike, see 'the face of God' and know our life assured in that vision alone?

4·7 Suffering Injustice

The Jews look back to the Dispersion, the ghettos, the pogroms and the holocaust. The Arabs look back to their oppression under the Turks, the broken promises of the western powers, the establishment of the State of Israel in 1948 and the traumatic defeat of 1967. Both people know the meaning of the word 'suffering' and 'injustice'.

The Quaker Report reminds us that the Middle East problem arises out of the sufferings of *both* the Jews *and* the Arabs, and out of their attempts to free themselves from oppression:

> The Jews and the Arabs are ancient and long-suffering peoples, and their sufferings continue. Both have been cruelly dealt with by peoples of other cultures, and both are still subject to manipulation by forces beyond their control. Both are distrustful of other peoples and of each other, as they seek to establish their own identity, their right to respect, freedom and national self-development.
>
> It is one of the great ironies of history that the roots of the present Arab-Jewish struggle should have grown, not in a poisoned soil of ancient mutual animosities, but in the mistreatment each has received at the hands of others. The Jews and the Arabs are Semitic cousins, share cultural traits and traditions, and through long centuries lived in relative peace with one another even during periods when Jews were subject to sustained persecution by the Christian West . . .
>
> The intensified struggle of Jews and Arabs has come since the end of World War I and most intensely since the end of World War II, as the two peoples, in their own ways, finally sought to put an end to persecution and to their common status as subject peoples – and ran head on into each other.
>
> Zionism, the most dynamic force of nineteenth-century Jewish nationalism, burst upon the world scene just as Arab nationalism was beginning to rise from the dying Turkish Empire. These simultaneously emerging nationalisms, unfortunately, were destined to fight for possession of the same territory in the Holy Land of Palestine.

We have already noticed how some of the prophets called for

justice. But is this all they had to say about injustice? Did they believe that if only they spoke out loudly enough, and if only the law courts did their job properly, all would be well?

Part of **Isaiah's** answer to the existence of injustice in his own nation and in other nations is the conviction that God will one day punish evildoers:

> The Lord looked and was displeased
>   that there was no justice.
> He saw that there was no-one,
>   and he was appalled that there
>   was no-one to intercede;
> so his own arm worked salvation for him,
>   and his own righteousness sustained him.
> He put on righteousness as his breastplate,
>   and the helmet of salvation on his head;
> he put on the garments of vengeance
>   and wrapped himself in zeal as in a cloak.
> According to what they have done,
>   so will he repay
>   wrath to his enemies
>   and retribution to his foes;
>   he will repay the islands their due . . .
>   Isaiah 59:15–18

In his vision of the future reign of God, the figure described as 'the Servant of the Lord' plays a special role in bringing 'justice to the nations';

> Here is my servant, whom I uphold,
>   my chosen one in whom I delight;
> I will put my Spirit on him
>   and he will bring *justice* to the nations.
> He will not shout or cry out,
>   or raise his voice in the streets.
> A bruised reed he will not break,
>   and a smouldering wick he will not snuff out.
> In faithfulness he will bring forth *justice*;
>   he will not falter or be discouraged
> till he establishes *justice* on earth.
>   In his law the islands will put their hope.
>   Isaiah 42:1–4

But when we ask *how* the Servant of the Lord is to establish justice on earth, the answer given is not the one we might have expected. Instead of dealing with injustice by force, and punishing evildoers, *the Servant himself suffers injustice*. Although he is totally innocent, and is not suffering for any wrong that he has done, he submits to all the injustice that is done to him:

> He was oppressed and afflicted,
> yet he did not open his mouth;
> he was led like a lamb to the slaughter,
> and as a sheep before her shearers is silent,
> so he did not open his mouth.
> By oppression and judgement, he was taken away.
> And who can speak of his descendants,
> For he was cut off from the land of the living;
> for the transgression of my people he was stricken.
> He was assigned a grave with the wicked,
> and with the rich in his death,
> though he had done no violence,
> nor was any deceit in his mouth.
> Isaiah 53:7–9

By accepting injustice and bearing undeserved suffering, he is in some mysterious way bearing the suffering and guilt of the whole people:

> Surely he took up our infirmities
> and carried our sorrows,
> yet we considered him stricken by God,
> smitten by him, and afflicted.
>
> But he was pierced for our transgressions,
> he was crushed for our iniquities;
> the punishment that brought us peace was upon him,
> and by his wounds we are healed.
> We all, like sheep, have gone astray,
> each of us has turned to his own way;
> and the Lord has laid on him
> the iniquity of us all.
> Isaiah 53:4–6

We may well want to ask with the Ethiopian eunuch 'Who is the prophet talking about, himself or someone else?' (Acts 8:34). This chapter in Isaiah has often proved to be an enigma, an embarrassment, and even at times a stumbling-block to Jews. If it is seen simply as a poetic expression of the value of vicarious suffering, there's no problem. But within the framework of traditional Jewish belief about God, it is hard to see how the suffering of an innocent person can actually be redemptive in the sense that it brings divine forgiveness for others.

Christians believe that this picture finds its supreme fulfilment in the person of Jesus of Nazareth, who, instead of calling down the judgement of God on those who condemned him so unjustly, was willing to suffer the injustice. But perhaps we are in danger of rushing too far ahead in seeking to identify the Suffering Servant of Isaiah with Jesus. At this stage it should be enough for us to notice that here in the Old Testament, we find the principle that judgement and condemnation aren't always the only answer to injustice. We can't make injustice disappear simply by finding a prophet to denounce what is evil and warn of judgement to come, or by bringing down the heavy arm of the law. Sometimes the way to overcome injustice is to suffer it. The divine answer to evil sometimes involves suffering.

Denys Baly points out the need to examine slogans like 'a just and durable peace':

> No peace can now be just. That is the lamentable fact, for whatever we do now will be unjust to somebody. If we confirm the Israeli immigrants in their homes, we shall be unjust to the Arab refugees, whose homes they once were, and who desperately long to return to them. If, however, we insist that justice shall be done to the Arabs, we shall be unjust to the Israeli immigrants, who cannot be held responsible for an exodus which took place before they set foot in the country . . . There are those on every side, it is true, who demand that justice be done to them and never mind about the others. But it is not this that 'justice' means.
>
> The Middle East is admittedly not peculiar in this, for in any problem area of the world, in Kashmir, in South Africa, in Germany, in Indochina and in North Africa, the issues have become so complex, and so much unrighted wrong has been done, that justice is no longer feasible. To pretend that it is is to make any forward step impossible, because if we have proclaimed that justice is our purpose, then we shall unfailingly be condemned for the inevitable injustice, and we shall have added to the number of those who feel themselves to be betrayed.

Reconciliation begins to be possible only when someone is willing to accept injustice:

> In a situation where justice is no longer possible reconciliation can come only if some men accept injustice. There is no other way. But the very thought of it is abhorrent, for whatever else men are ready to forgo, justice, it would seem, is a permanent

demand. This is, in fact, the root of nationalism. Only those in whom Christ lives can see the need to demand justice always for the other side and to accept injustice for themselves.

4·8 Repentance through Disaster

More often than not disaster leads to bitterness, anger and despair. Far from changing people's prejudices, it often hardens them or pushes them under the surface.

The message of the book of Lamentations, therefore, is all the more relevant because it shows how one person in particular refused to respond to a major national disaster in this way.

This short book, traditionally attributed to the prophet Jeremiah, was written some time after the Jews had witnessed the destruction of Jerusalem in 587 BC at the hands of the Babylonian army. According to tradition it was recited by the community in the remains of the temple in the following years. It has for many centuries held a special place in Jewish liturgical tradition, being read annually on the day commemorating the destruction of the temple (i.e. the Fast of the Ninth Ab).

What is specially significant about the way this prophet responds to the disaster? Firstly, instead of pouring out his anger on his enemies, the Babylonians, he is willing to ask the question: *why* has God allowed all this to happen? He points to particular leaders in the community who bear a large measure of responsibility for what has happened:

> The visions of your prophets
>   were false and worthless;
> they did not expose your sin
>   to ward off your captivity.
> The oracles they gave you
>   were false and misleading.
> Lamentations 2:14

> It happened because of the sins of her prophets
>   and the iniquities of her priests,
> who shed within her
>   the blood of the righteous.
> Lamentations 4:13

He also realizes that the people are reaping the consequences of the attitudes and actions of previous generations:

> Our fathers sinned and are no more,
>   and we bear their punishment.
> Lamentations 5:7

He admits that God has only done what he warned he would do if they didn't repent:

> The Lord has done what he planned;
>> he has fulfilled his word,
>> which he decreed long ago.
> Lamentations 2:17

He therefore encourages the people to examine themselves and turn to God in sincere repentance.

Secondly the writer recognizes that there is a difference between suffering that is *deserved* (that is suffering that comes as a judgement from God), and suffering that is *undeserved*. This means that if he and his people are willing to admit their share of responsibility and guilt for what has happened, they can then submit to God's heavy hand of judgement, knowing that he punishes only because he loves. When they have submitted to suffering that is deserved, they can begin to learn the secret of enduring suffering that is not deserved. In the midst of his suffering, therefore, he can overcome his feelings of despair, and face the future with hope and confidence.

These two themes are woven together in one key passage at the heart of the book:

> I remember my affliction and my wandering,
> the bitterness and the gall.
> I well remember them,
> and my soul is downcast within me.
> Yet this I call to mind
> and therefore I have hope:
>
> Because of the Lord's great love we are not consumed,
> for his compassions never fail.
> They are new every morning;
> great is your faithfulness.
> I say to myself, 'The Lord is my portion;
> therefore I will wait for him.'
>
> The Lord is good to those whose hope is in him,
> to the one who seeks him;
> it is good to wait quietly
> for the salvation of the Lord.
> It is good for a man to bear the yoke
> while he is young.
>
> Let him sit alone in silence,
> for the Lord has laid it on him.
> Let him bury his face in the dust–

there may yet be hope.
Let him offer his cheek to one who would strike him,
and let him be filled with disgrace.

For men are not cast off
by the Lord forever.
Though he brings grief, he will show compassion,
so great is his unfailing love.
For he does not willingly bring affliction
or grief to the children of men.

To crush underfoot
all prisoners in the land,
to deny a man his rights
before the most High,
to deprive a man of justice–
would not the Lord see such things?

Who can speak and have it happen
if the Lord has not decreed it?
Is it not from the mouth of the Most High
that both calamities and good things come?
Why should any living man complain
when punished for his sins?

Let us examine our ways and test them,
and let us return to the Lord.
Let us lift up our hearts and our hands
to God in heaven, and say:
'We have sinned and rebelled
and you have not forgiven.

'You have covered yourself with anger and pursued us;
you have slain without pity.
You have covered yourself with a cloud
so that no prayer can get through.
You have made us scum and refuse among the nations.

'All our enemies have opened their mouths
wide against us.
We have suffered terror and pitfalls,
ruin and destruction.'
Streams of tears flow from my eyes
because my people are destroyed.

My eyes will flow unceasingly,
without relief,
until the Lord looks down

from heaven and sees.
Lamentations 3:19—50

Denys Baly suggests two of the particular 'acts of repentance' that are necessary in the two main sides in the conflict in the Middle East:

> For any progress to be made in the Middle East two great acts of repentance are necessary: Israel must banish forever even secret thoughts of more territory, and therefore must renounce the concept of unlimited immigration; and the Arabs must admit the fact of Israel, and have the courage to tell the refugees that they have done so. Only those who have lived in the Middle East and count their friends on both sides of the Line can begin to estimate how great would be the cost of these two decisions. Men have died only because it was imagined that they held such opinions.

The La Grange Declaration II makes some specific suggestions as to what repentance might mean for American Christians:

> We are American Christians seeking to serve the cause of peace in the Middle East. We have heard the agonized cries of Palestinians – Christian and Muslim – who have been driven from their ancestral homes and/or deprived of their fundamental rights. We have heard from Jews of the fear which grips their hearts and the vision which inspires their hope. We have listened to the accounts of trial endured by the Christians of the holy land, whose churches have existed from the time of Christ. And with these laments in our ears, we have struggled to hear the word of God for this situation so that the church of Jesus Christ may fulfil its calling to be an agent of justice and a bearer of peace.
>
> In our quest, we are not striving to solve directly the public political questions of nation states, but rather to address fundamental human and religious concerns which affect the peoples of the Middle East and the world . . .

I *Questions for the American Church*

In our struggle to hear, discern, and to act, we have raised these questions.

A. We question biblically the vision of nationalism and statehood limited to any particular people as the means for building a durable and just peace in the holy land. We long, rather, for the vision of land and peoplehood secured for both Israeli people and Palestinian people in the holy land.

204 / WHOSE PROMISED LAND?

B. We question how Christians can believe that the Old Testament gives to the modern state of Israel divine and unconditional ownership of the land of Palestine, to the exclusion of the indigenous people. We believe that an honest, open, and comprehensive understanding of the Bible prohibits these claims and raises the priority of God's justice for all people as the means to nourish the hope of reconciliation between Israeli and Palestinian.

C. We have also come to question a United States foreign policy which restricts Palestinians from travelling to, speaking freely within, and remaining in the United States, limiting the opportunity of free expression of opinion to the American people; a foreign policy which directs 43 per cent of its foreign aid to the nation of Israel; and a foreign policy which refuses even to speak with representatives of the Palestinian people.

II Our commitments

Recognizing that our confession and faith must be grounded in our actions and lifestyles, we invite others to join us in the following commitments.

A. Hearing the cries of the people involved in the Israeli-Palestinian conflict we are called to pray daily for all our brothers and sisters who struggle in the Middle East.

B. Realizing the need for greater awareness and understanding of the current situation in Israel and Palestine, we will strive to make balanced information available to local media and the members of our communities and church families.

C. Recognizing that there can be no security and therefore no freedom for Jews, Christians, and Muslims in Israel or Palestine so long as people are afraid, we commit ourselves to working to overcome all fear.

1. Specifically, we pledge to root out any and all signs of anti-Semitism in our own lives, our culture, and our society.

2. We pledge to respond to any and all invitations from our Jewish and Palestinian brothers and sisters which will help us understand their concerns.

D. Confessing our share in the historical heritage which culminated in the holocaust and sent refugee Jews to Palestine rather than in providing them with safe and secure homes in Europe and the Americas, we are called to shoulder our fair burden in building a just peace.

1. Specifically, we pledge to use our persuasive powers to convince all parties to adopt nonviolent strategies to resolve their conflicts;

2. We pledge to lift up and denounce all forms of violence

whether covert military operations, overt military manoeuvres, or illegal seizures of property and intimidation of persons;

3. We pledge, if invited, to find US Christians willing to serve as peacemakers and agents of reconciliation in Israel and Palestine.

E. Recognizing United States complicity in the suffering of the Middle East, we are called to regularly contact our legislators and State Department officials, urging them to cease military aid and to equalize humanitarian aid to the Palestinian and Israeli peoples.

1. Specifically, we are called to persistently work to urge the US government to curtail subsidies to the government of Israel until Israel ceases all illegal seizures of property, establishment of settlements on Palestinian lands, and expulsion of Palestinians.

4·9 The Temptation of Taking Sides and Throwing Stones

Surely you've got to be on one side or the other? Haven't you sooner or later got to come down on the side of the Jews or the Arabs?

The following quotation is from a full-page advertisement in *The New York Times* in July 1976, sponsored by the American Board of Mission to the Jews. It included the names of 105 churches in the US which 'fully believe in God's promises to Israel and in his everlasting love for her':

God's Timepiece

If you want to know where we are in history, look at the Jewish people.

They are, God's timepiece and people of prophecy. Part of an eternal clock ticking away as an everlasting reminder that although other peoples or nations may come or go, these people will remain forever.

Because that's the way God wants it. Promised it. And planned it. Long ago.

He made a covenant with Abraham, promising a large portion of the Middle East as an inheritance for him and his descendants.

No mortgage. No lease. And no divine right of eminent domain to ever pop up later.

The covenant was unconditional. Just like his love. And because of God's love he made another promise through

Abraham. That through his seed all the nations of the earth would be blessed.

This is history past. For the seed which came through Abraham, Isaac and Jacob . . . Ruth, Jesse and David . . . came to fruition as the Messiah of Israel.

We, as believers in the Messiah, know him to fulfil ancient promises while bringing love, joy and peace to us now.

This is history today.

And as the Jewish people continue to return to their promised land by the thousands, they take part in fulfilling prophecy today. And history tomorrow. Bringing us one step closer to the most important event of all. The return of the Messiah.

Because the Jewish people are the people of prophecy, they are the people of the land.

And we, knowing him who made the promise, totally support the people and land of Israel in their God-given, God-promised, God-ordained right to exist.

Any person or group of nations opposed to this right isn't just fighting Israel. But God and time itself.

The following article entitled *America's Evangelicals: More Zionist than Zionists* by William Claiborne appeared in the Washington Post:

Estimated at 40 million members and embracing Abraham's Covenant as fervently as the most impassioned Zionists, the burgeoning Evangelical Christian movement in the United States is fast becoming one of Israel's most potent allies in its conflict with the Arab world.

They range in ideology from political moderates who simply view Israel as an underdog in a lopsided struggle for survival, to infatuated rightists who are convinced that the Jewish state will play the central role in that final apocalyptical chapter of history that climaxes with the Second Coming of Christ.

Some of them make pilgrimages to the Holy Land and pay homage to the leaders of Prime Minister Begin's government as adoringly as they visit the shrines along the Via Dolorosa, where Jesus is believed to have walked to his crucifixion. They issue warnings with beatific certainty that a great conflagration with the Soviet Union in the Middle East is a biblical prophecy, but promise that the United States will come to Israel's rescue . . .

'For these people, the Bible is a political guide to their activities. They understand that the land of Israel was promised by God to Abraham. They have no problem with the (occupied) West Bank. There's no question in their minds that the Bible is accurate in its geographical and historical description of the Jews' right to the Land of Israel', said Zeey Chafets, director of Israel's Government Press Office. 'Not only do they support Israel, but they particularly support Begin and the Likud government. How could we be displeased with that kind of friendship?' he added.

Israeli officials are keenly aware of the growing Evangelical movement in the United States, which according to public opinion analyst George Gallup, includes one in three Americans who acknowledge having been 'born again', and 38 per cent of the nation that believes the Bible is the actual word of God and should be taken literally.

An aide to Mr Begin said that the Evangelicals 'are a pillar that Israel has in the United States. They number 10 times the Jews in America, and they are outspoken. Naturally, we look kindly on what they are doing . . .'

Some Evangelical leaders deny that the movement is particularly disposed to the Likud government's rightist policies, although Dr. Larry Samuels, an American medical professor at Hadassah Hospital here said that he once told Mr. Begin, 'You know, I think you have more supporters among Evangelical Christians in North America than you have Jews supporting Israel.' . . .

The first of the following two incidents in the life of Jesus illustrates the danger of immediately taking sides in a conflict. The second explains why we need to be very careful about 'throwing stones'.

'Who made me a judge or divider over you?'

Luke records a revealing incident in which Jesus was invited to intervene in a family dispute:

Someone in the crowd said to him, 'Teacher, tell my brother to divide the inheritance with me.'

Jesus replied, 'Man, who appointed me a judge or an arbiter between you?' Then he said to them, 'Watch out! Be on your guard against all kinds of greed; a man's life does not consist in the abundance of his possessions.'

And he told them this parable . . .
Luke 12:13-16

If this was a simple case of injustice, with the older brother refusing to give his younger brother his legitimate share of the family property, we might expect Jesus to support the younger brother in his demand for justice. This is precisely what Jesus did *not* do. Luke's account is remarkably brief, and we are left wondering if this is all that Jesus said. Did he, for example, begin by asking more questions and investigating the case in greater detail? Or did he refuse to get involved in any way? We don't know because Luke doesn't tell us.

What is clear, however, from this account is that Jesus did not immediately take sides – not, presumably, because he wasn't concerned about justice, but because he wanted to tackle the deeper issue of covetousness which lay beneath the surface. But who was doing the coveting? Was it the older brother who was holding on to the whole property? Or was it the younger brother who, even though he had a legitimate right to the property, was motivated primarily by selfishness and greed? Again, we don't know. It could have been either, or it could have been both.

A modern version of the same incident might read like this: 'An Israeli in the crowd said to him, "Master, tell my Arab neighbours to let me live in peace in the land of my fathers . . ."' Or it might begin: 'An Arab in the crowd said to him, "Master, tell the Israelis to give us back the land which they have taken from us . . ."' It is hard to imagine that Jesus is not concerned about the rights and wrongs of every human situation – not least in the land today. But if he were approached in this way, he would probably see more clearly than we do the rights and wrongs on both sides (or rather on *all* sides); and before taking sides in any way with one group against the other, he would no doubt want to deal with some of the underlying issues and have something to say to *every* party involved in the conflict.

'If any one of you is without sin, let him be the first to throw a stone.'

The story of Jesus' dealings with the woman taken in adultery underlines the need to be careful in passing judgement on others. Jesus does not in any way condone the woman's adultery, since it is still described as 'sin'. There is, therefore, no blurring of the moral issue. But he refuses to approve of stoning the woman or to condemn her in the same tones that his audience expected. He simply says to her, 'Neither do I condemn you . . . go now and leave your life of sin' (John 8:11).

There is one reason why the Christian church needs to be particularly careful about pointing the prophetic finger at the Jewish people over this issue of the land. Every Christian today ought to blush with shame when he reads what some of the greatest names in church history have said about the Jews. We may protest that we ourselves have no anti-Semitic feelings whatsoever, and that we cannot be held responsible for what Christians said and did in the

Middle Ages. As far as the Jew is concerned, however, we are inevitably identified with them, just as members of the same family are identified with each other in the eyes of the world. If we do not want to forget all the good that has been done in the name of Christ, the Jew can hardly forget all the suffering that Christians have brought to Jews in the name of Christ.

Does this mean that Christians, like those who tried to get Jesus to condemn the woman taken in adultery, must 'go away one at a time' (John 8:9)? Or are there ways of challenging wrong and helping the wrong-doer that are more Christ-like than taking up stones in order to carry out the final sentence ourselves?

If we try to embark on this task, we have to be willing to admit with the psalmist 'We have sinned, even as our fathers did' (Psalm 106:6), and confess with the prophet Isaiah, 'I am a man of unclean lips, and I live among a people of unclean lips . . .' (Isaiah 6:5). For the message of Jesus to all would-be prophets is: 'First take the plank out of your own eye, and then you will see clearly to remove the speck from your brother's eye' (Matthew 7:5).

The writers of the Quaker Report explain what it meant for them to write about justice in the Middle East:

> Despite our best efforts to treat this issue with objectivity and candour and to win the widest possible agreement for a peaceful solution, we face these realities:
>
> a. It is impossible to come to a fair and responsible judgement on the Arab-Israeli conflict on the basis of endorsing the Israeli government position or the positions of the Arab governments or of the Palestinian Arab organizations. No side has a case so right and just that all its past or present actions can be defended.
>
> b. Many on each side will denounce any comment which does not support their position on the grounds that 'if you are not for us, you are against us'.
>
> c. It is impossible to reach an even-handed judgement on the basis of some neat compromise. On some issues, we believe, the Arabs have been clearly wrong and on other issues, the Israelis have been clearly wrong.

They state their conviction that it is possible to be 'both pro-Jewish and pro-Arab':

> We wish to make clear to all, particularly to our countrymen of Jewish and Arab backgrounds, that our position is one of concern for both peoples and is based on the conviction that the rights and interests of both must be recognized and

reconciled on some just and peaceful basis. We believe that to ignore or to deny the essential rights of one group will lead to the ultimate destruction of the rights of the other. Peace and decent living conditions, if not available to both, will be unavailable to either. We firmly believe that it is possible to be both pro-Jewish and pro-Arab. And for both the essential need is peace.

Denys Baly points out why people who are prejudiced cannot do anything to bring about reconciliation:

The New Testament presents the reconciliation of God and man as possible only when there is someone who can properly be identified with both God and man . . . Political reconciliation can come about only when there are those who struggle earnestly to belong to both sides . . . It is fatally easy in the circumstances of increasing polarization to become so vividly aware of the sufferings and the injustice done to one side that we become wholly identified with them, and see no virtue at all in the other side . . . Certainly it may be right to go to the defence of those who seem to be the underdogs (though we should beware always of a merely emotional and superficial assessment), but our concern for the underdog should not prevent us from entering fully into the hopes and fears even of those who seem to be the oppressors, of struggling to comprehend why they are doing what they are doing . . . and think in their terms. To neglect this task is utterly to fail to speak the word of reconciliation and to betray the cause of Christ. I use the strongest words that I know, partly because every effort will be made by those who are embroiled in the battle to obtain your one-hundred per cent allegiance and to deny it to the other side, and partly also because this is a polarised world. . . . A necessary part of the defence against the betrayal of Christ is the rejection of absolute moral standards as a basis for positive political action.

He also explains why the Christian church bears a considerable measure of responsibility for anti-Semitism:

We may squirm and wriggle as much as we like, but we cannot escape the charge that Zionism would never have been if we had not persecuted the Jews. No one can study the history of the Zionist movement and remain unconvinced of this. If Herzl had not found himself reporting the Dreyfus Case for the Vienna paper, the *Neue Freie Presse*, and if he had not been faced in carefree Vienna itself with occasional outbursts of anti-

Semitic venom, he would possibly have remained an assimilationist to the day of his death. It is a strange fact that the man who was able to write in his diary, 'At Basle I founded the Jewish State,' became convinced of the need for a Jewish state by no teaching of those who already held such convictions, but by the naked truth of anti-Semitism alone. It is a fact also that the Zionists could make little headway where the Jews were at peace. It was the pogroms and the persecution which convinced the doubters. Century after century has had its discrimination, its bloody massacres, its fantastic accusations, its hysteria. We may forget this tragic story, but the Jews never can. It is their story. Much of the persecution has been done in the name of the Christian faith, and almost all has been done by those who profess and call themselves Christian. And what have we to set against it? Some glorious stories of charity, of mercy to the refugees, of noble protest, it is true; but they are only pages in the whole book. Every discussion with the Zionists is determined by this history. It is a story which they cannot forget and we cannot escape.

4·10 The Cost of being a Peace-Maker

Both parties in any conflict usually think they are totally in the right, and that their cause is totally just. Any admission of guilt means loss of face, and any concession means accepting something that is unjust. Anyone who wants to bring the two parties together has to try to identify with both sides, and runs the risk of being hated and rejected by both. Peace-making is a costly business.

Edward Said explains something of the 'despair and pessimism' felt by Jews and Arabs in the conflict:

Much of the despair and pessimism that one feels at the whole Palestinian-Zionist conflict is each side's failure in a sense to reckon with the existential power and presence of *another* people with its land, its unfortunate history of suffering, its emotional and political investment in that land, and worse, to pretend that the Other is a temporary nuisance that, given time and effort (and punitive violence from time to time), will finally go away. The actuality is that Palestinian and Israeli Jews are now fully implicated in each others' lives and political destinies.

In this kind of situation what can we learn from the Bible about peace-making?

'Blessed are the peace-makers'

The Beatitudes taken as a whole (Matthew 5:2–12) paint a picture of the only kind of people who are qualified to undertake this delicate task:

● they are those who are poor in spirit, because they're acutely conscious of their own shortcomings and weaknesses (5:3);

● they mourn over the sins of others, instead of gloating over them and compiling statistics of them (5:4);

● they are meek, and don't throw their weight around (5:5);

● in their hunger and thirst for righteousness, they are not only concerned to have a right relationship with God, but also to see right prevail (5:6);

● they are merciful, because they realize that the application of law by itself cannot bring peace and reconciliation (5:7);

● they are pure in heart because their motives are utterly unselfish (5:8);

● they are concerned not only to talk about peace, but also to make peace and to bring enemies together (5:9);

● they know that they're likely to get hurt in the process, but are willing to suffer and pay the price of being peace-makers (5:10).

'He himself is our peace'

As a Jew, Paul was acutely conscious of the feelings of the Jewish people towards Gentiles in his own day. He believed, however, that God's intention was to create 'one new man', instead of two kinds of men – Jew and Gentile – and that God had begun to bring this about through the death of Jesus on the cross. This is the kind of relationship which God wanted to exist between Jews and Gentiles:

> He himself is our peace, who has made the two (Jew and Gentile) one and has destroyed the barrier, the dividing wall of hostility, by abolishing in his flesh the law with its commandments and regulations. His purpose was to create in himself one new man out of the two, thus making peace, and in this one body to reconcile both of them to God through the cross, by which he put to death their hostility. He came and preached peace to you who were far away and peace to those who were near. For through him we both have access to the Father by one Spirit.
>
> Consequently, you are no longer foreigners and aliens, but fellow-citizens with God's people and members of God's household, built on the foundation of the apostles and prophets, with Christ Jesus himself as the chief corner-stone.
>
> . . . through the gospel the Gentiles are heirs together with

Israel, members together of one body, and sharers together in
the promise in Christ Jesus.
Ephesians 2:14–20, 36

'And so all Israel will be saved'

One of the recurring themes in books about prophecy today is the
conviction that one day there will be a large-scale conversion of
Jews. Their return to the land and the establishment of the Jewish
state are regarded as specially significant in the sequence of events
which will eventually lead them to acknowledge Jesus as Messiah.
The conversion of large numbers of Jews (or even perhaps of all
Jews) will in turn lead to a time of unparalleled blessing for the
Gentiles.

These hopes are built largely on Paul's discussion about the
Jewish people in Romans 9–11, supported by many individual verses
from the Old Testament prophets. There is one particular sentence
in Paul's argument which is crucial, and which has caused a great
deal of controversy: '. . . and so all Israel will be saved . . .' In order
to understand this sentence, we need at the very least to notice the
context and the verses immediately before and after it:

> I do not want you to be ignorant of this mystery, brothers, so
> that you may not become conceited: Israel has experienced a
> hardening in part until the full number of the Gentiles has come
> in. And so all Israel will be saved, as it is written:
> 'The deliverer will come from Zion;
>   he will turn godlessness away from Jacob.
> And this is my covenant with them,
>   when I take away their sins.'
> Romans 11:25–27

The following is offered as a brief summary of one way of interpreting this difficult passage.

1. 'Israel' means 'the Jewish people', and not 'the Church'. In all the
other thirteen instances in these three chapters where he uses
'Israel', he clearly means 'the Jewish people' (Romans 9:4, 6, 27, 31;
10:1, 16, 19, 21; 11:1, 2, 7, 11, 25). If we insist that 'Israel' here means
the church, we must accept that Paul uses the word in two consecu-
tive sentences with two completely different meanings: 'Israel (i.e.
the Jewish people) has experienced a hardening . . .' (Romans 11:25).
'And so all Israel (i.e. the church, the people of God, including both
Jews and Gentiles) will be saved . . .' (11:26).

Paul is at pains to point out to his Gentile Christian readers that
God has *not* rejected the people of Israel. The Jews are *still* heirs to
all the promises made to their forefathers. Simply by virtue of being

the physical descendants of Abraham, the privileges and blessings of
the covenant are still theirs:

> I ask then, Did God reject his people? By no means! ... God
> did not reject his people whom he foreknew.
>
> Romans 11:1–2

> ... the people of Israel. Theirs is the adoption as sons; theirs the
> divine glory, the covenants, the receiving of the law, the temple
> worship and the promises. Theirs are the patriarchs, and from
> them is traced the human ancestry of Christ, who is God over
> all, for ever praised! Amen.
>
> Romans 9:4–5

> ... as far as election is concerned, they are loved on account of
> the patriarchs, for God's gifts and his call are irrevocable.
>
> Romans 11:28–29

2. 'All' does not mean every single individual among the Jewish
people either in the past, present or future. Earlier in the letter Paul
has insisted that being a real Jew is not simply a matter of physical
descent:

> Not all who are descended from Israel are Israel. Nor because
> they are his descendants are they all Abraham's children ...
>
> Romans 9:6–7

> Circumcision has value if you observe the law, but if you break
> the law, you have become as though you had not been
> circumcised ... A man is not a Jew if he is only one outwardly,
> nor is circumcision merely outward and physical. No, a man is a
> Jew if he is one inwardly; and circumcision is circumcision of
> the heart, by the Spirit, not by the written code. Such man's
> praise is not from men, but from God.
>
> Romans 2:25, 28–29

Since the majority of the Jewish people of his own time had rejected
Jesus as their promised Messiah, they had forfeited the privileges of
the covenant through their unbelief. Paul uses several vivid expressions to describe the unbelief of the Jews and its results:

> Israel has experienced a hardening in part ...
>
> Romans 11:25 (compare 11:7)

> their transgressions ... their loss ...
>
> Romans 11:12

> they were broken off because of unbelief ... God did not spare
> the natural branches ...
>
> Romans 11:20, 21

If Paul has said earlier 'not all who are descended from Israel are Israel' (Romans 9:6) it would be strange for him to say now (in 11:26) that at some stage in the future *all* the Jewish people who are alive at that time will turn to Christ. He could hardly say in one breath that *not all* who are descended from Israel are real Jews, and in the next breath to say that *all* Jews who are alive at some future date will 'be saved'.

3. 'All Israel' means 'the full number of Israel'. In contrast to the 'hardening *in part*' which Israel has experienced (Romans 11:25), Paul seems to be saying that what we can now look forward to is the salvation of *the full number* of the Jews. This would mean a larger proportion than those who had already believed in Jesus, but it would still not mean every individual Jew who would be living at the time he is speaking about.

The 'hardening in part' which has already taken place will eventually lead to 'the full number of the Gentiles' coming in; and this in turn will lead to the full number of the Jews (i.e. 'all Israel') being saved. The expression 'all Israel' therefore has the same meaning as the expression 'their fulness' ('their coming to full strength' Romans 11:12, New English Bible).

Some have argued that the quotation from the Old Testament which follows implies that Paul looked forward to a total conversion of the Jewish people at the time of the second coming of Christ. It would seem, however, that rather than supporting any idea about the *number* of Jews who would be saved ('all Israel') this Old Testament quotation illustrates the theme of *salvation* by giving content to the idea that all Israel 'will be saved'. Since Paul is so insistent elsewhere that Jesus the Messiah has already come as deliverer and made a covenant to deal with the sins of his people, he could hardly be suggesting that Jesus has to come once again to complete the special salvation of the Jews.

Although Paul does not think in terms of the conversion of the whole Jewish people at some state in the future, he does look forward to the time when a larger proportion of Jews will recognize Jesus as Messiah. *There is* a better future, a more glorious future for the Jewish people to look forward to, although Paul doesn't describe in any detail what that future will be like.

His argument can be set out in the following way:

Romans 11:12
   if [i.e. since]
   'their transgression' and 'their loss'
   means 'riches for the world' and 'riches for the Gentiles'
   then

'their fulness' [i.e. 'their coming to full strength'] (New
English Bible)
will bring 'how much greater riches'

Romans 11:15
if [since]
'their rejection' [i.e. the fact that the majority have not
believed and have therefore been rejected, cut off]
has led to 'the reconciliation of the world'
then
'their acceptance' [i.e. the acceptance of the 'full number'
of the Jews]
will mean 'life from the dead'

Romans 11:23
if
'they did not persist in unbelief'
then
'they will be grafted in'

His message to the largely Gentile church in Rome can therefore be
paraphrased as follows: 'Don't assume that since the majority of the
Jewish people have now rejected their Messiah, this will always be
the case. The refusal of the Jews to recognize Jesus has meant that
the gospel has spread all over the Gentile world. So think what kind
of a future we can look forward to when the full number of Jewish
believers is brought into the kingdom! Don't write off the Jews!'

4. Paul's main concern in this passage is not to predict the future, but
to correct wrong attitudes towards the Jewish people. Paul does not
unfold any detailed plan of how the full number of the Jews will one
day come to believe. He is not presenting a grand blue-print for the
future of the Jewish people. He says nothing about the land; and
says nothing about political or national issues. His main concern is to
correct wrong attitudes to the Jewish people which he knew were
there in the minds of many Gentile Christians. They had concluded
that since the majority of the Jews had failed to accept Jesus as their
Messiah, God had totally rejected them as a people, and they no
longer had any role to play in the plan of God for the world. Paul is
concerned to use every argument he can to correct these attitudes of
pride and superiority:

I am talking to you Gentiles . . . If some of the branches have
been broken off, and you, though a wild olive shoot, have been
grafted in among the others and now share in the nourishing
sap from the olive root, *do not boast* over those branches. If you
do, consider this: you do not support the root, but the root

supports you. You will say then, 'Branches were broken off so that I could be grafted in.' Granted. But they were broken off because of unbelief, and you stand by faith. *Do not be arrogant*, but be afraid.
Romans 11:13, 17–20

I do not want you to be ignorant of this mystery, brothers, *so that you may not be conceited.*
Romans 11:25

Paul ends the discussion by expressing the hope that Jews will turn to God and receive mercy through seeing evidence of God's mercy in the Gentiles:

Just as you who were at one time disobedient to God have now received mercy as a result of their disobedience, so they too have now become disobedient in order that they too may now receive mercy as a result of God's mercy to you. For God has bound all men over to disobedience so that he may have mercy on them all.
Romans 11:30–32

If only Christians in the past had listened to Paul's warning and challenged and corrected every attitude of arrogance and superiority towards the Jews whenever it raised its ugly head!

If only John Chrysostom, Augustine, Aquinas and Luther had soaked themselves in these chapters, and not written the Jewish people off as being beyond the pale!

If only they had seen that these chapters were not intended as a theological treatise about predestination and freewill, but as a challenge to think in a truly Christian way about the people who are 'loved on account of the patriarchs' (Romans 11:28)!

If only they had got Paul's point and tried to look forward to the time – even if it wasn't to be in their day – when the full number of the Jews 'would be grafted into their own olive' (Romans 11: 24)!

If only Christians today would use Paul's words for the purpose of correcting wrong attitudes to the Jews, and not for speculating about how and when the Jews are going to join the church in large numbers!

Kenneth E. Bailey, a New Testament scholar, who was born in Egypt and has lived most of his life in different parts of the Middle East suggests what the Christian gospel has to say about peace-making and reconciliation in a poem entitled

Resurrection
(Ode on a Burning Tank: The Holy Lands, October 1973)

I am a voice,
   the voice of spilt blood
      crying from the land.

The life is in the blood
   and for years my life flowed in the veins of a young man.
      My voice was heard through his voice
         and my life was his life.

Then our volcano erupted
and for a series of numbing days
   all human voices were silenced
      amid the roar of the heavy guns,
      the harsh clank of tank tracks,
         the bone-jarring shudder of sonic booms,
            as gladiators with million-dollar swords
            killed each other high in the sky.

Then suddenly – suddenly
   there was the swish of a rocket launcher –
   a dirty yellow flash –
   and all hell roared.
The clanking of the great tracks stopped.
   My young man staggered screaming from his inferno,
   his body twitched and flopped in the sand

And I was spilt into the earth –
   into the holy earth
      of the Holy Land.

The battle moved on.
   The wounded vehicles burned,
      scorched,
         and cooled.
The 'meat wagons' carried the bodies away as
      the chill of the desert night
      settled on ridge and dune,
 And I stiffened and blackened in the sand.

And then – and then
As the timeless silence
   of the now scarred desert returned,
there – there congealed in the land,
   in the land of prophet, priest and king –
I heard a voice –
   a voice from deep in the land,
   a voice from an ageless age,

a voice from other blood
    once shed violently in the land.

The voice told me this ancient story;
    precious blood intoned this ancient tale.

'A certain man had two sons.
One was rich and the other was poor.
    The rich son had no children
    while the poor son was blessed with many sons and many
    daughters.

In time the father fell ill.
    He was sure he would not live through the week
    so on Saturday he called his sons to his side
      and gave each of them half of the land of their inheritance.
    Then he died.

Before sundown the sons buried their father with respect
    as custom required.

That night the rich son could not sleep.
    He said to himself,
      'What my father did was *not just*.
    I am rich, my brother is poor.
    I have bread enough and to spare,
      while my brother's children eat one day
        and trust God for the next.
I must move the landmark which our father has set in the
middle of the land
so that my brother will have the greater share.
    Ah – but he must not see me.
    If he sees me he will be shamed.
    I must arise early in the morning before it is dawn and
move the landmark!'
With this he fell asleep
    and his sleep was secure and peaceful.

Meanwhile, the poor brother could not sleep.
    As he lay restless on his bed he said to himself,
      'What my father did was *not just*.
    Here I am surrounded by the joy of my many sons and
      many daughters,
    while my brother daily faces the shame
      of having no sons to carry on his name
        and no daughters to comfort him in his old age.
    He should have the land of our fathers.

Perhaps this will in part compensate him
for his indescribable poverty.
Ah – but if I give it to him he will be shamed.
I must awake early in the morning before it is dawn
and move the landmark which our father has set!'
With this he went to sleep
and his sleep was secure and peaceful.

On the first day of the week –
very early in the morning,
a long time before it was day,
the two brothers met at the ancient landmarker.
They fell with tears into each other's arms.
And on that spot was built the city of Jerusalem.'

4·11 Some Conclusions

1. Any Christian who is concerned about the problem of the land
should demonstrate his concern by doing all he can to find out the
truth about the land. We have no right to turn to the Bible for
guidance if we don't know the whys and wherefores of the return of
Jews to the land and the establishment of the State of Israel, or if
we've been fed a very one-sided version of what happened.

2. If the Jew appeals to the Abrahamic promise as the title deeds
which give him and his people the right to the land for all times, he
automatically puts himself under the authority of the Law of Moses.
He cannot have the one without the other. The more he seeks to
interpret what has happened in the land in the light of the divine
promise, the more he should be willing for his actions to be judged in
the light of the divine Law. The more he wants to see recent history
as the fulfilment of prophecy, the more he should be prepared to
submit himself and his people to the demands of the Law.

It is not out of place to ask questions like these about *how* the
Jews have acquired the land, and *how* they have treated the Arabs:

• how much of the land has been acquired legally?

• how much has been acquired by war?

• how much has been acquired illegally – by being stolen, con-
fiscated or expropriated?

• are the Jews treating the Arabs as if they are their own native
born, or are they oppressing them and ill-treating them?

3. Interpreting the Old Testament prophets today should mean very
much more than trying to find how their predictions have been
fulfilled in history. If, in addition to predicting future events, the
prophets sought to interpret what was going on around them, our

study of the prophets today should encourage and enable us to make moral judgements about all that has happened in the land in the last 100 years.

If God judges individuals for breaking his Law, he also judges nations for the ways in which they break his Law in their relationships with each other. Since God is the lord of history, his judgement is not confined to what happens on the day of judgement; it is rather a process of judgement which is going on all the time in the lives of individuals and of nations.

4. If the prophets were concerned about justice for all who were oppressed, we ought to have the same concern for every individual and community in the Middle East which feels that it is oppressed and denied the justice for which it longs. If we are not interested in working for justice and peace, we are like curious, but frivolous spectators watching other people suffer.

5. God is not selective in his judgement. Instead of enjoying immunity from judgement because of their special relationship with God, the Jewish people have a special responsibility before God, and must expect to be judged in the light of their own Law. Furthermore it is not only terrorists – whether Jewish or Arab – who need to be singled out for judgement, but also:

- the Christians who contributed so much to anti-Semitism
- the European governments which used anti-Semitism as a political weapon
- the great powers which carved up the defeated Ottoman Empire in 1918 to serve their own ends
- the great powers today which are more concerned to protect and extend their own influence and power in the world than to fight for human rights
- the Arab countries whose weaknesses and failings have been so cruelly exposed through the creation of an alien state in their midst . . .

All in their own way are suffering for their own sins and for the sins of their fathers. And all in their own way are suffering as a result of the sins of the others.

But when God acts in judgement, he also longs to act in mercy. So the more we understand of how God is at work in judging the nations, the more we should pray 'O Lord, in wrath remember mercy' (Habakkuk 3:2).

6. Jews today believe that Zionism is one valid expression of Judaism in the modern world. It is hard to see, however, how the concept of a Jewish state in Palestine can be reconciled with the universalist vision presented by several of the prophets. If these prophetic visions were more than pious hopes for the future, they challenge the whole idea of a modern state in which citizenship is based primarily on being Jewish.

7. There should be something different and unique about the way in which the people of God respond to injustice. In some situations the way to *overcome* evil and injustice is to *suffer* it.

8. One of the most distinctive marks of a *Christian* response to the conflict over the land should be repentance. Instead of simply pointing the finger of accusation at others, the Christian should be willing to admit the guilt of *all* the parties in the conflict and say 'both we and our fathers have sinned' (Psalm 106:6).

9. When outsiders take their stand very openly with one side or the other in any conflict they tend to become so prejudiced and partisan in their approach that they lose the right and the opportunity to say anything positive to the other side. If the Christian wants to have anything to say about the conflict, he ought, even at the risk of being misunderstood, to resist the temptation to become totally and blindly committed to one side or the other.

Because of the shameful way in which Christians have treated Jews in the past, the Christian church bears a large measure of responsibility for the situation which forced so many Jews to emigrate to Palestine. If the Jew feels that the Christian church is responsible in this way, he will not find it easy to listen to the Christian (especially if he is a westerner) denouncing the crimes of Israel and the Jews.

10. The example of Jesus is not an impossible ideal. Not only can it change fundamental attitudes; it can also be translated into action in very practical terms by those who are willing to be his disciples and follow in his footsteps.

If Christian communities in the Middle East and throughout the world can feel with those who suffer in and around the land today, they may be one step nearer to understanding the mystery of the land. If we can interpret the message, the example and the achievement of the Suffering Servant to ourselves, to the Muslim and the Jew, we may make it easier for everyone to believe that 'he is our peace'.

5

EPILOGUE
WHOSE PROMISED LAND?
ONE POSSIBLE ANSWER

We began by looking at the *history* of the land, and only then went on to look at what the *Bible* says about the land. I'm quite sure that some of my Christian friends will tell me that I've made a basic mistake, and that I should have begun with the Bible.

If we were talking about events which we've all lived through, I would agree. If, for example, we were a group of older people from many different countries in Europe, meeting to discuss the significance of World War II, we could take the history for granted, because we had all lived through the war. Apart from exchanging stories about personal experiences, we could quickly get down to discussing the significance of these events.

But this is just what we *cannot* do with a typical group of Christians anywhere in the world in the 1980s who are discussing the problem of the land. Many of us have *not* lived through all the major events – and even if we have, it's been as spectators rather than as actors. We've been dependent on the media with their own political bias, and on Christian writers who nearly always have some particular axe to grind. So we can't begin to discuss what these events mean until we're sure that we're talking the same language, and talking about the same events.

The Jews have seen their *Aliyah* as a 'return' – a return to the land of their forefathers. From the point of view of the Arabs, however, the Jews came in as immigrants settling in a foreign country. The Jews from the Dispersion felt they were united to the Jews of Palestine by strong ties of race and religion. But the Arabs had good reason to feel that because the whole immigrant movement was encouraged by the western colonial powers, the Arabs were being made to suffer for the crimes of Europe. Is one view right and the other wrong? Or is the truth somewhere in between? We cannot, we dare not, identify ourselves so completely with one viewpoint that we become totally insensitive to the other.

When, however, we begin to look at the philosophy of Zionism and its achievements in more detail, we are forced to make up our minds and to make some kind of judgement. We cannot for ever sit on the fence and say 'both the Jews and the Arabs were right'. Is it possible, therefore, for me to explain my basic uneasiness with the philosophy of Zionism without being accused of anti-Semitism? I would not want to argue that Jewish immigration to the land was in itself wrong. I have nothing but admiration for the achievement of the Jews in the land – the resettlement of Jews from all over the world, the reclaiming of so much soil, the revival of the Hebrew language, the incredible social, cultural and technological achievement of the nation. But I *do* have problems with the original vision of many Zionists to establish a Jewish homeland or a state in Palestine which would be exclusively or near-exclusively Jewish.

Given the situation of Palestine at the end of the nineteenth century – with 5 per cent Jews and 95 per cent Arabs living under the Ottoman Empire – there were bound to be acute problems in realizing such a dream. Herzl and Weizmann *did know*, at least in general terms, what Palestine was like. They *did know* that, for all its backwardness after centuries of neglect under the Turks, most of the land was inhabited. If they had wanted to, they could easily have found out about the aspirations of the people who were already living there.

I can appreciate the feelings of desperation which led Herzl to conceive of the idea of 'the Jews' state' as the final answer to the Jewish question in Europe. But I cannot see how he can be excused for describing Palestine to European audiences as 'a land without a people'. And when I read that Weizmann openly declared that he wanted to establish a society in Palestine which would be 'as Jewish as England is English, or America is American', I sympathize with the Palestinian Arab who sees this as an example of typical nineteenth-century European imperialism. If I'm looking for biblical parallels or precedents, the achievements of Zionism, *taken as a whole over the last hundred years*, seem to me to have more in common with the conquest of the land under Joshua than the peaceful return from the exile under Zerubbabel.

Even if I had no problem with the original vision, I would still feel compelled as a Christian, to ask questions about *how* it has been realized. Weizmann's repeated assurances to the Arabs have a curiously hollow ring when we read them today: 'Palestine must be built up without violating the legitimate rights of the Arabs – not a hair of their heads shall be touched.' 'It is not our aim to get hold of the supreme power and administration in Palestine, nor to deprive any native of his possession.' If he really meant what he said and was not deliberately misleading his audience, the kindest thing we can say is that the whole enterprise which he and others began with such high ideals was soon taken over by others who didn't have the same standards. The logic of the Zionist dream, when faced with the realities of the situation in Palestine, demanded a much less gentle approach.

Although many of the Jewish settlers wanted to settle peacefully and were sensitive to the reactions of the Arab population, the leaders of the Zionist movement, the politicians and the soldiers who have played the most decisive roles at each stage have been less sensitive to the feelings of the Arab majority. The State of Israel could never have been created, nor could it have survived and reached its present size by purely peaceful means. Conflict and violence were almost inevitable. So when I ask *how* the vision of a Jewish state has been realized, and when I see the price that has been paid – especially by others – I cannot help suspecting that there was something wrong with the original vision.

If once again I am looking for biblical parallels and precedents, I must note that much of the land has been acquired by Jews in ways that were just as legal as Abraham's purchase of the cave of Macpelah (Genesis 23). But I cannot be blind to the fact that much land has been acquired in something like the way that Ahab acquired Naboth's vineyard (1 Kings 21). So if God judged Ahab, and if he judged the nation of Israel and all the surrounding nations in the way that the Old Testament describes, I must assume that he is judging and will continue to judge the Jews, the Arabs and the world powers in the same way today. What I cannot do is to suspend moral judgement and say that because God wanted the Jews back in the land, we can draw a veil over the question of *how* they got themselves there and *how* they established the Jewish state.

This is not to suggest that the Arabs were totally innocent. The presence of an increasing number of aliens in their midst exposed their weaknesses ruthlessly. They were often disunited, and individuals and groups were sometimes more concerned with their own interests than with those of the whole Arab community. If they hadn't constantly adopted an all-or-nothing approach, and if they had shown half the tactical skill and flexibility of a man like Weizmann they might have found ways of establishing some kind of peaceful co-existence with the Jews. They made many mistakes, they committed many crimes, and in many different ways contributed to the deepening tragedy. But their reaction to the threat of being dominated by a Jewish minority was *utterly natural. Any other people* would have reacted in exactly the same way – if not with even greater violence.

It's not just the benefit of hindsight which enables a person to make judgements of this kind today. Some of the Jews in the earliest days obviously *did* have a conscience about what they were doing to the Arabs. If Ahad Ha-Am could say that it was already evident in 1891 that 'the day would come when the Arabs would stand up against us'; if Max Nordau could run to Herzl on hearing for the first time that there were Arabs in Palestine and say 'then we are committing an injustice'; if Najib Azuri could see in 1905 that Arab nationalism and Jewish nationalism 'are destined to be in permanent conflict', then I conclude that even in these early days, long before the holocaust, the writing was already on the wall. The seeds of conflict had already been sown.

Does this sound like seeing the speck in my brother's eye, or casting the first stone? If it does, I hasten to add that the more I find myself questioning the ideals and achievements of Zionism in this way, the more I have to confess the guilt of those who had treated the Jews in such a way that they felt they *had* to seek a homeland in another country. Must we not say that anti-Semitism is one of the greatest crimes of Europe? Could it not even be described as *the* greatest?

Jesus had something to say to Pilate about degrees of responsibility and guilt: 'You would have no power over me if it were not given to you from above. Therefore *the one who handed me over to you is guilty of a greater sin*' (John 19:11). Was it not the Christian west (or the so-called 'Christian west', if this description makes it easier for us to take the point) which put the Jews into this position, which 'handed them over', so to speak, and is therefore 'guilty of a greater sin'?

So much for history. How do I understand the significance of the land in the Bible? According to the Old Testament, the land is *God's land*, for 'the land is mine . . .' (Leviticus 25:23). He chose to give it to Abraham's descendants as a gift, not as something that they should possess by right. It was intended to be the scene of God's gradual revelation of himself, which would lead eventually to the coming of Jesus, and so to blessing for all peoples of the world.

Since the New Testament speaks of all followers of Jesus as 'Abraham's seed and heirs according to the promise' (Galatians 3:29), it must mean that all four aspects of the covenant – the land, the nation, the covenant relationship between God and his people, and the blessing for all peoples of the world – find their fulfilment in Jesus and in those who put their faith in him. As a Christian, I feel bound to conclude that the promise of the land to Abraham and his descendants 'as an everlasting possession' does *not* give the Jews a divine right to possess the land for all time.

When I read the Gospels, I see Jesus of Nazareth, a Jew, presenting himself as the fulfilment of *all* the hopes and longings (which means both spiritual and political) of the Jewish nation. And although his disciples at first had typically Jewish hopes about the establishment of the kingdom of God through an independent Jewish state in the land, after the ascension they ceased to think and speak in these terms.

If therefore I am asked: is the state of Israel 'of God or of men'? I have to answer that I believe it *is* 'of God' in the sense that it is something which has happened under the sovereignty of God. God has been at work in all that has happened. These events *do* have some special significance; they are not an accident. But I *don't* believe that the State of Israel is 'of God' in the sense that it is the fulfilment (or even a preliminary stage in the fulfilment) of all that God promised and predicted in the Old Testament about the future of the land and its people.

I would go further and suggest that for Christians to interpret these events simply as the fulfilment of prophecy represents a kind of regression. It is a return to a way of thinking which the disciples abandoned once and for all when they grasped the kind of kingdom that Jesus had inaugurated through his death and resurrection. Instead of helping the Jew to come nearer to believing in Jesus as the Messiah, it may have the opposite effect and harden him in his unbelief.

What then is God doing with the Jewish people? If all we have witnessed is not the fulfilment of prophecy, what does it mean? For fear of simply rejecting one popular view and having nothing to put in its place, I must dare to rush in where angels fear to tread:

● Could it be that God is recalling the Jewish people to their scriptures? When politicians appeal to the Old Testament and justify Israeli claims to the West Bank, calling it 'Judaea and Samaria'; when children read the book of Joshua in the classroom to understand their own history and their own roots as a people; when young soldiers who have fought in several wars read the Old Testament out of curiosity, wondering why their people should have to suffer and fight year after year ... When they read the Old Testament, they are being recalled in different ways to 'the very words of God' which have been entrusted to their people (Romans 3:2).

● Could it be that God is giving them a severe test of their obedience? The presence of the Arabs, within Israel and on their borders, presents the Jews in Israel with what could be one of the greatest challenges they have faced in their history. How are they going to come to terms with these neighbours, these aliens, these strangers, these enemies? The Jews themselves have mostly come out of situations where they were, or were made to feel, aliens and strangers, and so they ought to 'know the heart of a stranger'. Are they therefore going to love these Arabs as themselves, to settle peacefully alongside them, and give those who live in the Jewish state the same rights that they have demanded for themselves? Or are they going to drive them out, to take over their land, to oppress them, to keep them as second-class citizens and as 'hewers of wood and drawers of water', to deny that they exist as a people and to pour scorn on their nationalistic feelings? Is God's motive anything like that behind the fearful wanderings in the wilderness: 'the Lord your God led you all the way in the desert these forty years, to humble you and to test you in order to know what was in your heart, whether or not you would keep his commands' (Deuteronomy 8:2).

• Could it be that God is challenging the whole Jewish people to think again about their destiny as a people? What is the whole enterprise of settling Jews in the land and setting up a Jewish state doing to the soul of Judaism? Did God really intend that they should be 'a peculiar people' for ever and ever? Is there no alternative to the choice between traditional orthodox Judaism, assimilation and Zionism? Is there no other way by which the Jews can live securely among the nations without ceasing to be Jews?

• Could it be that God is trying to bring the Jews face to face with the person of Jesus? Whether it's through Bethlehem, Nazareth, Galilee or Jerusalem, whether it's through the constant flow of Christian tourists and pilgrims who come to see the holy sites, whether it's through the Christian churches or the foreign missionaries in their midst, Jews are being reminded, whether they like it or not, of Jesus of Nazareth. Is God therefore putting to them even more forcefully today the question which Jesus put to the Jews of his day: 'what do you think about the Christ?' (Matthew 22:42).

Perhaps it's naive or arrogant to put such thoughts on paper. They certainly don't offer a neat and tidy blue-print of history between now and the second coming of Christ. But I believe they may do more justice to history, to the Bible, to the nature of the church's task, and to the present dilemma of the Jewish people than the popular answer which says: 'Now at last the land belongs to the Jews! Now at last prophecy has been fulfilled! All we have to do is to watch the predicted sequence of events unfold before our eyes in and around Jerusalem and the Jewish state. Now that they're back in the land, and back in Jerusalem, it's only a matter of time before the Jewish people as a whole turn to acknowledge their Messiah and become a blessing to the world.'

For obvious reasons this book has not attempted to make specific recommendations about how the land should be divided between the Jews and the Palestinians. That is something for them to decide together – hopefully by direct negotiation in which each recognizes the rights of the other. It has, however, tackled some of the basic attitudes and prejudices which affect the thinking of Jews and Arabs and of the many spectators who watch the conflict. I hope therefore that it has pointed clearly to some of the ways in which all the parties may have to think again, to change their minds – in other words, to repent – before any practical solutions can be found.

Repentance for the Jews in Israel and Jews elsewhere who support Israel might mean developing a conscience about what the Jews have done and are still doing to the Palestinian people. Repentance for the great powers might mean recognizing the injustices that have been done to the Jews in Europe before 1945 and to the Palestinian Arabs since 1880. It might mean being less selfish in safeguarding their own national interests, and more concerned to redress obvious injustices. Repentance for the Arabs might mean facing up to their own weaknesses, and admitting their own share of responsibility for all that has happened. It might also mean finding a way of responding to injustice which doesn't use the same weapons as their oppressors and so cause even more suffering and injustice.

But isn't this asking rather a lot from human nature? Of course it is! But asking anything less may put us in the position of the false prophets who

> . . . dress the wound of my people
> as though it were not serious.
> 'Peace, peace, they say,
> when there is no peace.'
> Jeremiah 8:11

It's hard for the Jew to be told that the Jewish people may find their true identity not in the establishment of a Jewish state which welcomes Jews from all over the world, but only within 'the Israel of God', the new people of God which embraces people of all races.

It's hard for the Jew to take such words from a Christian whom he inevitably identifies with the Christian church of the past 2,000 years which has been responsible for such despicable attitudes and such murderous actions towards his people.

It's hard for the proud Britisher or American to face up to the facts of history and admit the large measure of responsibility which his country bears for creating the problem in the first place, and doing so little to solve it since then.

It's hard for the Muslim Arab to believe that there are times when the only way to overcome injustice is to suffer it, because Islam encourages him to believe that when a person's cause is just, he can expect God to vindicate him with 'a mighty victory'.

It's hard for the Christian Arab to believe that the Jewish people *are* (and not only *were*) 'loved on account of the patriarchs' (Romans 11:28). It's hard for them to lie down meekly and accept injustice without any protest, because this inevitably gives the impression that the injustice wasn't all that serious in the first place, and that it's easy to swallow one's personal and national pride.

It's hard for Christians looking on from outside to admit the extent to which Christians in the past contributed to anti-Semitism, and to admit that their political attitudes and their biblical interpretation may have been influenced more than they realize by national prejudices and by one-sided interpretations of history.

It's hard for every party in the conflict, and for every spectator. But this only reminds us that at the heart of the gospel of Jesus Christ there is something which challenges, which disturbs, which shocks and which offends all men everywhere. If the message of Jesus in the first century was 'a stumbling block to the Jews and foolishness to Gentiles' (1 Corinthians 1:23), it's just as much a stumbling block and foolishness to the Jew, the Arab and the watching world today.

We therefore end with a passage from the *Jewish* scriptures. It's a passage which speaks about a figure described as 'the Servant of the Lord'. If these words tie together some of the strands of this book – rejection, sorrow, suffering, wounds, transgressions, oppression, violence, and deceit – they may make it easier for us to see how Jesus of Nazareth could be *for us all* that 'Servant of the Lord'.

> He was despised and rejected by men.
> a man of sorrows, and familiar with suffering . . .
>
> Surely he took up our infirmities
> and carried our sorrows . . .
>
> But he was pierced for our transgressions,
> he was crushed for our iniquities;
> the punishment that brought us peace was upon him,
> and by his wounds we are healed.
> We all, like sheep, have gone astray,
> each of us has turned to his own way;
> and the Lord has laid on him
> the iniquity of us all.

He was oppressed and afflicted,
  yet he did not open his mouth;
he was led like a lamb to the slaughter,
  and as a sheep before her shearers is silent,
so he did not open his mouth.

By oppression and judgement
  he was taken away . . .
And who can speak of his descendants?
For he was cut off from the land of the living;
  for the transgression of my people he was stricken.
He was assigned a grave with the wicked,
  and with the rich in his death,
though he had done no violence,
  nor was any deceit in his mouth.

Yet it was the Lord's will to
  crush him and cause him to suffer . . .

. . . he poured out his life unto death,
  and was numbered with the transgressors.
For he bore the sin of many,
  and made intercession for the transgressors.
Isaiah 53:3–12

6

APPENDIX
CHRISTIAN INTERPRETATION
OF
OLD TESTAMENT PROPHECY

6·1 Principles of Interpretation

If we are to establish any agreed principles of interpreting prophecy, and in particular prophecies about the return to the land and the future of the nation, these are some of the questions we will need to ask:

Q What kind of language is the prophet using?

Sometimes the prophet is making *a simple prediction of an event* which doesn't need any interpretation. For example:

> This is what the Sovereign Lord says . . . 'I will take you out of the nations; I will gather you from all the countries and bring you back into your own land.'
> **Ezekiel 36:24**

At other times he describes *a future event in poetic language*. For example:

> The desert and the parched land will be glad;
> the wilderness will rejoice and blossom . . .
> and the ransomed of the Lord will return . . .
> **Isaiah 35:1, 10**

In many cases the prophet is describing *a vision*. Thus, for example, the book of Ezekiel begins with an explanation of where and when the prophet saw his 'visions of God':

> In the thirtieth year, in the fourth month on the fifth day, while I was among the exiles by the Kebar River, the heavens were opened and I saw visions of God.
> **Ezekiel 1:1**

The prophet sometimes describes what he sees, and is then given an interpretation of what he sees. For example:

vision	**interpretation**
'I saw a great many bones on the floor of the valley, bones that were very dry.' (Ezekiel 37:2)	'these bones are the whole house of Israel.' (Ezekiel 37:11)

vision	**interpretation**
'the bones came together, bone to bone . . . and breath entered them; they came to life and stood up on their feet – a vast army.' (Ezekiel 37:7, 10)	'I am going to open your graves and bring you up from them; I will bring you back to the land of Israel.' (Ezekiel 37:12)

In other cases we are not given any interpretation of the details of the visions. For example, Ezekiel's vision of the new Jerusalem contains details like these:

> The remaining area, 5,000 cubits wide and 25,000 cubits long, will be for the common use of the city, for houses and for pasture-land. The city will be in the centre of it, and will have these measurements: the north side 4,500 cubits, the south side 4,500 cubits, the east side 4,500 cubits, and the west side 4,500 cubits . . .
> Ezekiel 48:15–16

Does the prophet really intend to give us an architect's blueprint of the new Jerusalem? If so, we must interpret the visions very literally and see them as a kind of visual preview of history. The alternative is to try to interpret the language of the vision and translate it into a message which was relevant to the original hearers and is relevant to anyone who wants to listen today.

Q When were these prophecies delivered, and can we see any fulfilment of them during or soon after the time of the prophet?

The writer of 2 Chronicles and Ezra wants us to understand that the return to the land in 537 BC was the fulfilment of the prophecies of Jeremiah. This doesn't present any problems.

It's more complicated when we come to Zechariah's prophecy of a return of exiles *both* from the southern kingdom of Judah, *and* from the northern kingdom of Israel (Zechariah 10:6–10). If he was writing around 520 BC, the first wave of exiles of the people of Judah had already returned from Babylon seventeen years before; and more exiles were to return many years later with Ezra and

Nehemiah. It's therefore easy to see how this part of the prophecy was fulfilled soon after his lifetime.

But what of the prophecy of a return of exiles from the northern kingdom of Israel, which implies the eventual union of the two kingdoms of Israel and Judah (Zechariah 10:6–10; compare Ezekiel 37:15–23)? There is nothing in the history of the centuries immediately following Zechariah's time which could by any stretch of the imagination be described as the fulfilment of these prophecies.

When we are faced with this kind of dilemma, we have to make a choice:

either	**or**
we insist that we must continue to look for a literal fulfilment in history – in which case we may see the return of Jews to the land in the twentieth century and the establishment of the State of Israel as the intended fulfilment.	we look for other ways in which these prophecies could have been fulfilled already in the past or could yet be fulfilled in the future.

 Q Do the prophecies themselves contain any clues which help us to interpret them?

One important clue is that in many of the prophecies there are echoes of the four promises which made up the original covenant with Abraham. For example:

● *the land:* 'you will live in the land I gave your forefathers' (Ezekiel 36:28)

● *the nation:* 'I will make their people as numerous as sheep' (Ezekiel 36:37)
'I will redeem them; they will be as numerous as before' (Zechariah 10:8)

● *the covenant relationship:* 'you will be my people, and I will be your God' (Ezekiel 36:28)
'they will be my people and I will be their God' (Jeremiah 24:7)
'they will be my people, and I will be faithful and righteous to them as their God' (Zechariah 8:8)

● *blessing for all people:* 'then the nations will know . . .' (Ezekiel 36:36)

This suggests that the fulfilment of the promises about the land must be seen in the context of the fulfilment of the whole covenant with Abraham.

Q How are these prophecies related to other divine promises in the Old Testament?

Several of these prophecies contain the phrase 'for ever', which is associated in other parts of the Old Testament with the continuation of the line of David and the line of Aaron, and the presence of God in the temple:

● *the promise of a king in the line of David:* 'Your house and your kingdom shall endure *for ever* before me; your throne shall be established *for ever*.' (2 Samuel 7:16; compare Psalm 89:3–4)

● *the commissioning of Aaron and his descendants* 'Aaron was set apart, he and his descendants *for ever*, to consecrate the most holy things, to offer sacrifices before the Lord, to minister before him and to pronounce blessings in his name *for ever*.' (1 Chronicles 23:13)

● *the promise concerning the temple built by Solomon:* 'I have heard the prayer and plea you have made before me; I have consecrated this temple, which you have built, by putting my Name there *for ever*. My eyes and my heart will always be there.' (1 Kings 9:3)

In Ezekiel 37 the phrase 'for ever' is linked to four out of the fifteen themes:

● 'they and their children's children will live there *for ever*' (37:25)

● 'my servant David will be their prince *for ever*' (37:25)

● 'it will be an everlasting covenant' or 'this covenant shall be theirs *for ever*' (New English Bible) (37:26)

● 'I will put my sanctuary among them *for ever*' (37:26)

If God promised that the descendants of Abraham would live in the land for ever, he also promised that the royal line of David would continue for ever, that the priestly line of Aaron would continue for ever, and that the temple in Jerusalem would bear the name of God for ever. Do we therefore have any right to separate these promises and interpret one of them very literally (the one about the land), but interpret all the others in a totally different way?

If we insist on a *literal* interpretation of everything that the Old Testament says about the land, we ought to be consistent and give a literal interpretation to *all* the other promises in the Old Testament. But the mind boggles at the thought of a descendant of David being installed as king in Jerusalem, the temple being rebuilt and the whole sacrificial system reinstituted . . . Since it hasn't happened yet, is it still to happen in the future?

If, however, we interpret everything about the land in a *literal* and *spiritual* way at the same time, once again we have to be consistent and interpret *all* the promises in the same way. But the Davidic monarchy did *not* continue in Jerusalem after 587 BC; and although sacrifices were offered in the temple after the exile, the temple was destroyed in AD 70 and completely obliterated in AD 135. So how can we combine a spiritual and literal interpretation of these promises if the literal interpretation makes nonsense of history? There is no reason why we should be content with a *spiritual* interpretation of the Davidic monarchy, the temple and its sacrifices, but at the same time insist that the teaching about the land has both a *spiritual* and a *literal* meaning.

The only solution to this problem is to link all these Old Testament promises and prophecies together and see them in the same light. When we do this, it begins to look as if their fulfilment may also somehow be bound up together.

Q How did Jesus and the biblical writers interpret these prophecies?

This question is hardly relevant for the Jew. But for the Christian it's crucial, because he feels bound to try to read the Old Testament through the eyes of Jesus and the apostles.

There are basically three different ways in which the writers of the Old and New Testaments understood the fulfilment of prophecy. These can be indicated by the symbols F1, F2 and F3:

F1 **Fulfilment in the original context in which the prophet spoke**
i.e. fulfilment in historical events at, or soon after, the time of the prophet
e.g. the return of the exiles from Babylon in 539 BC is described in 2 Chronicles 36:22 and Ezra 1:1 as the fulfilment of the prophecies of Jeremiah.

F2 **Fulfilment in the first coming of Jesus Christ**
i.e. fulfilment in the birth, life, death, resurrection and ascension of Jesus Christ, and therefore also in the new age which has been inaugurated through his coming
e.g. the angel announcing the birth of Jesus told Mary that Jesus would be the fulfilment of the promise that a descendant of David would sit on his throne 'for ever' (Luke 1:30–33).

F3 **Fulfilment in the second coming of Jesus Christ**
i.e. fulfilment in events in the future associated with the second coming of Jesus Christ and the end of the world
e.g. The apostle John saw the final fulfilment of Ezekiel's vision of the new Jerusalem and the new temple in 'a new heaven and a new

earth' (Revelation 21:1—22:6).

The prophet

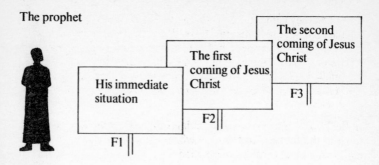

These three ways of understanding the fulfilment of prophecy are not mutually exclusive. We are not forced in every case to choose between these different kinds of fulfilment. Some prophecies can be interpreted as referring to *all three periods* of time, while others can be related to *two different periods* – for example, the immediate future (F1) and the first coming of Jesus (F2), or the first coming of Jesus (F2) and the second coming (F3).

The following words, for example, are found in a passage in the prophet Zechariah which speaks about the whole people of Judah and Jerusalem returning to God in a spirit of deep repentance;

> And I will pour out on the house of David and the inhabitants of Jerusalem a spirit of grace and supplication. *They will look on me, the one they have pierced*, and *they will mourn for him* as one mourns for an only child, and grieve bitterly for him as one grieves for a firstborn son.
> Zechariah 12:10

There is a clear echo of these words in Matthew's version of the saying about the coming of the Son of man. If the coming of the Son of man refers primarily to the vindication of Jesus in the years immediately following his death (see section 3:8), the mourning of all the nations of the earth must also refer primarily to this period:

> At that time the sign of the Son of Man will appear in the sky, and all nations of the earth *will mourn. They will see* the Son of Man coming on the clouds of the sky, with power and great glory.
> Matthew 24:30

The words are also quoted in John's Gospel, in his description of the crucifixion, and related to the piercing of the side of Jesus' body with a spear:

> When they came to Jesus and found that he was already dead, they did not break his legs. Instead, one of the soldiers pierced Jesus' side with a spear, bringing a sudden flow of blood and water. . . These things happened so that the Scripture would be fulfilled: 'Not one of his bones will be broken,' and, as another Scripture says, *'They will look on the one they have pierced.'*
> John 19:33–37

In the book of Revelation John relates the same prophecy to something in the future – to the time when Jesus comes with the clouds and is seen by all those who crucified him:

> Look, he is coming with the clouds,
> and *every eye will see him,*
> *even those who pierced him;*
> *and all the peoples of the earth will mourn because of him.*
> So shall it be! Amen.
> Revelation 1:5–7

6·2 Applying the Principles

Because of this flexibility in the New Testament's interpretation of Old Testament prophecy, we need to reckon that in many cases there may be more than one way of interpreting a particular passage of prophecy. We now approach four passages from Old Testament prophets with three questions in mind:

● Were these words fulfilled in any way during the time of the prophet or soon after? (F1)

● Were these words fulfilled in any way in the first coming of Jesus Christ? Is there any indication that Jesus regarded himself, or that his disciples regarded him, as the fulfilment of this prophecy? (F2)

● Are these words to be fulfilled in the future at the second coming of Jesus Christ? Is there any indication that either Jesus himself or the disciples related these prophecies to the end of the world? (F3)

When we have attempted to answer these questions, we will not have exhausted the meaning of these prophecies. They may have much to teach us about Christian history between the first and second comings of Jesus Christ. But we shall see how difficult it is, if not impossible, to relate the prophecy to specific events in the twentieth century in the way that many are suggesting today. We dare not try to reduce the whole of biblical prophecy to a neat and tidy system. But we do need to make sure that we have understood how the New Testament writers handled Old Testament prophecy *before* we start using it to interpret contemporary events in detail.

In each passage all the words, phrases or sentences which are quoted or echoed in other parts of the Old Testament or the New Testament are in italics, and the references to the relevant passages are in the column on the right.

The Planting of Israel in the Land   Amos 9:8–15

'Surely the eyes of the Sovereign Lord
are on the sinful kingdom.
I will destroy it
   from the face of the earth –
yet I will not totally destroy
   the house of Jacob', declares the Lord.
'For I will give the command,
   and I will shake the house of Israel among all the nations
as corn is shaken in a seive,
   but not an ear will fall to the ground.
All the sinners among the people
   will die by the sword,
all those who say,
"Disaster will not overtake or meet us."

'In that day *I will restore*   Acts 15:16–17
  David's fallen tent.
I will repair its broken places,
  restore its ruins,
   and build it as it used to be,
so that they may possess the remnant of Edom
  and all the nations that bear my name,'
   declares the Lord, who will do these things.
'The days are coming,' declares the Lord,
  'when the reaper will be overtaken by the ploughman
  and the planter by the one treading grapes.
New wine will drip from the mountains
  and flow from all the hills.
I will bring back my exiled people Israel;
  they will rebuild the ruined cities and live in them.
They will plant vineyards and drink their wine;
  they will make gardens and eat their fruit.
I will plant Israel in their own land,
  never again to be uprooted

from the land I have given them,'
says the Lord your God.

F1. The prophet Amos came from the *southern* kingdom of Judah, but was called to exercise his prophetic ministry in the *northern* kingdom of Israel. After preaching in the capital of Samaria from approximately 760 to 750 BC, he was ordered to return home to Judah. He warned the people of the northern kingdom of a severe judgement to come (Amos 9:8), and this was fulfilled in 721 BC when Samaria was captured and the people taken into exile in Assyria.

Most commentators find it difficult to point to any clear fulfilment of this prophecy of a return from the exile in Assyria. It would seem that the exiles were scattered all over the Assyrian Empire, and that the vast majority were assimilated with the local population. Even if a few individuals were able to return to their land, there was nothing resembling the return of the exiles from Babylon to Judah in the mid sixth century BC.

F2. At the Council of Jerusalem described in Acts 15, Peter and Paul argue that the way in which the Gentiles had received the gospel message and the way in which God had given his Spirit and worked signs and wonders among them proved beyond doubt that he intended them to be accepted as full members of the church. James, apparently acting as a kind of chairman to the Council, accepted their argument, and went on to quote from Amos 9:11–12 to support his position.

The two verses quoted cannot be isolated from the rest of the passage. So, for example, verse 11 ('I will ... restore its ruins, and build it as it used to be') is echoed in verse 14 ('they will rebuild the ruined cities and live in them'.) The original passage in Amos speaks about the restoration of the *people* of Israel to the land, the rebuilding of the ruined cities, and the permanent replanting of the people in the land. When James quotes the passage, he is trying to show that the inclusion of the Gentiles in the church is *a* fulfilment – or should we not rather say *the* fulfilment? – of the prophecies of Amos.

The restoration of Israel is not understood as something still in the future, but as something that has already taken place. And the inclusion of the Gentiles in the church is described as a result of the restoration of Israel (. . .*that* the remnant of men may seek the Lord, and all the Gentiles who bear my name . . .' Acts 15:17).

Hopes for the Restored Nation Ezekiel 37:15–28:

The word of the Lord came to me: 'Son of man, take a
stick of wood and write on it, "Belonging to Judah and
the Israelites associated with him." Then take another

stick of wood, and write on it, "Ephraim's stick,
belonging to Joseph and all the house of Israel
associated with him." Join them together into one stick
so that they will become one in your hand.
'When your countrymen ask you, "Won't you tell us
what you mean by this?" say to them, "This is what the
Sovereign Lord says; I am going to take the stick of
Joseph – which is in Ephraim's hand – and of the
Israelite tribes associated with him, and join it to
Judah's stick, making them a single stick of wood, and
they will become one in my hand." Hold before their
eyes the sticks you have written on and say to them,
"This is what the Sovereign Lord says: I will take the
Israelites out of the nations where they have gone. I will
gather them from all around and bring them back into
their own land. I will make them *one nation* in the land,   John 10:16
on the mountains of Israel. There will be *one king* over   11:51–52
all of them and they will never again be two nations or
be divided into two kingdoms. They will no longer
defile themselves with their idols and vile images or
with any of their offences, for I will *save them from all
their sinful backsliding*, and I will *cleanse them. They* will   Hebrews 9:14
be my people, and I will be their God. "My servant   1 John 1:7
David will be king over them, and they will all have one   1 Peter 2:9–10
shepherd. They will *follow my laws and be careful to keep*   Luke 1:31–33
my decrees. They will live in the land I gave to my   John 10:11
servant Jacob, the land where your fathers lived. They   Hebrews
and their children and their children's children will live   8:7–13
there for ever, and *David my servant will be their prince*   Luke 22:20
for ever. I will make a *covenant* of peace with them;   Hebrews 13:20
it will be *an everlasting covenant.* I will establish them
and increase their numbers, and I will put *my sanctuary*   John 2:18–22
among them for ever ... *My dwelling-place will be with*   John 1:14
them; I will be their God, and they will be my people.   Revelation
Then the nations will know that I the Lord make *Israel*   21:3
holy, when *my sanctuary is among them for ever*."'   1 Peter 2:9

F1. Some of these words found their immediate fulfilment in the
return of the Jewish exiles from Babylon to Jerusalem beginning in
537 BC.

F2. The reference to the 'one shepherd' (Ezekiel 37:24) and the
'one nation' (37:22) are echoed in Jesus' claim that he is 'the good
shepherd' who brings together 'one flock' (John 10:11, 14, 16). John
believed that Jesus had died not only for the Jewish nation, 'but also

for the scattered children of God, to bring them together and make them one' (John 11:51–52).

The promise about the Davidic king who will rule over his people for ever (37:22, 24, 25), is fulfilled in the person of Jesus and his kingly rule (Luke 1:31–33). Since the rule of the Davidic king is inevitably associated with the land (37:22, 25), we must assume that the promise about his people living in the land 'for ever' (37:25) must also be related to Jesus Christ and his church.

Jesus spoke of his death as the inauguration of a new covenant (Luke 22:20), and the writer to the Hebrews relates the 'everlasting covenant' (Ezekiel 37:26) to this same covenant (Hebrews 13:20).

John sees Jesus as the new temple in which the glory of God has been revealed (John 1:14, 2:26).

Peter describes all Christian believers as being 'a holy nation' (1 Peter 3:9), and thus fulfilling the promise that God would make Israel 'holy' (Ezekiel 37:28).

It demands an impossible kind of surgery to cut out and isolate references to the land in this passage (Ezekiel 37:22, 25) and expect them to be fulfilled in a literal way (and not only in the sixth century BC but also in the twentieth century AD), while accepting that every other aspect of the prophecies has been fulfilled in Jesus Christ and his people.

Jerusalem Under Attack Zechariah 12:1–10:

This is the word of the Lord concerning Israel. The Lord, who stretches out the heavens, who lays the foundation of the earth, and who forms the spirit of man within him, declares: 'I am going to make Jerusalem a cup that sends all the surrounding peoples reeling. Judah will be beseiged as well as Jerusalem. On that day, when *all the nations of the earth are gathered against her*, I will make Jerusalem an immovable *rock* for all the nations. All who try to move it will *injure themselves*. On that day I will strike every horse with panic and its rider with madness,' declares the Lord. 'I will keep a watchful eye over the house of Judah, but I will blind all the horses of the nations. Then the leaders of Judah will say in their hearts, "The people of Jerusalem are strong, because the Lord Almighty is their God."

'On that day I will make the leaders of Judah like a firepot in a woodpile, like a flaming torch among sheaves. They will consume right and left all the surrounding people, but Jerusalem will remain intact in

Revelation
20:7–9
Matthew 21:44

her place. 'The Lord will save the dwellings of Judah
first, so that the honour of the house of David and of
Jerusalem's inhabitants may not be greater than that of
Judah. On that day the Lord will shield those who live
in Jerusalem, so that the feeblest of them will be like
David, and the house of David will be like God, like
the Angel of the Lord going before them. On that day *I*   Matthew
will set out to destroy all the nations that attack Jerusalem.'   16:18

    'And I will pour out on the house of David and the   Revelation
inhabitants of Jerusalem a spirit of grace and   20:7–10
supplication. They will *look on me, the one they have*   John 19:37
pierced, and *mourn* for him as one mourns for an   Revelation 1:7
only child, and grieve bitterly for him as one grieves   Matthew 24:30
for a firstborn son.'

F1. Some of Zechariah's earlier prophecies could be regarded as having been fulfilled in the Maccabean struggle for independence from Seleucid rule in 165 BC. But he is not writing here about the immediate future, but about a more distant time, which he speaks of as 'that day'.

F2. Jesus relates the picture of the rock (Zechariah 12:3) to himself in Matthew 21:24.

In Matthew 24:30 there is an echo of Zechariah 12:10, when he says that all nations of the earth will 'mourn' at the coming of the Son of man, i.e. in the period immediately after his death (see section 3:8).

John connects verse 10 with the crucifixion of Jesus (John 19:37).

F3. John also relates the vision of all nations of the earth mourning to the second coming of Jesus Christ (Revelation 1:7).

When he later takes up the picture of all nations attacking Jerusalem, he describes it as 'the camp of God's people, the city he loves' (Revelation 20:9). This could hardly refer to the Jewish people or the city of Jerusalem, and must therefore refer to the church.

If Jesus and the apostles relate these verses so clearly to the first and second comings of Jesus, it is difficult to believe that they could *also* be applied to the modern city of Jerusalem as the capital of Israel withstanding attacks from all nations of the world. If we insist on this kind of literal interpretation, we must lengthen the list to include *every other occasion* on which Jerusalem has withstood attacks – for example during the Muslim conquest in the seventh century, the Crusades in the eleventh and twelfth centuries, the Byzantine wars, and World War I.

'The Day of the Lord' Zechariah 14:1–9, 21:

A day of the Lord is coming when your plunder will be

divided among you. *I will gather all the nations to*
Jerusalem to fight against it; the city will be captured,   Revelation 20:7–9
the houses ransacked, and the women raped. Half
of the city will go into exile, but the rest of the people
will not be taken from the city.

    Then *the Lord will go out and fight against those*   Revelation 20:7–9
nations, as he fights in the day of battle. On that day
his feet will stand on the Mount of Olives, east of
Jerusalem, and the Mount of Olives will be split in two
from east to west, forming a great valley, with half of
the mountain moving north and half moving south.
You will flee by my mountain valley, for it will extend
to Azel. You will flee as you fled from the earthquake
in the days of Uzziah king of Judah. Then the Lord
my God will come, and *all the holy ones with him*.   Matthew 16:27;
    On that day there will be no light, no cold or frost.   25:31
It will be a unique day, *without daytime or night-time*   Revelation 22:5
– a day known to the Lord. When evening comes,
there will be light. On that day *living water will flow from*   Joel 13:18
Jerusalem, half to the eastern sea and half to the   John 7:37–39
western sea, in summer and in winter. *The Lord*   Revelation 22:1–2
will be king over the whole earth. On that day there   Revelation 11:15–17
will be one Lord, and his name *the only name*.   Acts 4:12

And on that day there will no longer be a Canaanite   Mark 11:15–17
(*or* merchant) in the house of the Lord Almighty.   John 2:13–17

F1. The capture of Jerusalem described in Zechariah 14:2 could
perhaps be related to the capture of Jerusalem in AD 70 by the
Romans.

F2. Mark summarizes the message preached by Jesus in the
words: 'The time has come ... The kingdom of God is near ...'
(Mark 1:15). All his teaching about the coming of the kingdom
(compare Mark 9:1) must be related to Zechariah's prophecy 'The
Lord will be king over the whole earth' (Zechariah 14:9).

    The cleansing of the temple by Jesus is a clear fulfilment of the
words 'there will no longer be a Canaanite (or merchant) in the
house of the Lord Almighty' (Zechariah 14:21) (compare Mark
11:15–17 and John 2:13–19).

    The picture of living water flowing from Jerusalem (Zechariah
14:8) is found in two other prophets (Ezekiel 47:1–12 and Joel 3:18).
It must be to this that Jesus was referring when he said, 'Whoever
believes in me, as the Scripture has said, streams of living water will
flow from within him' (John 7:37). There is no other passage in the
Old Testament which could account for his using the phrase 'as the

Scripture has said'. Jesus therefore takes the original vision of living water flowing from the temple in Jerusalem down to the Dead Sea and interprets it as a picture of the life-giving influence of the believer who is filled with the Holy Spirit, or of himself as the one through whom the Spirit is given.

The words 'On that day there will be one Lord, and his name the only name' (Zechariah 14:9) are echoed by Peter's claim about Jesus: 'Salvation is found in no one else, for there is no other name under heaven given to men by which we must be saved' (Acts 4:12).

F3. There is an echo of Zechariah 14:5 in Jesus' words about the coming of the Son of man (Matthew 16:27 and 25:31), since 'the holy ones' are probably to be understood as 'angels'.

Several of the themes that are mentioned here are taken up by John in his vision of 'a new heaven and a new earth' (Revelation 21:1ff.) – for example the defeat of the nations attacking Jerusalem (Zechariah 14:2–3, compare Revelation 20:7–9), and the unique day in which there is no day or night (Zechariah 14:7, compare Revelation 22:5). The picture of living water flowing from the temple is here given a completely different interpretation: it now becomes 'the river of the water of life, as clear as crystal, flowing from the throne of God and of the Lamb' (Revelation 22:1–2).

However closely, therefore, some of Zechariah's words seem to correspond to events in and around Jerusalem since 1948, we must resist the temptation to draw the connection *until and unless* we have answered these two basic questions:

● How do the New Testament writers understand the fulfilment of the prophecies of Zechariah?

● Do the New Testament writers encourage us in any way to relate Zechariah's words to historical events in Jerusalem between the first and second comings of Jesus Christ?

Since they relate Zechariah's prophecies at so many points to the first and second comings of Jesus, and since they give us no encouragement whatsoever to relate them to events in the city of Jerusalem between the two comings, is there any good reason why we in the twentieth century should want to do so? When the New Testament writers have opened our eyes to see how Jesus fulfilled some of Zechariah's prophecies in his first coming, and when they have given us a vision of how others will be fulfilled at his second coming, the attempt to relate them, for example, to Arab attacks on the State of Israel seems to be a step backward rather than forward. It's rather like lighting a candle when the sun is already shining.

NOTES

1

John H. Davis, *The Evasive Peace, A Study of the Zionist-Arab Problem*, John Murray, 1968

2

Najib Azuri, *Le réveil de la nation Arabe*, Libraire Plon, Paris, 1905, quoted in Lucas Grollenberg, *Palestine Comes First*, SCM Press, 1980, p.6

Asher Ginsberg (Ahad Ha'Am), quoted in Moshe Menuhin, *The Decadence of Judaism in Our Time*, Institute of Palestinian Studies, Beirut, 1969

Moshe Dayan, in *Ha'olam Hazeh*, 8 July 1968

2.1

Theodor Herzl, quoted in John Bagot Glubb, *Peace in the Holy Land, An Historical Analysis of the Palestine Problem*, Hodder and Stoughton, 1971, p. 258

Max Nordau, quoted in David Vital, *The Origins of Zionism*, Oxford University Press, 1975, pp. 362-64

Dagobert D. Runes, *The Jew and the Cross*, Philosophical Library, New York, 1965, pp. 12, 14-15, 87, 61, 62, 40, 41, 25

James Parkes, *The Emergence of the Jewish Problem* (1878-1939), Oxford University Press, 1946, pp. 195-98

2.2

Denys Baly, *Multitudes in the Valley, Church and Crisis in the Middle East*, Seabury Press, New York, 1957, pp. 22ff.

David Vital, *The Origins of Zionism*, © Oxford University Press 1975, by permission of Oxford University Press, pp. 118-19, 128-31

Noah Lucas, *A Modern History of Israel*, Weidenfeld and Nicolson, 1974, pp. 24-25, 27

Theodor Herzl, *The Jewish State*, Henry Pordes, fifth edition, 1967

The Basle Programme, quoted in Walid Khalidi, *From Haven to Conquest, Readings in Zionism and the Palestine Problem until 1948*, The Institute for Palestine Studies, Beirut, 1971

Ahad Ha'Am, quoted in David Vital, *The Origins of Zionism*, p. 373

David Vital, *The Origins of Zionism*, pp. 371-73

Theodor Herzl, *Complete Diaries*, Herzl Press and Thomas Yoseloff, New York, 1960

Chaim Weizmann, 'States must be built up . . .' quoted in *Palestine, A Study of Jewish, Arab and British Policies*, ESCO Zionist Institute, Yale University Press, vol. 1, pp. 98-99; 'The Balfour Declaration . . .' and 'I trust to God . . .' from *Chaim Weizmann: Excerpts from his Historic Statements, Writings and Addresses*, The Jewish Agency for Palestine, New York, 1952, pp. 302, 48; 'All fears . . .', 'I need hardly say . . .' and 'The Zionists are not demanding . . .' quoted in John Bagot Glubb, *Peace in the Holy Land*, pp. 277, 266, 267; 'Palestine must be built up . . .' and 'It is not our objective . . .' quoted in David Hirst, *The Gun and the Olive Branch*, p. 39

Sir Charles Webster, 'The Art and Practice of Diplomacy' in *The Listener*, 28 February 1952

2.3

David Hirst, *The Gun and the Olive Branch*, reprinted by permission of Faber and Faber, pp. 29, 78-79, 79-80

David Ben-Gurion, *The History of the Haganah*, World Zionist Organization, 1954

Joseph Weitz, *My Diary and Letters to the Children*, Tel Aviv: Massada, 1965, vol. 2, pp. 181-82

Moshe Dayan, in *Jerusalem Post*, 10 August 1967

2.4

Najib Azuri, *Le réveil de la nation Arabe*, Librarie Plon, Paris, 1905, pp. 6ff, quoted in Lucas Grollenberg, *Palestine Comes First*, p. 31

Asher Ginsberg, 'Palestine is not an uninhabited country . . .' and 'As to the war . . .' quoted in *The Decadence of Judaism in Our Time*, Institute of Palestinian Studies, Beirut, 1969; 'We abroad . . .' quoted in H. Kohn, *Nationalism and Imperialism in the Hither East*, London, 1923, p. 126 footnote

The Emir Faisal, quoted in John H. Davis, *The Evasive Peace*, pp. 14-15, 46

Moshe Sharett, as above, p. 149

David Ben-Gurion, as above, pp. 141-42

Commander Hogarth, as above, p. 58

Herbert Samuel, as above, p. 61

Gilbert Clayton, as above, pp. 28-29

2.5

Arthur Balfour, quoted in Oskar K. Rabinowicz, *Winston Churchill on Jewish Problems*, Thomas Yoseloff, New York, 1960, p.167

Arthur Koestler, *Promise and Fulfilment*, Macmillan, 1949, p. 4

Hussein-McMahon Correspondence, quoted in George Antonius, *The Arab Awakening*, pp. 435-36

Anglo-French Declaration, as above, pp. 435-36

Sir Edward Grey, quoted in Walid Khalidi, *From Haven to Conquest*, pp. 219-20

Lord Balfour, quoted in Doreen Ingrams, *Palestine Papers 1917-1922*, John Murray, 1972, p. 73

Erskine Childers, writing in the Jubilee Volume of the Netherlands-Arabia Association 1955-1966, E.J. Brill, Leiden 1966

2.6

David Hirst, *The Gun and the Olive Branch*, pp. 131-32

President Truman, 'I am sorry . . .' quoted in William Eddy, *F.D.R. Meets Ibn Saud*, American Friends of the Middle East, New York, 1954, p. 36; 'The facts were . . .' from *Memoirs*, Doubleday, 1958, vol. 2, pp. 158ff.

David Hirst, *The Gun and the Olive Branch*, p. 132

Maxime Rodinson, 'Israel, fait colonial?' in *Les Temps Modernes*, no. 253, 1967, quoted in Lucas Grollenberg, *Palestine Comes First*, p. 54

British Council of Churches Report, *Towards Understanding the Arab-Israeli Conflict*, London, 1982

Edward Said, *The Question of Palestine*, Vintage Books, New York, 1980

The Quaker Report, *Search for Peace in the Middle East*, Friends Peace and International Relations Committee, London, 1970

Erskine Childers, in the Jubilee volume of the Netherlands-Arabia Association 1955-1966, quoted in Lucas Grollenberg, *Palestine Comes First*, p. 10

2.7

Denys Baly, *Multitudes in the Valley*, p. 85

John Bagot Glubb, *Peace in the Holy Land, An Historical Analysis of the Palestine Problem*, Hodder and Stoughton, 1971, pp. 299-300

Jon and David Kimche, *A Clash of Destinies: The Arab-Jewish War and the Founding of the State of Israel*, Praeger Publishers, New York, 1960, p. 92

David Ben-Gurion, *Rebirth and Destiny of Israel*, Philosophical Library, New York, 1954, pp. 530-31

Menachem Begin, quoted in John Bagot Glubb, *Peace in the Holy Land*, p. 299

David Hirst, *The Gun and the Olive Branch*, p. 124

Jacques de Reynier, *A Jerusalem un Drapeau Flottait sur la Ligne de Feu*, Editions de la Beconnière, Neuchatel, 1950, pp. 71-76

Larry Collins and Dominique Lapierre, *O Jerusalem!* Simon and Schuster, 1972, pp. 299-307

Edgar O'Ballance, *The Arab-Israeli War of 1948*, Faber and Faber, 1956, p. 64

I.F. Stone, quoted in *Zionism, A Preliminary Memo*, Department of Information and Interpretation of the Middle East Council of Churches, published by the Commission of the Churches on International Affairs, WCC, Geneva, 1976, pp. 30-31

Menachem Begin, quoted in David Hirst, *The Gun and the Olive Branch*, p. 128-29

Yigal Allon, *Ha Sepher La Palmach*, vol. 2, p. 286 and 43

Chaim Weizmann, quoted in James McDonald, *My Mission to Israel*, Simon and Schuster, New York, 1952, p. 176

John H. Davis, *The Evasive Peace*, p. 121

2.8

David Ben-Gurion, quoted in John H. Davis, *The Evasive Peace*, p. 84

Abba Eban, *An Autobiography*, 1978, p. 609

Moshe Davis, *I Am A Jew*, Mowbray, 1978, p. 88

Moshe Dayan, *Story of My Life*, Weidenfeld and Nicolson, 1976, p. 58-59

W. Laqueur, *A History of Zionism*, Schocken Books, New York, 1978, p. 595-97

2.9

The Ecumenical Theological Research Fraternity in Israel, *An Appeal to the Churches around the World*, Commission of the Churches on International Affairs of the World Council of Churches, Geneva, 1976

The Times, May 1917

Asher Ginsberg, quoted in Hans Kohn, 'Zion and the Jewish National Idea', *Menorah Journal*, Autumn-Winter 1958, p. 39ff.

Albert Einstein, *Out of My Later Years*, Philosophical Library, New York, 1950, p. 262ff.

Rabbi Benjamin, quoted in James and Marti Hefley, *Arabs, Christians and Jews*, Logos International, 1978, p. 149

Rabbi Yosef Becher, quoted by Ghassan Bishara in 'Praying for the "Peaceful Disappearance" of Israel', *Monday Morning*, 25 May 1981, Beirut, p. 55ff.

2.10

Statistics from *The Sunday Times*, 22 August 1982

Everett Mendelsohn, *A Compassionate Peace*, Penguin, 1982, p. 40, copyright © American Friends Service Committee, 1982, reprinted by permission of Penguin Books Ltd

Edward Said, *The Question of Palestine,* p. 117-18, 51

Fawaz Turki, *The Disinherited,* Monthly Review Press, New York, 1974, p. 168

Edward Said, *The Question of Palestine,* p. 125-26

Tawfiq Zayyad, *Enemy of the Sun: Poetry of Palestinian Resistance,* edited by Naseer Arari and Edmund Ghareeb, Drum and Spear Press, Washington, 1970, p. 66

Kamal Nasr, *Jirah Tughanni,* Beirut, 1960

British Council of Churches Report, *Towards Understanding the Arab-Israeli Conflict,* pp. 62-63

Everett Mendelsohn, *A Compassionate Peace,* p. 42-43, 47-48, 44

Yasser Arafat, quoted in *Middle East,* November 1981, p. 24

Everett Mendelsohn, as above, p. 46

Edward Said, *The Question of Palestine,* p. 140, 223-24

3

W.D. Davies, *The Gospel and the Land,* University of California Press, 1974, p. 375

3.2

Alan Millard, *The Lion Handbook to the Bible,* Lion Publishing, 1973, p. 213

3.4

Philo, quoted in W.D. Davies, *The Gospel and the Land,* p. 122

3.7

Kittel Theological Dictionary of the New Testament, vol. VI, p. 36

R.T. France, *Old Testament Prophecy and the Future of Israel: A Study in the Teaching of Jesus,* Tyndale Bulletin no. 26, 1975, pp. 58, 73, 68

R.T. France, *Jesus and the Old Testament,* Tyndale Press, 1971, pp. 227-39

4.1

Statement from the Israeli embassy, quoted in Edward Said, *The Question of Palestine,* p.43

Walter Barker, writing in *Third Way,* February 1981, p. 24

Lance Lambert, *Battle for Israel,* Kingsway Publications, 1976, pp. 122-23

George Antonius, *The Arab Awakening,* Hamish Hamilton, 1938, pp. 387-89

William Zuckerman, from the *Jewish Newsletter,* 7 December 1958

General Carl von Horn, *Soldiering for Peace,* Cassell, 1966, p. 85

Levi Eshkol, in *Newsweek*, February 1969

Israeli Minister of Education, in *Haaretz*, 9 September 1974

The Quaker Report, *The Search for Peace in the Middle East*, pp. 5-7

General Carl von Horn, *Soldiering for Peace*, pp. 282ff.

Denys Baly, *Multitudes in the Valley*, pp. 96, 281-83, 268

Graham Hoskins, in *Interchange*, no. 18, 1976, Australian Fellowship of Evangelical Students

4.2

Chaim Weizmann, 'In all humbleness . . .' from Report of the UN Special Committee on Palestine, Document A/364, 1947, p. 77; 'I am certain . . .' quoted in John H. Davis, *The Evasive Peace*, p. 19

Simha Flapan, *Zionism and the Palestinians*, Croom Helm, 1979, pp. 78-79, 83, 12

David Ben-Gurion, quoted in I.F. Stone, *For a New Approach to the Israeli-Arab Conflict*, The New York Review of Books, 3 August 1967

Golda Meir, *The Sunday Times*, 15 June 1969

Samuel Katz, *The Jewish Presence in Palestine*, Israel Academic Committee on the Middle East, p.35

Menachem Begin, *The History of the Haganah*, World Zionist Organization, 1954

Nahum Goldmann, quoted in Simha Flapan, *Zionism and the Palestinians*, p. 126

W. Brunn, quoted in *Zionism, A Preliminary Memo*, Department of Information and Interpretation of the Middle East Council of Churches, p.30

4.3

Mike Evans, *Israel – America's Key to Survival*, Logos International, 1981, pp. 103-4

Max Nordau, quoted in David Hirst, *The Gun and the Olive Branch*, p.19

Moshe Dayan, in *Haaretz*, 4 April 1969

Joseph Weitz, *My Diary and Letters to the Children*, vol. III, p. 302

Nathan Chofshi, in *The Jewish Newsletter*, 9 February 1959

Rabbi Elmer Berger, 'Prophecy, Zionism and the State of Israel', an address delivered at the University of Leiden, Holland, 20 March 1968, published by Arnold J. Toynbee, p. 17

4.4

Saul Bellow, *To Jerusalem and Back*, Penguin, 1977, pp. 135-36

Raja Shehadeh and Jonathan Kuttab, *The West Bank and the Rule of Law*, International Commission of Jurists, Geneva, 1980

The La Grange Declaration, quoted in *The Jordan Times,* 21 December 1981

4.5

Denys Baly, *Multitudes in the Valley,* p. 258

4.6

Status Law, quoted in John H. Davis, *The Evasive Peace,* p. 75
    Haim Cohen, quoted in Joseph Badi, *Fundamental Laws of the State of Israel,* Twaine Publishers, New York, 1960, p. 156
    I.F. Stone, quoted in *Zionism, A Preliminary Memo,* pp. 31-32
    Rabbi Yoseph Becher, in *Monday Morning,* Beirut
    Kenneth Cragg, in *Bible Lands,* Jerusalem and the Middle East Church Association, Spring 1982, pp. 24-26

4.7

The Quaker Report, *Search for Peace in the Middle East,* pp. 8-9
    Denys Baly, *Multitudes in the Valley,* pp. 277-78, 300

4.8

Denys Baly, *Multitudes in the Valley,* p. 297

4.9

The Quaker Report, *Search for Peace in the Middle East,* p. 7
    Denys Baly, 'The Things that Belong unto Peace', The Sprigg Lectures 1971, quoted in Johan Bouman, *Biblical Interpretation . . . and the Middle East,* World Council of Churches, Geneva, 1974, pp. 40-41; 'We may squirm . . .' from *Multitudes in the Valley,* p.30

4.10

Edward Said, *The Question of Palestine,* p. 49
    Kenneth Bailey, *Through Peasant Eyes, More Lucan Parables,* Eerdmans, 1980, pp. 71-73, reprinted by permission of Eerdmans Publishing Co.